THE HARP AND LAUREL WREATH

THE HARP
AND
LAUREL WREATH

Poetry and Dictation
for the Classical Curriculum

Edited by Laura M. Berquist

Illustrated by Christopher J. Pelicano

IGNATIUS PRESS   SAN FRANCISCO

About the title:
The harp is traditionally associated with one who sings, often on his way from one place to another. The wandering minstrels of the Middle Ages took their harps with them. Additionally, in classical times a poet was seen as a type of singer. In Plato's *Republic*, for example, the considerations made about music include poetry. Hence the harp is an appropriate image for the young 'singer', who is on a journey, the end of which is truth.

The laurel wreath is the historic symbol of victory and excellence. Such a wreath was given to the victorious athletes of the Olympic Games. Our children are pursuing a course that will lead to spiritual and intellectual excellence, and to the victory that is attendant on that achievement.

Cover design by Riz Boncan Marsella

© 1999 Ignatius Press, San Francisco
ISBN 978-0-89870-716-8
Library of Congress catalogue number 98-73638
Printed in the United States of America ∞
Manufactured by Thomson-Shore, Dexter, MI (USA); RMA574LS701, June, 2011

CONTENTS

INTRODUCTION

The Importance of Poetry

It is a temptation for a person who is homeschooling children to save fine arts appreciation for days when religion, English, mathematics, science, history, geography, literature, and penmanship are all finished. The problem, of course, is that all of these things seldom get done. Therefore the introduction of beautiful pictures, great music, and excellent poetry remains an activity to do "someday".

This is a mistake, because the appreciation of fine arts is formative for the soul. The old adage "You are what you eat" could be changed truthfully to say "You are what you see and hear." The models in one's imagination and memory become a part of the soul and affect all the rest of life.

If the soul holds good, true, beautiful, noble, and heroic images, it will be inclined to love those things. Additionally, since whatever is true is also beautiful, an appreciation of the beautiful prepares the way for an appreciation of the true. If children love the beautiful they will be disposed to love the truth, *as truth*, when they are older. Thus, even in terms of intellectual formation, fostering the fine arts is important. Socrates, in *The Republic*, says it pretty clearly:

> And further, because omissions and the failure of beauty in things badly made or grown would be most quickly perceived by one who was properly educated in music ["music" here includes all the fine arts], and so, feeling distaste rightly, he would praise beautiful things

and take delight in them and receive them into his soul to foster its growth and become himself beautiful and good. The ugly he would rightly disapprove of and hate while still young and yet unable to apprehend the reason, but when reason came the man thus nurtured would be the first to give her welcome, for by this affinity he would know her.

We should foster in our children a love of the beautiful and true and a corresponding distaste for what is ugly and false. Children's sense of beauty can be encouraged in various ways; those of us who are homeschooling may include beautiful art, music, and literature regularly in our curricula, in ways that are appropriate to the various stages of the intellectual formation of the child. Attention to such things will aid in the kind of intellectual formation that is the object of a classical education because it will strengthen and inform the imagination, which must be developed in the right way to do its job well.

Poetry is one of the forms of the beautiful that is relatively accessible to children. Children respond to patterns of sound and enjoy the rhythm of poetry, if they are introduced to it before someone tells them they shouldn't like it. Poetry is naturally pleasant to the ordinary child, and pleasure is a sign teachers and parents should never ignore.

Children are very good at imitation because it is the way God intends them to learn. We need to keep this in mind for all areas of our children's development, moral *and* intellectual. Children need models of right behavior and of excellence in all the scholastic areas that are appropriate for them to pursue. The right use and richness of language is an area that is most appropriate for the formation of children. For this reason they should be exposed to the best examples of the use of language that we can give them. Beautiful word patterns and sounds, the right choice of words, and methods of producing particular responses can be imitated by children who have had good models. Language development is significantly enriched by exposure to good poetry.

Additionally, in all of the fine arts, one of the chief benefits of appreciation is seeing the world through the eyes of the artist. His gift of observation is given to the student when the work is studied. It is as though the artist said, "Look, here is something really beautiful that I saw and want to share. Perhaps you missed it." For this reason a painting can be better than a photograph in drawing the viewer's attention to certain aspects of a particular scene, for example, the lighting or the composition of the figures. Similarly, poetry can be a better way to draw attention to certain truths or make some facet of an experience stand out. Excellent poetry will both direct the student's attention to these aspects of reality and model the best way to share that experience.

Also, poetry appeals to the emotions, as does music, and, like music, beautiful and rightly ordered poetry can habituate or train the soul to the right kind of internal movement. Familiarity with truly good poetry will encourage children to love the good, to hope for its victory, and to feel sad at its demise. The opposite habituation is very clear to see in children who watch or read stories in which the grotesque is taken for granted. They cease to be shocked by what is really disgusting. That is a great loss to the soul.

In addition to these reasons, which are true for all age levels, there are other, more specific, developmental considerations:

In the earliest years, the object of our curricula should be twofold. We need to teach basic reading, writing, and arithmetic, and we should encourage memory and observation. The basic skills are the tools of all further learning; memorization and observation are what children do naturally at this stage of development. It is through the use of natural inclinations that the intelligence is formed at every stage of development.

When babies are ready to crawl, you encourage and help them do just what they want to do. You put attractive objects where they can see them, so they will practice crawling. You don't put the toy too far out of reach, because that would be discouraging for the child. You don't put it too close, because that wouldn't provide enough practice. Instead, you make a judgment about just the right distance and make adjustments as the baby's ability grows.

Teaching children is like that. Little children are good at memorization; they pick up jumping-rope rhymes and doggerel verses without effort. Encourage this inclination and ability by having the children memorize fine poetry, among other things. This will strengthen the imagination and memory, as well as prepare the children for the subsequent stages of intellectual development. Since poetry draws attention to specific aspects of experience, regular exposure to poetry will reinforce children's observational powers.

In the middle years, seventh through ninth grade, children are ready to analyze. Summaries, grammatical exercises, both in Latin and English, and various categorization activities will encourage and improve analytic ability, as will the close examination of well-reasoned arguments. With respect to poetry, the student at this level should try to turn poetry into prose. This exercise in simple analysis also begins to focus the mind on what is specific to poetry that differentiates it from other forms of speech. The teacher should lay this question before the child and not give him the answer too soon. Let him learn inductively, through many examples. This is how the mind is trained to think. If the answer is given too quickly, the student exercises his memory but not his intelligence. Left to himself, he will eventually come to see that poetry is not primarily intended to impart information, but to evoke a particular emotional response. The student who has come to see this about poetry on his own, through directed exploration, will have a much fuller and richer appreciation of the fact than one who has simply been told that this is so.

Though poetry is not intended primarily to impart information or to make an intellectual argument, there is a quasi-argument in the poem nonetheless. The poet moves the mind of the reader from ignorance to knowledge. The student's attention should be directed to trying to find and articulate that movement.

Further, continued practice in memorization will stretch the faculty of imagination. Like any power of the soul, repeated use of the power will improve it. Children who memorize regularly find it easy to do, and a good memory is a real asset to the intellectual life.

In the upper grades, tenth to twelfth, students should concentrate on learning how to present the logical arguments they are now able to make. They need to learn rhetorical patterns, and imitation remains an excellent way to learn. But there should also be a study of the method employed by others. Ask *how* an author achieves the effects he achieves, and have the students study those techniques in detail.

This is a good example of a general principle in education. First supply experience of the various types of whatever you are studying, exposing the children to many instances of the category. Then when they are ready, turn to a detailed study, which will be much more effective, and easier, because of the early exposure. This is not necessary to a good understanding, but it makes it significantly easier to acquire that understanding. Teaching Latin in high school to someone who has already memorized vocabulary and paradigms and is familiar with grammar is a breeze compared to teaching it to a student who has never done any Latin or whose grammatical knowledge is shaky. The same thing is true about teaching philosophy to students who have a wide acquaintance with history and literature. They are properly prepared to undertake the more difficult study, having experiences that give a content to the philosophical ideas which are now introduced.

In the study of poetry, the high school years are the right time to bring up basic poetical information, such as figures of speech, meter and rhyme scheme, and the classes of poems. Familiarity with many poems makes this an easier study, though one may undertake it without the earlier preparation. I have included, in the ending sections of this book, poems of increasing difficulty, with information on terms and concepts to know in the study of poetry, as well as study questions and answers.

How to Use This Book

Poetry

The poems included in this collection consist of the poems I recommend in *Designing Your Own Classical Curriculum*, with substantial additions for the high school years.

In the early years, have the children work on memorizing a number of poems each year. Poetry is more easily memorized when it is heard, so start by reading the poem to your child. Then work on one or two stanzas per week. On the first day introduce the poem, reading it and talking about it. On the second day spend five minutes going over the first stanza with the child, having him repeat the lines as they are read to him. On the following two days repeat this procedure, and on the fifth day have the student recite the first stanza.

In the next week start studying the second stanza, reading the lines to your child and having him repeat them. Also review the first stanza. This should not take more than five minutes per day. Again, on the last day have the child recite the stanzas he now knows. Continue this process until the poem is learned. Thus a four-stanza poem will take four weeks to learn, or two weeks if the student learns two stanzas per week. Children can learn poetry more quickly than this, but it tends not to stay with them if they learn it too rapidly.

Once the poem is learned, enter it in a "Poetry Notebook". This can be a plain-paper or lined notebook. Write the poem down and invite the child to illustrate it. (As he gets older, he can do the writing.) Do this with each poem as it is mastered, and eventually the student will have his own personal anthology, full of poetry he knows and enjoys.

In the analytic period, have the children continue to memorize poems and add to their "anthology", but also use the poems as matter for analysis.

When a new poem is introduced, have the child turn it into prose. Ask him which he likes better, his retelling of the information of the poem or the poem itself. Do they produce the same effect? Let him try to express the movement from ignorance to knowledge in the poem. Ask him, "What does the poet lead you to see? How do you respond to that?"

In the high school years a study of the power and beauty of language and the uses to which it can be put should be central to the curriculum. This book is intended to aid the home-school teacher in reaching that end. There are numerous poetry selections included that are appropriate for high school students, as well as study questions that can be used to help students investigate the various ways in which poetry achieves its effects.

The poetry for the rhetorical stage, usually tenth through twelfth grade, is divided into three sections, each section containing more than enough poems for a poetry unit per year. The number of poems included is deliberately greater than necessary so that the student may choose among them for the poems that appeal to him.

The first section concentrates on the figures of speech used in poetry. The terms used in such a study, and their meanings, are given at the beginning of the section, and then poems are presented that illustrate these figures, along with study questions about the material. The second section turns the student's attention to the types of meter used in poetry, while still incorporating the information on figures of speech. Again, there are study questions to go with each poem. The third section consists of a presentation of the various types of poetry, with some of their distinguishing characteristics. Study questions are included. All three sections constitute only a beginning of the study of poetry, but they will set the high school student on the road to an intelligent, informed appreciation of poetry, encourage thinking skills, and point out various, effective ways in which language can be used.

There are answers included for all the study questions, but I suggest that you use them sparingly. They might be helpful when a question is unclear, because then the answer may illuminate the point of the question. In general, however, it is better to ignore the answers given, which are, after all, only one interpretation, and let the student exercise his mind looking for the answers himself. If you give him the answers, he will exercise his memory, but not his mind, as mentioned above. It is better to let the child struggle with something, reflect on it, and come back to it later, than it is to give him the answer.

Dictation

At the end of the earlier sections of poetry in this book, you will find a number of prose selections. These selections are included for those who want to incorporate dictation exercises in their curriculum but don't want to use the available full programs that have such activities.

Studied dictation is a useful tool in the development of children's writing ability. First, the children are working from models of good writing. They see and study correct usage, punctuation, and spelling, as well as excellent writing of various styles. In the old days of Catholic education, schools were financially poorer, but they turned out excellent scholars, as well as faithful Catholics. One reason for this was that neither the children nor the schools could afford books, so lessons were copied and then worked on. This meant that the children were continuously exposed to models of correctly written material. This is another example of the truth that children learn by imitation.

In a studied dictation, the teacher goes through the passage with the child, line by line, noting and giving a reason for every capital, comma, semicolon, colon, period, question mark, exclamation mark, and quotation mark. Difficult spellings are gone over as well. The teacher then dictates the passage to the child, who writes it from the dictation. This way the student gives concentrated attention to the mechanics of writing in a situation where he is writing material that has been put together because it goes together, as opposed to material artificially put together to try to highlight examples of writing mechanics.

In an unstudied dictation, the teacher reads a passage that the child has not yet seen. The student writes the passage down as best he can from simply hearing it. This is an excellent opportunity to put together all the various spelling and mechanics rules he has learned. He has to concentrate his attention on what he hears and think about how it should be written. Such an exercise reveals whether the student has mastery in these areas or not. It is a much better indication of spelling proficiency than a weekly spelling test. All that is required for that is a good short-term memory.

Whether studied or unstudied, the method of doing the dictation is the same. First, read the selection at a normal speed. Then, say the first five or so words of the initial sentence and have the child repeat those words and write them without saying anything else. My children often want to offer a comment at this point, but I have found that, if they do, they lose their focus and can't remember what they're supposed to be writing. The dictation takes twice as long that way and is not as effective. As soon as the student finishes the first set of words, read the rest of the sentence, have him repeat it and write it, and then move on to the next set of words. The dictation doesn't take long this way, but it does provide a model of good writing and practice in spelling and punctuation. Further, over the years the student becomes familiar with many styles of writing and is prepared to think about the differences in technique between such writers as Jane Austen and Charles Dickens.

Poetry is important in the intellectual development of children, and it is a pleasure as well; these are not unrelated phenomena. It is my hope that this book will be of use to Catholic homeschoolers as they raise their children to be faithful, informed, intelligent people who will put their talents to use in the service of God.

The Early Years

POETRY SELECTIONS

Whole Duty of Children

by Robert Louis Stevenson

A child should always say what's true
And speak when he is spoken to,
And behave mannerly at table:
At least as far as he is able.

At the Seaside

by Robert Louis Stevenson

When I was down beside the sea
A wooden spade they gave to me
    To dig the sandy shore.

My holes were empty like a cup.
In every hole the sea came up,
    Till it could come no more.

Rain

by Robert Louis Stevenson

The rain is raining all around,
It falls on field and tree,
It rains on the umbrellas here,
And on the ships at sea.

Happy Thought

by Robert Louis Stevenson

The world is so full of a number of things,
I'm sure we should all be as happy as kings.

Singing

by Robert Louis Stevenson

Of speckled eggs the birdie sings
And nests among the trees;
The sailor sings of ropes and things
In ships upon the seas.

The children sing in far Japan,
The children sing in Spain:
The organ with the organ man
Is singing in the rain.

Time to Rise

by Robert Louis Stevenson

A birdie with a yellow bill
Hopped upon the window sill,
Cocked his shining eye and said:
"Ain't you 'shamed, you sleepyhead!"

Singing Time

by Rose Fyleman

I wake in the morning early
And always, the very first thing,
I poke out my head and I sit up in bed
And I sing and I sing and I sing.

Once I Saw a Little Bird

an old nursery rhyme

Once I saw a little bird
Come hop, hop, hop:
So I cried, "Little bird,
Will you stop, stop, stop?"

And was going to the window,
To say, "How do you do?"
But he shook his little tail
And far away he flew.

I'm Glad

Anonymous

I'm glad the sky is painted blue,
   And the earth is painted green,
With such a lot of nice fresh air
   All sandwiched in between.

Bird Talk

by Aileen Fisher

"Think . . . ," said the robin,
"Think . . . ," said the jay,
sitting in the garden,
talking one day.

"Think about people—
the way they grow:
they don't have feathers
at all, you know.

"They don't eat beetles,
they don't grow wings,
they don't like sitting
on wires and things."

"Think!" said the robin.
"Think!" said the jay.
"Aren't people funny
to be that way?"

The Little Turtle

by Vachel Lindsay

There was a little turtle.
He lived in a box.
He swam in a puddle.
He climbed on the rocks.

He snapped at a mosquito.
He snapped at a flea.
He snapped at a minnow.
And he snapped at me.

He caught the mosquito.
He caught the flea.
He caught the minnow.
But he didn't catch me.

Animal Crackers

by Christopher Morley

Animal crackers, and cocoa to drink,
That is the finest of suppers, I think;
When I'm grown up and can have what I please
I think I shall always insist upon these.

What do *you* choose when you're offered a treat?
When Mother says, "What would you like best
    to eat?"

Is it waffles and syrup, or cinnamon toast?
It's cocoa and animals that *I* love the most!

The kitchen's the cosiest place that I know:
The kettle is singing, the stove is aglow,
And there in the twilight, how jolly to see
The cocoa and animals waiting for me.

Daddy and Mother dine later in state,
With Mary to cook for them, Susan to wait;
But they don't have nearly as much fun as I
Who eat in the kitchen with Nurse standing by;
And Daddy once said he would like to be me
Having cocoa and animals once more for tea!

Merry Sunshine

Anonymous

"Good morning, Merry Sunshine,
　How did you wake so soon,
You've scared the little stars away
　And shined away the moon.
I saw you go to sleep last night
　Before I ceased my playing;
How did you get 'way over there?
　And where have you been staying?"

"I never go to sleep, dear child,
　I just go round to see
My little children of the East,
　Who rise and watch for me.
I waken all the birds and bees
　And flowers on my way,
And now come back to see the child
　Who stayed out late at play."

There Once Was a Puffin

by Florence Page Jaques

Oh, there once was a Puffin
Just the shape of a muffin,
And he lived on an island
In the
    bright
      blue sea!

He ate little fishes,
That were most delicious,
And he had them for supper
And he
   had
     them
       for tea.

But this poor little Puffin,
He couldn't play nothin',
For he hadn't anybody
To
    play
        with
            at all.

So he sat on his island
And he cried for a while, and
He felt very lonely,
And he
    felt
        very small.

Then along came the fishes,
And they said, "If you wishes,
You can have us for playmates,
Instead
    of
        for
            tea!"

So they now play together,
In all sorts of weather,
And the Puffin eats pancakes,
Like you
    and
        like
            me.

Windy Nights

by Robert Louis Stevenson

Whenever the moon and stars are set,
   Whenever the wind is high,
All night long in the dark and wet,
   A man goes riding by.
Late in the night when the fires are out,
Why does he gallop and gallop about?

Whenever the trees are crying aloud,
   And ships are tossed at sea,
By, on the highway, low and loud,
   By at the gallop goes he:
By at the gallop he goes, and then
By he comes back at the gallop again.

Bed in Summer

by Robert Louis Stevenson

In winter I get up at night
And dress by yellow candlelight.
In summer, quite the other way,
I have to go to bed by day.

I have to go to bed and see
The birds still hopping on the tree,
Or hear the grown-up people's feet
Still going past me in the street.

And does it not seem hard to you,
When all the sky is clear and blue,
And I should like so much to play,
To have to go to bed by day?

Where Go the Boats?

by Robert Louis Stevenson

Dark brown is the river,
    Golden is the sand.
It flows along forever,
    With trees on either hand.

Green leaves a-floating,
    Castles of the foam,
Boats of mine a-boating—
    Where will all come home?

On goes the river
    And out past the mill,
Away down the valley,
    Away down the hill.

Away down the river,
    A hundred miles or more,
Other little children
    Shall bring my boats ashore.

Foreign Lands

by Robert Louis Stevenson

Up into the cherry tree
Who should climb but little me?
I held the trunk with both my hands
And looked abroad on foreign lands.

I saw the next door garden lie
Adorned with flowers, before my eye,
And many pleasant places more
That I had never seen before.

I saw the dimpling river pass
And be the sky's blue looking glass;
The dusty roads go up and down
With people tramping into town.

If I could find a higher tree
Farther and farther I should see,
To where the grown-up river slips
Into the sea among the ships,

To where the roads on either hand
Lead onward into fairyland,
Where all the children dine at five,
And all the playthings come alive.

The Land of Counterpane

by Robert Louis Stevenson

When I was sick and lay abed,
I had two pillows at my head,
And all my toys beside me lay
To keep me happy all the day.

And sometimes for an hour or so,
I watched my leaden soldiers go,
With different uniforms and drills,
Among the bedclothes, through the hills;

And sometimes sent my ships in fleets
All up and down among the sheets;
Or brought my trees and houses out,
And planted cities all about.

I was the giant great and still
That sits upon the pillow-hill,
And sees before him, dale and plain,
The pleasant Land of Counterpane.

My Shadow

by Robert Louis Stevenson

I have a little shadow that goes in and out with me,
And what can be the use of him is more than I can
see.
He is very, very like me from the heels up to the head;
And I see him jump before me, when I jump into my
bed.

The funniest thing about him is the way he likes to
grow—
Not at all like proper children, which is always very
slow;
For he sometimes shoots up taller like an India-
rubber ball,
And he sometimes gets so little that there's none of
him at all.

He hasn't got a notion of how children ought to play,
And can only make a fool of me in every sort of way.
He stays so close beside me, he's a coward you can see;
I'd think shame to stick to nursie as that shadow sticks
to me!

One morning, very early, before the sun was up,
I rose and found the shining dew on every buttercup;
But my lazy little shadow, like an arrant sleepyhead,
Had stayed at home behind me and was fast asleep in
bed.

The Wind

by Robert Louis Stevenson

I saw you toss the kites on high
And blow the birds about the sky;
And all around I heard you pass,
Like ladies' skirts across the grass—
    O wind, a-blowing all day long,
    O wind, that sings so loud a song!

I saw the different things you did,
But always you yourself you hid.
I felt you push, I heard you call,
I could not see yourself at all—
    O wind, a-blowing all day long,
    O wind, that sings so loud a song!

O you that are so strong and cold,
O blower, are you young or old?
Are you a beast of field and tree,
Or just a stronger child than me?
    O wind, a-blowing all day long,
    O wind, that sings so loud a song!

The Moon

by Robert Louis Stevenson

The moon has a face like the clock in the hall;
She shines on thieves on the garden wall,
On streets and field and harbor quays,
And birdies asleep in forks of the trees.

The squalling cat and the squeaking mouse,
The howling dog by the door of the house,
The bat that lies in bed at noon,
All love to be out by the light of the moon.

But all of the things that belong to the day
Cuddle to sleep to be out of her way;
And flowers and children close their eyes
Till up in the morning the sun shall arise.

The Early Years: Poetry Selections

The Hayloft

by Robert Louis Stevenson

Through all the pleasant meadowside
    The grass grew shoulder-high,
Till the shining scythes went far and wide
    And cut it down to dry.

Those green and sweetly smelling crops
    They led in wagons home;
And they piled them here in mountaintops
    For mountaineers to roam.

Here is Mount Clear, Mount Rusty-Nail,
    Mount Eagles and Mount High;—
The mice that in these mountains dwell,
    No happier are than I!

Oh! what a joy to clamber there,
    Oh, what a place for play,
With the sweet, the dim, the dusty air,
    The happy hills of hay!

The Land of Story-Books

by Robert Louis Stevenson

At evening when the lamp is lit,
Around the fire my parents sit;
They sit at home and talk and sing,
And do not play at anything.

Now, with my little gun, I crawl
All in the dark along the wall,
And follow round the forest track
Away behind the sofa back.

There, in the night, where none can spy,
All in my hunter's camp I lie,
And play at books that I have read
Till it is time to go to bed.

These are the hills, these are the woods,
These are my starry solitudes;
And there the river by whose brink
The roaring lions come to drink.

I see the others far away
As if in firelit camp they lay,
And I, like to an Indian scout,
Around their party prowled about.

So, when my nurse comes in for me,
Home I return across the sea,
And go to bed with backward looks
At my dear land of Story-Books.

The Swing

by Robert Louis Stevenson

How do you like to go up in a swing,
　Up in the air so blue?
Oh, I do think it the pleasantest thing
　Ever a child can do!

Up in the air and over the wall,
　Till I can see so wide,
Rivers and trees and cattle and all
　Over the countryside—

Till I look down on the garden green,
　Down on the roof so brown—
Up in the air I go flying again,
　Up in the air and down!

The Lamplighter

by Robert Louis Stevenson

My tea is nearly ready and the sun has left the sky.
It's time to take the window to see Leerie going by;
For every night at teatime and before you take your
    seat,
With lantern and with ladder he comes posting up
    the street.

Now Tom would be a driver and Maria off to sea,
And my papa's a banker and as rich as he can be;
But I, when I am stronger and can chose what I'm
    to do,
O Leerie, I'll go round at night and light the lamps
    with you!

For we are very lucky, with a lamp before the door,
And Leerie stops to light it as he lights so many more;
And oh! before you hurry by with ladder and with
    light;
O Leerie, see a little child and nod to him tonight!

The Cow

by Robert Louis Stevenson

The friendly cow all red and white,
   I love with all my heart;
She gives me cream with all her might,
   To eat with apple tart.

She wanders lowing here and there,
   And yet she cannot stray,
All in the pleasant open air,
   The pleasant light of day;

And blown by all the winds that pass
   And wet with all the showers,
She walks among the meadow grass
   And eats the meadow flowers.

The Christening

by A. A. Milne

What shall I call
   My dear little dormouse?
His eyes are small,
   But his tail is e-nor-mouse.

I sometimes call him Terrible John,
'Cos his tail goes on—
And on—
And on.
And I sometimes call him Terrible Jack,
'Cos his tail goes on to the end of his back.
And I sometimes call him Terrible James,
'Cos he says he likes me calling him names. . . .

   But I think I shall call him Jim,
   'Cos I *am* so fond of him.

Some One

by Walter de la Mare

Some one came knocking
   At my wee, small door;
Some one came knocking,
   I'm sure—sure—sure;
I listened, I opened,
   I looked to left and right,

But nought there was a-stirring
  In the still dark night.
Only the busy beetle
  Tap-tapping in the wall,
Only from the forest
  The screech-owl's call,
Only the cricket whistling
  While the dewdrops fall,
So I know not who came knocking,
  At all, at all, at all.

Furry Bear

by A. A. Milne

If I were a bear,
  And a big bear too,
I shouldn't much care
  If it froze or snew;
I shouldn't much mind
  If it snowed or friz—
I'd be all fur-lined
  With a coat like his!

For I'd have fur boots and a brown fur wrap,
And brown fur knickers and a big fur cap.
I'd have a fur muffle-ruff to cover my jaws,
And brown fur mittens on my big brown paws.
With a big brown furry-down up to my head,
I'd sleep all the winter in a big fur bed.

At the Zoo

by A. A. Milne

There are lions and roaring tigers, and enormous
    camels and things,
There are biffalo-buffalo-bisons, and a great big bear
    with wings,
There's a sort of tiny potamus, and a tiny nosserus
    too—
But *I* gave buns to the elephant when *I* went down to
    the Zoo!

There are badgers and bidgers and bodgers, and a
    Superintendent's House,
There are masses of goats, and a Polar, and different
    kinds of mouse,
And I think there's a sort of something which is
    called a wallaboo—
But *I* gave buns to the elephant when *I* went down to
    the Zoo!

If you try to talk to the bison, he never quite
    understands;
You can't shake hands with a mingo—he doesn't like
    shaking hands.
And lions and roaring tigers *hate* saying , "How do
    you do?"—
But *I* give buns to the elephant when *I* go down to
    the Zoo!

The Owl and the Pussy-cat

by Edward Lear

The Owl and the Pussy-cat went to sea
   In a beautiful pea-green boat,
They took some honey, and plenty of money
   Wrapped up in a five-pound note.
The Owl looked up to the stars above,
   And sang to a small guitar,
"O lovely Pussy, O Pussy, my love,
   What a beautiful Pussy you are,
      You are,
      You are!
   What a beautiful Pussy you are!"

Pussy said to the Owl, "You elegant fowl,
　　How charmingly sweet you sing!
Oh! let us be married; too long we have tarried:
　　But what shall we do for a ring?"
They sailed away, for a year and a day,
　　To the land where the bong-tree grows;
And there in a wood a Piggy-wig stood,
　　With a ring at the end of his nose,
　　　　His nose,
　　　　His nose,
　　With a ring at the end of his nose.

"Dear Pig, are you willing to sell for one shilling
　　Your ring?" Said the Piggy, "I will."
So they took it away, and were married next day
　　By the Turkey who lives on the hill.
They dined on mince, and slices of quince,
　　Which they ate with a runcible spoon;
And hand in hand, on the edge of the sand,
　　They danced by the light of the moon,
　　　　The moon,
　　　　The moon,
　　They danced by the light of the moon.

The Duel

by Eugene Field

The gingham dog and the calico cat
Side by side on the table sat;
'T was half-past twelve, and (what do you think!)
Nor one nor t' other had slept a wink!
   The old Dutch clock and the Chinese plate
   Appeared to know as sure as fate
There was going to be a terrible spat.
     (I wasn't there; I simply state
     What was told to me by the Chinese plate!)

The gingham dog went, "bow-wow-wow!"
And the calico cat replied, "mee-ow!"
The air was littered, an hour or so,
With bits of gingham and calico,
   While the old Dutch clock in the chimney-place
   Up with its hands before its face,
For it always dreaded a family row!
     (Now mind: I'm only telling you
     What the old Dutch clock declares is true!)

The Chinese plate looked very blue,
And wailed, "Oh, dear! what shall we do!"
But the gingham dog and the calico cat
Wallowed this way and tumbled that,
   Employing every tooth and claw
   In the awfullest way you every saw—
And, oh! how the gingham and calico flew!

(Don't fancy I exaggerate—
I got my news from the Chinese plate!)

Next morning, where the two had sat
They found no trace of dog or cat;
And some folks think unto this day
That burglars stole that pair away!
 But the truth about the cat and pup
 Is this: they ate each other up!
Now what do you really think of that!
(The old Dutch clock it told me so,
And that is how I came to know.)

The Song of Mr. Toad

by Kenneth Grahame

The world has held great Heroes,
 As history-books have showed;
But never a name to go down in fame
 Compared with that of Toad!

The clever men at Oxford
 Know all that there is to be knowed.
But they none of them knew one half as much
 As intelligent Mr. Toad!

The animals sat in the Ark and cried;
 Their tears in torrents flowed.
Who was it said, "There's land ahead"?
 Encouraging Mr. Toad!

The Army all saluted
   As they marched along the road.
Was it the King? Or Kitchener?
   No. It was Mr. Toad!

The Queen and her Ladies-in-waiting
   Sat at the window and sewed.
She cried, "Look! who's that *handsome* man?"
   They answered, "Mr. Toad."

A Christmas Carol

by G. K. Chesterton

The Christ-child lay on Mary's lap,
His hair was like a light.
(O Weary, Weary were the world,
But here is all aright.)

The Christ-child lay on Mary's breast,
His hair was like a star.
(O stern and cunning are the Kings,
But here the true hearts are.)

The Christ-child lay on Mary's heart,
His hair was like a fire.
(O Weary, Weary is the world,
But here the world's desire.)

The Christ-child stood at Mary's knee,
His hair was like a crown,
And all the flowers looked up at Him,
And all the stars looked down.

Stopping by Woods on a Snowy Evening

by Robert Frost

Whose woods these are I think I know.
His house is in the village, though;
He will not see me stopping here
To watch his woods fill up with snow.

My little horse must think it queer
To stop without a farmhouse near
Between the woods and frozen lake
The darkest evening of the year.

He gives his harness bells a shake
To ask if there is some mistake.
The only other sound's the sweep
Of easy wind and downy flake.

The woods are lovely, dark, and deep,
But I have promises to keep,
And miles to go before I sleep,
And miles to go before I sleep.

Psalm 23

A Psalm of David

The LORD is my shepherd, I shall not want;
   he makes me lie down in green pastures.
He leads me beside still waters;
   he restores my soul.
He leads me in paths of righteousness
   for his name's sake.

Even though I walk through the valley of the
      shadow of death,
   I fear no evil;
for thou art with me;
   thy rod and thy staff,
   they comfort me.

Thou preparest a table before me
   in the presence of my enemies;
thou anointest my head with oil,
   my cup overflows.
Surely goodness and mercy shall follow me
   all the days of my life;
and I shall dwell in the house of the LORD
   for ever.

Psalm 100

A Psalm of David

Make a joyful noise to the LORD, all the lands!
  Serve the LORD with gladness!
  Come into his presence with singing!

Know that the LORD is God!
  It is he that made us, and we are his;
  we are his people, and the sheep of his pasture.

Enter his gates with thanksgiving,
  and his courts with praise!
Give thanks to him, bless his name!

For the LORD is good;
  his steadfast love endures for ever,
  and his faithfulness to all generations.

Our Brother Is Born

by Harry and Eleanor Farjeon

Now every child that dwells on earth,
Stand up, stand up and sing;
The passing night has given birth
Unto the children's king.
Sing sweet as the flute,
Sing clear as the horn,
Sing joy for the children,
Come Christmas morn:

  Little Christ Jesus
  Our brother is born.

BIBLE VERSES FOR MEMORIZATION AND DICTATION

To be used for memorization, penmanship, and reference

- Let us go to the house of the Lord! (Psalm 122:1).

  Thou dost show me the path of life; in thy presence there is fullness of joy, in thy right hand are pleasures for evermore (Psalm 16:11).

- The Lord is my shepherd (Psalm 23:1).

- Make me to know thy ways, O Lord; teach me thy paths (Psalm 25:4).

  One thing have I asked of the Lord, that will I seek after; that I may dwell in the house of the Lord all the days of my life (Psalm 27:4).

- How great are thy works, O Lord! (Psalm 92:5).

- Thy word is a lamp to my feet and a light to my path (Psalm 119:105).

- Let thy steadfast love, O Lord, be upon us, even as we hope in thee (Psalm 33:22).

  You will not fear the terror of the night, nor the arrow that flies by day, nor the pestilence that stalks in darkness, nor the destruction that wastes at noonday (Psalm 91:5–6).

  May he have dominion from sea to sea, and from the River to the ends of the earth! (Psalm 72:8)

  Be still, and know that I am God (Psalm 46:10).

It is a holy and wholesome thought to pray for the dead, that they may be loosed from their sins (2 Maccabees 12:46, Douay-Rheims Version).

For God alone my soul waits in silence; from him comes my salvation (Psalm 62:1).

O God, come to my assistance; O Lord, make haste to help me (Psalm 69:1, Douay-Rheims Version).

They who wait for the Lord shall renew their strength (Isaiah 40:31).

I will satisfy the weary soul, and every languishing soul I will replenish (Jeremiah 31:25).

My presence will go with you, and I will give you rest (Exodus 33:14).

May the God of hope fill you with all joy and peace in believing, so that by the power of the Holy Spirit you may abound in hope (Romans 15:13).

I will sing of thy might; I will sing aloud of thy steadfast love in the morning (Psalm 59:16).

A tranquil mind gives life to the flesh (Proverbs 14:30).

And the peace of God, which passes all understanding, will keep your hearts and your minds in Christ Jesus (Philippians 4:7).

All that the Lord has spoken we will do, and we will be obedient (Exodus 24:7).

The wise man also may hear and increase in learning, and the man of understanding acquire skill (Proverbs 1:5).

Children, obey your parents in everything, for this pleases the Lord (Colossians 3:20).

It is good to give thanks to the Lord (Psalm 92:1).

DICTATION SELECTIONS

From *American Cardinal Readers*, volume one

1. It was morning. It was time for Father to go to his work.

2. Jean worked hard that day getting the surprise ready.

3. John helped her all he could. Sometimes Mother had to help her.

4. Long ago there lived some wise men. They were good men who loved God above all things.

5. God's promise was that a King should be born.

6. This King was to rule over all people. He was to help the people love and obey God in all ways.

7. One night the wise men were watching the stars.

8. It was near the time God said the King should come.

9. So the wise men got ready to go in search of the new-born King.

10. Mother said, "God forgives us when we tell Him we are sorry for not doing as He wishes us to do."

11. Joseph said, "I have a big brother who could put out your big flag. Shall I run home for him?

From *The Angels' Alphabet, by Hilda van Stockum*

B IS FOR BALAAM'S ASS

12. When Balaam went to prophesy
    An angel barred the way
    And Balaam's donkey balked the reins—
    He could no more obey.

13. He could no more, he would no more
    His master's blows in spite
    Who, blind and angry, failed to guess
    What caused the donkey's fright.

14. And so the prophet Balaam
    For all he was so wise
    Missed what was plainly visible
    To a little donkey's eyes.

15. O little donkeys everywhere
    Cheer up—if you are kind
    You may behold what all the wise
    Have vainly tried to find.

E IS FOR ETERNITY

16. My days are round as pennies
    And roll as merrily
    And they are all the wealth I need
    To win Eternity.

17. But then I'll have to polish them
    And keep them free from sin
    For if my days are grubby
    Saint Peter won't let me in.

18. Perhaps I'll even have enough
    To help another boy
    Who may have wasted all his days
    Upon a silly toy.

19. I'll ask Saint Peter at the gate:
    "Please, will you let him through?
    I know he hasn't much to show,
    But I've enough for two!"

J IS FOR JACOB'S LADDER

20. The sun had gone down
    And stars were peeping
    Over the head
    Of Jacob sleeping.

21. Who saw a ladder
    Raised to God
    And up and down it
    Angels trod,

22. While God Himself
    On the ladder leant
    Talking to Jacob's
    Wonderment.

23. And Jacob, listening,
    Dimly guessed
    How his offspring
    Would be blessed.

24. Dimly guessed, for
    From afar
    He could see the
    Christmas Star.

From "O is for Obedience"

25. Is there no way for us at all
    To be holy when we're small?

26. Yes, in God's eyes it's purest gold
    Always to do as you are told
    Nor poutingly or in a rage
    But like God's loving little page.

From *The Fussy Angel*, by Mary Arnold

27. "Blow out your lanterns," he ordered the shepherds. "The baby needs some sleep."

28. The angel strode outside again:—"No, no, no! Brother angels, have pity on him. He's a human and he needs his sleep. Turn the volume down!"

From *American Cardinal Readers*, volume two

29. Every day Robert went to this town to sell the little cakes his mother made. Sometimes he took fresh eggs to sell, too.

30. "This is not my ax head," he said. "It is finer than the one I lost. This one is made of silver. Mine was made of steel."

31. The king's friends tried the riddles, but they could not guess them. The king's servants could not guess them. People came from near and far to hear the riddles. When they had heard them, they could not guess them.

32. "You have all seen the bell in the market place. I have had it placed there to help you. You are to ring it whenever any wrong is done to you. Then I shall come to the market place and have the wrong made right."

The Grammatical Stage

POETRY SELECTIONS

The Flag Goes By
by Henry Holcomb Bennett

Hats off!
Along the street there comes
A blare of bugles, a ruffle of drums,
A flash of color beneath the sky:
    Hats off!
The flag is passing by!

Blue and crimson and white it shines,
Over the steel-tipped, ordered lines.
    Hats off!
The colors before us fly;
But more than the flag is passing by.

Sea-fights and land-fights, grim and great,
Fought to make and to save the State:
Weary marches and sinking ships;
Cheers of victory on dying lips;

Days of plenty and years of peace;
March of a strong land's swift increase;
Equal justice, right and law,
Stately honor and reverend awe;

Sign of a nation, great and strong
To ward her people from foreign wrong:

Pride and glory and honor,—all
Live in the colors to stand or fall.

   Hats off!
Along the street there comes
A blare of bugles, a ruffle of drums;
And loyal hearts are beating high:
   Hats off!
The flag is passing by!

The Children's Hour

by Henry Wadsworth Longfellow

Between the dark and the daylight,
   When the light is beginning to lower,
Comes a pause in the day's occupations
   That is known as the Children's Hour.

I hear in the chamber above me
   The patter of little feet,
The sound of a door that is opened,
   And voices soft and sweet.

From my study I see in the lamplight,
   Descending the broad hall stair,
Grave Alice and laughing Allegra,
   And Edith with golden hair.

A whisper, and then a silence;
   Yet I know by their merry eyes,
They are plotting and planning together
   To take me by surprise.

A sudden rush from the stairway,
    A sudden raid from the hall!
By three doors left unguarded
    They enter my castle wall!

They climb up into my turret,
    O'er the arms and back of my chair;
If I try to escape, they surround me;
    They seem to be everywhere.

They almost devour me with kisses,
    Their arms about me entwine,
Till I think of the Bishop of Bingen
    In his Mouse Tower on the Rhine.

Do you think, O blue-eyed banditti,
    Because you have scaled the wall,
Such an old mustache as I am
    Is not a match for you all?

I have you fast in my fortress,
    And will not let you depart,
But put you down into the dungeon
    In the round-tower of my heart.

And there will I keep you forever,
    Yes, forever and a day,
Till the wall shall crumble to ruin,
    And moulder in dust away!

The Village Blacksmith

by Henry Wadsworth Longfellow

Under a spreading chestnut-tree
    The village smithy stands;
The smith, a mighty man is he,
    With large and sinewy hands;
And the muscles of his brawny arms
    Are strong as iron bands.

His hair is crisp and black and long;
    His face is like the tan;
His brow is wet with honest sweat,—
    He earns whate'er he can;
And looks the whole world in the face,
    For he owes not any man.

Week in, week out, from morn till night,
    You can hear his bellows blow;
You can hear him swing his heavy sledge,
    With measured beat and slow,
Like a sexton ringing the village bell
    When the evening sun is low.

And children, coming home from school,
    Look in at the open door;
They love to see the flaming forge,
    And hear the bellows roar,
And catch the burning sparks that fly
    Like chaff from a threshing-floor.

He goes on Sunday to the church,
    And sits among his boys;
He hears the parson pray and preach,

He hears his daughter's voice,
Singing in the village choir,
    And it makes his heart rejoice.

It sounds to him like her mother's voice
    Singing in Paradise!
He needs must think of her once more,
    How in the grave she lies;
And with his hard, rough hand he wipes
    A tear out of his eyes.

Toiling, rejoicing, sorrowing,
    Onward through life he goes;
Each morning sees some task begin,
    Each evening sees it close;
Something attempted, something done,
    Has earned a night's repose.

Thanks, thanks to thee, my worthy friend,
    For the lesson thou hast taught!
Thus at the flaming forge of life
    Our fortunes must be wrought;
Thus on its sounding anvil shaped
    Each burning deed and thought.

Christmas Bells

by Henry Wadsworth Longfellow

I heard the bells on Christmas Day
Their old, familiar carols play,
        And wild and sweet
        The words repeat
Of peace on earth, good-will to men!

And thought how, as the day had come,
The belfries of all Christendom
    Had rolled along
    The unbroken song
Of peace on earth, good-will to men!

Till, ringing, singing on its way,
The world revolved from night to day,
    A voice, a chime,
    A chant sublime
Of peace on earth, good-will to men!

Then from the black, accursèd mouth
The cannon thundered in the South,
    And with the sound
    The carols drowned
Of peace on earth, good-will to men!

It was as if an earthquake rent
The hearth stones of a continent,
    And made forlorn
    The households born
Of peace on earth, good-will to men!

And in despair I bowed my head;
"There is no peace on earth," I said;
    "For hate is strong,
    And mocks the song
Of peace on earth, good-will to men!"

Then pealed the bells more loud and deep:
"God is not dead; nor doth He sleep!
    The Wrong shall fail,
    The Right prevail,
With peace on earth, good-will to men!"

The Tide Rises, the Tide Falls

by Henry Wadsworth Longfellow

The tide rises, the tide falls,
The twilight darkens, the curlew calls;
Along the sea-sands damp and brown
The traveler hastens toward the town,
    And the tide rises, the tide falls.

Darkness settles on roofs and walls,
But the sea, the sea in darkness calls;
The little waves, with their soft, white hands,
Efface the footprints in the sands,
    And the tide rises, the tide falls.

The morning breaks; the steeds in their stalls
Stamp and neigh, as the hostler calls;
The day returns, but nevermore
Returns the traveler to the shore.
    And the tide rises, the tide falls.

Casey at the Bat

by Ernest Lawrence Thayer

It looked extremely rocky for the Mudville nine that day,
The score stood four to six with but an inning left to play.
And so, when Cooney died at first, and Burrows did the same,
A pallor wreathed the features of the patrons of the game.

A straggling few got up to go, leaving there the rest,
With the hope which springs eternal within the human breast.
For they thought if only Casey could get a whack at that,
They'd put up even money now, with Casey at the bat.

But Flynn preceded Casey, and likewise so did Blake,
And the former was a pudding, and the latter was a fake;
So on that stricken multitude a death-like silence sat,
For there seemed but little chance of Casey's getting to the bat.

But Flynn let drive a single to the wonderment of all,
And the much-despised Blakey tore the cover off the ball,
And when the dust had lifted and they saw what had occurred,
There was Blakey safe on second, and Flynn a-hugging third.

Then from the gladdened multitude went up a joyous yell—
It bounded from the mountaintop and rattled in the dell,
It struck upon the hillside, and rebounded on the flat,
For Casey, mighty Casey, was advancing to the bat.

There was ease in Casey's manner as he stepped into his place,
There was pride in Casey's bearing and a smile on Casey's face,
And when responding to the cheers he lightly doffed his hat,
No stranger in the crowd could doubt 'twas Casey at the bat.

Ten thousand eyes were on him as he rubbed his hands with
    dirt,
Five thousand tongues applauded as he wiped them on his
    shirt;
And while the writhing pitcher ground the ball into his hip—
Defiance gleamed from Casey's eye—a sneer curled Casey's
    lip.

And now the leather-covered sphere came hurtling through
    the air,
And Casey stood a-watching it in haughty grandeur there;
Close by the sturdy batsman the ball unheeded sped—
"That ain't my style," said Casey—"Strike one," the umpire
    said.

From the bleachers black with people there went up a muffled
    roar,
Like the beating of the storm waves on a stern and distant
    shore.
"Kill him! kill the umpire!" shouted some one from the
    stand—
And it's likely they'd have done it had not Casey raised his
    hand.

With a smile of Christian charity great Casey's visage shone,
He stilled the rising tumult and he bade the game go on;
He signaled to the pitcher and once more the spheroid flew,
But Casey still ignored it and the umpire said, "Strike two."

"Fraud!" cried the maddened thousands, and the echo answered, "Fraud,"
But one scornful look from Casey and the audience was awed;
They saw his face grow stern and cold; they saw his muscles strain,
And they knew that Casey would not let that ball go by again.

The sneer is gone from Casey's lip; his teeth are clenched in hate,
He pounds with cruel violence his bat upon the plate;
And now the pitcher holds the ball, and now he lets it go,
And now the air is shattered by the force of Casey's blow.

Oh! somewhere in this favored land the sun is shining bright,
The band is playing somewhere, and somewhere hearts are light,
And somewhere men are laughing, and somewhere children shout;
But there is no joy in Mudville— mighty Casey has "Struck out."

Old Ironsides

by Oliver Wendell Holmes

Ay, tear her tattered ensign down!
  Long has it waved on high,
And many an eye has danced to see
  That banner in the sky;
Beneath it rung the battle-shout,
  And burst the cannon's roar:
The meteor of the ocean air
  Shall sweep the clouds no more!

Her deck, once red with heroes' blood,
    Where knelt the vanquished foe,
When winds were hurrying o'er the flood
    And waves were white below,
No more shall feel the victor's tread,
    Or know the conquered knee:
The harpies of the shore shall pluck
    The eagle of the sea!

O better that her shattered hulk
    Should sink beneath the wave!
Her thunders shook the mighty deep,
    And there should be her grave:
Nail to the mast her holy flag,
    Set every threadbare sail,
And give her to the god of storms,
    The lightning and the gale!

Hiawatha's Childhood
by Henry Wadsworth Longfellow

By the shores of Gitche Gumee,
By the shining Big-Sea-Water,
Stood the wigwam of Nokomis,
Daughter of the Moon, Nokomis.
Dark behind it rose the forest,
Rose the black and gloomy pine-trees,
Rose the firs with cones upon them;
Bright before it beat the water,
Beat the clear and sunny water,
Beat the shining Big-Sea-Water.
    There the wrinkled old Nokomis
Nursed the little Hiawatha,

Rocked him in his linden cradle,
Bedded soft in moss and rushes,
Safely bound with reindeer sinews;
Stilled his fretful wail by saying,
"Hush! the Naked Bear will hear thee!"
Lulled him into slumber, singing,
"Ewa-yea! my little owlet!
Who is this, that lights the wigwam?
With his great eyes lights the wigwam?
Ewa-yea! my little owlet!"
    Many things Nokomis taught him
Of the stars that shine in heaven;
Showed him Ishkoodah, the comet,
Ishkoodah, with fiery tresses;
Showed the Death-Dance of the spirits,
Warriors with their plumes and war-clubs,
Flaring far away to northward
In the frosty nights of Winter;
Showed the broad, white road in heaven,
Pathway of the ghosts, the shadows,
Running straight across the heavens,
Crowded with the ghosts, the shadows.
    At the door on Summer evenings
Sat the little Hiawatha;
Heard the whispering of the pine-trees,
Heard the lapping of the water,
Sounds of music, words of wonder;
"Minne-wawa!" said the pine-trees,
"Mudway-aushka!" said the water.
    Saw the fire-fly, Wah-wah-taysee,
Flitting through the dusk of evening,
With the twinkle of its candle
Lighting up the brakes and bushes,
And he sang the song of children,

Sang the song Nokomis taught him:
"Wah-wah-taysee, little fire-fly,
Little, flitting, white-fire insect,
Little, dancing, white-fire creature,
Light me with your little candle,
Ere upon my bed I lay me,
Ere in sleep I close my eyelids!"
    Saw the moon rise from the water,
Rippling, rounding from the water,
Saw the flecks and shadows on it,
Whispered, "What is that, Nokomis?"
And the good Nokomis answered:
    "Once a warrior, very angry,
Seized his grandmother, and threw her
Up into the sky at midnight;
Right against the moon he threw her;
'T is her body that you see there."
    Saw the rainbow in the heaven,
In the eastern sky, the rainbow,
Whispered, "What is that, Nokomis?"
And the good Nokomis answered:
" 'T is the heaven of flowers you see there;
All the wild-flowers of the forest,
All the lilies of the prairie,
When on earth they fade and perish,
Blossom in that heaven above us."

When he heard the owls at midnight,
Hooting, laughing in the forest,
"What is that?" he cried in terror;
"What is that?" he said, "Nokomis?"
And the good Nokomis answered:
"That is but the owl and owlet,
Talking in their native language,
Talking, scolding at each other."
Then the little Hiawatha
Learned of every bird its language,
Learned their names and all their secrets,
How they built their nests in Summer,
Where they hid themselves in Winter,
Talked with them whene'er he met them,
Called them "Hiawatha's Chickens."
Of all beasts he learned the language,
Learned their names and all their secrets,
How the beavers built their lodges,
Where the squirrels hid their acorns,
How the reindeer ran so swiftly,
Why the rabbit was so timid,
Talked with them whene'er he met them,
Called them "Hiawatha's Brothers."

Ye who love a nation's legends,
Love the ballads of a people,
That the voices from afar off
Call to us to pause and listen,
Speak in tones so plain and childlike,
Scarcely can the ear distinguish
Whether they are sung or spoken;—
Listen to this Indian Legend,
To this Song of Hiawatha!

The Grammatical Stage: Poetry Selections

Columbus

by Joaquin Miller

Behind him lay the gray Azores,
    Behind the Gates of Hercules;
Before him not the ghost of shores,
    Before him only shoreless seas.
The good mate said: "Now must we pray,
    For lo! the very stars are gone.
Brave Adm'r'l, speak, what shall I say?"
      "Why, say: 'Sail on! sail on! and on!' "

"My men grow mutinous day by day;
    My men grow ghastly wan and weak."
The stout mate thought of home; a spray
    Of salt wave washed his swarthy cheek.
"What shall I say, brave Adm'r'l, say
    If we sight naught but seas at dawn?"
"Why, you shall say, at break of day:
      'Sail on! sail on! sail on! and on!' "

They sailed and sailed, as winds might blow,
    Until at last the blanched mate said:
"Why, now not even God would know
    Should I and all my men fall dead.
These very winds forget their way,
    For God from these dread seas is gone.
Now speak, brave Adm'r'l; speak and say"—
    He said: "Sail on! sail on! and on!"

They sailed. They sailed. Then spake the mate:
    "This mad sea shows his teeth to-night;
He curls his lips, he lies in wait,
    With lifted teeth, as if to bite:

Brave Adm'r'l, say but one good word;
　　What shall we do when hope is gone?"
The words leapt like a leaping sword:
　　"Sail on! sail on! sail on! and on!"

Then pale and worn, he kept his deck,
　　And peered through darkness. Ah, that night
Of all dark nights! And then a speck—
　　A light! a light! a light! a light!
It grew, a starlit flag unfurled!
　　It grew to be Time's burst of dawn.
He gained a world; he gave that world
　　Its grandest lesson: "On! sail on!"

America for Me

by Henry Van Dyke

'Tis fine to see the Old World, and travel up and down
Among the famous palaces and cities of renown,
To admire the crumbly castles and the statues of the kings,—
But now I think I've had enough of antiquated things.

So it's home again, and home again, America for me!
My heart is turning home again, and there I long to be,
In the land of youth and freedom beyond the ocean bars,
Where the air is full of sunlight and the flag is full of stars.

Oh, London is a man's town, there's power in the air;
And Paris is a woman's town, with flowers in her hair;
And it's sweet to dream in Venice, and it's great to study
　　Rome;
But when it comes to living there is no place like home.

I like the German fir-woods, in green battalions drilled;
I like the gardens of Versailles with flashing fountains filled;

But, oh, to take your hand, my dear, and ramble for a day
In the friendly western woodland where Nature has her way!

I know that Europe's wonderful, yet something seems to lack:
The Past is too much with her, and the people looking back.
But the glory of the Present is to make the Future free,—
We love our land for what she is and what she is to be.

Oh, it's home again, and home again, America for me!
I want a ship that's westward bound to plough the rolling sea,
To the blessed Land of Room Enough beyond the ocean bars,
Where the air is full of sunlight and the flag is full of stars.

Sea Fever

by John Masefield

I must go down to the seas again, to the lonely sea and the sky,
And all I ask is a tall ship and a star to steer her by;
And the wheel's kick and the wind's song and the white sail's
    shaking,
And a grey mist on the sea's face, and a grey dawn breaking.

I must go down to the seas again, for the call of the running
    tide
Is a wild call, and a clear call that may not be denied;
And all I ask is a windy day with the white clouds flying,
And the flung spray and the blown spume, and the sea-gulls
    crying.

I must go down to the seas again, to the vagrant gypsy life,
To the gull's way and the whale's way, where the wind's like a
    whetted knife;
And all I ask is a merry yarn from a laughing fellow-rover,
And quiet sleep and a sweet dream when the long trick's over.

Christmas Everywhere

by Phillips Brooks

Everywhere, everywhere, Christmas tonight!
Christmas in lands of the fir-tree and pine,
Christmas in lands of the palm-tree and vine,
Christmas where snow peaks stand solemn and white,
Christmas where cornfields stand sunny and bright.
Christmas where children are hopeful and gay,
Christmas where old men are patient and gray,
Christmas where peace, like a dove in his flight,
Broods o'er brave men in the thick of the fight;
Everywhere, everywhere, Christmas tonight!

For the Christ-child who comes is the Master of all;
No palace too great, no cottage too small.

The Fool's Prayer

by Edward Rowland Sill

The royal feast was done; the King
    Sought some new sport to banish care,
And to his jester cried: "Sir Fool,
    Kneel now, and make for us a prayer!"

The jester doffed his cap and bells,
    And stood the mocking court before;
They could not see the bitter smile
    Behind the painted grin he wore.

He bowed his head, and bent his knee
    Upon the monarch's silken stool;
His pleading voice arose: "O Lord,
    Be merciful to me, a fool!

The Grammatical Stage: Poetry Selections

"No pity, Lord, could change the heart
   From red with wrong to white as wool;
The rod must heal the sin: but, Lord,
   Be merciful to me, a fool!

" 'T is not by guilt the onward sweep
   Of truth and right, O Lord, we stay;
'T is by our follies that so long
   We hold the earth from heaven away.

"These clumsy feet, still in the mire,
   Go crushing blossoms without end;
These hard, well-meaning hands we thrust
   Among the heart-strings of a friend.

"The ill-timed truth we might have kept—
   Who knows how sharp it pierced and stung!
The word we had not sense to say—
   Who knows how grandly it had rung!

"Our faults no tenderness should ask,
   The chastening stripes must cleanse them all;
But for our blunders—oh, in shame
   Before the eyes of heaven we fall.

"Earth bears no balsam for mistakes;
   Men crown the knave, and scourge the tool
That did his will; but Thou, O Lord,
   Be merciful to me, a fool!"

The room was hushed; in silence rose
   The King, and sought his gardens cool,
And walked apart, and murmured low,
   "Be merciful to me, a fool!"

The Bells

by Edgar Allan Poe

Hear the sledges with the bells—
Silver bells!
What a world of merriment their melody foretells!
How they tinkle, tinkle, tinkle,
In the icy air of night!
While the stars that oversprinkle
All the heavens, seem to twinkle
With a crystalline delight;
Keeping time, time, time,
In a sort of Runic rhyme,
To the tintinnabulation that so musically wells
From the bells, bells, bells, bells,
Bells, bells, bells,—
From the jingling and the tinkling of the bells.

Hear the mellow wedding bells,
Golden bells!
What a world of happiness their harmony foretells!
Through the balmy air of night
How they ring out their delight!
From the molten-golden notes,
And all in tune,
What a liquid ditty floats
To the turtle dove that listens, while she gloats
On the moon!
Oh, from out the sounding cells,
What a gush of euphony voluminously wells!
How it swells!
How it dwells
On the Future! how it tells
Of the rapture that impels

To the swinging and the ringing
  Of the bells, bells, bells,
  Of the bells, bells, bells, bells,
    Bells, bells, bells,—
To the rhyming and the chiming of the bells!

  Hear the loud alarum bells—
    Brazen bells!
What a tale of terror now their turbulency tells!
  In the startled ear of night
  How they scream out their affright!
  Too much horrified to speak
  They can only shriek, shriek,
    Out of tune,
In a clamorous appealing to the mercy of the fire,
In a mad expostulation with the deaf and frantic fire,
  Leaping higher, higher, higher,
  With a desperate desire,
    And a resolute endeavor,
    Now—now to sit or never,
  By the side of the pale-faced moon.
    Oh, the bells, bells, bells!
    What a tale their terror tells
        Of despair!
  How they clang, and clash, and roar!
  What a horror they outpour
On the bosom of the palpitating air!
  Yet the ear it fully knows,
    By the twanging,
    And the clanging,
  How the danger ebbs and flows;
  Yet the ear distinctly tells,
    In the jangling,
    And the wrangling,

How the danger sinks and swells,
By the sinking or the swelling in the anger of the bells—
Of the bells—
Of the bells, bells, bells, bells,
Bells, bells, bells,—
In the clamor and the clangor of the bells!

Hear the tolling of the bells—
Iron bells!
What a world of solemn thought their monody compels!
In the silence of the night,
How we shiver with affright
At the melancholy menace of their tone!
For every sound that floats
From the rust within their throats
Is a groan.
And the people—ah, the people—
They that dwell up in the steeple,
All alone,
And who tolling, tolling, tolling,
In that muffled monotone,
Feel a glory in so rolling
On the human heart a stone—
They are neither man nor woman—
They are neither brute nor human—
They are Ghouls:
And their king it is who tolls;
And he rolls, rolls, rolls,
Rolls
A paean from the bells!
And his merry bosom swells
With the paean of the bells!
And he dances, and he yells;
Keeping time, time, time,

In a sort of Runic rhyme,
  To the paean of the bells—
    Of the bells:
Keeping time, time, time,
In a sort of Runic rhyme,
  To the throbbing of the bells—
    Of the bells, bells, bells,—
  To the sobbing of the bells;
Keeping time, time, time,
      As he knells, knells, knells,
In a happy Runic rhyme,
    To the rolling of the bells—
Of the bells, bells, bells—
    To the tolling of the bells,
Of the bells, bells, bells, bells—
    Bells, bells, bells—
To the moaning and the groaning of the bells!

Spring

(From *In Memoriam*)

by Alfred Lord Tennyson

LXXXIII

Dip down upon the northern shore,
  O sweet new-year, delaying long:
  Thou doest expectant Nature wrong;
Delaying long, delay no more.

What stays thee from the clouded noons,
  Thy sweetness from its proper place?
  Can trouble live with April days,
Or sadness in the summer moons?

Bring orchis, bring the foxglove spire,
    The little speedwell's darling blue,
    Deep tulips dashed with fiery dew,
Laburnums, dropping-wells of fire.

O thou, new-year, delaying long,
    Delayest the sorrow in my blood,
    That longs to burst a frozen bud,
And flood a fresher throat with song.

CVX

Now fades the last long streak of snow;
    Now bourgeons every maze of quick
    About the flowering squares, and thick
By ashen roots the violets blow.

Now rings the woodland loud and long,
    The distance takes a lovelier hue,
    And drowned in yonder living blue
The lark becomes a sightless song.

Now dance the lights on lawn and lea,
    The flocks are whiter down the vale,
    And milkier every milky sail,
On winding stream to distant sea;

Where now the seamew pipes, or dives
    In yonder greening gleam, and fly
    The happy birds, that change their sky
To build and brood, that live their lives

From land to land; and in my breast
    Spring wakens too; and my regret
    Becomes an April violet,
And buds and blossoms like the rest.

Requiem

by Robert Louis Stevenson

Under the wide and starry sky
Dig the grave and let me lie.
Glad did I live and gladly die,
     And I laid me down with a will.
This be the verse you grave for me:
Here he lies where he longed to be;
Home is the sailor, home from the sea,
     And the hunter home from the hill.

Captain Kidd

by Stephen Vincent Benét

This person in the gaudy clothes
Is worthy Captain Kidd.
They say he never buried gold.
I think, perhaps, he did.

They say it's all a story that
His favorite little song
Was "Make these lubbers walk the plank!"
I think, perhaps, they're wrong.

They say he never pirated
Beneath the Skull-and-Bones.
He merely traveled for his health
And spoke in soothing tones.
In fact, you'll read in nearly all
The newer history books
That he was mild as cottage cheese
—But I don't like his looks!

Christopher Columbus

by Stephen Vincent Benét

There are lots of queer things that discoverers do
But his was the queerest, I swear.
He discovered our country in One Four Nine Two
By thinking it couldn't be there.

It wasn't his folly, it wasn't his fault,
For the very best maps of the day
Showed nothing but water, extensive and salt,
On the West, between Spain and Bombay.

There were monsters, of course, every watery mile,
Great krakens with blubbery lips
And sea-serpents smiling a crocodile-smile
As they waited for poor little ships.

There were whirlpools and maelstroms, without any doubt
And tornadoes of lava and ink.
(Which, as nobody yet had been there to find out,
Seems a little bit odd, don't you think?)

But Columbus was bold and Columbus set sail
(Thanks to Queen Isabella, her pelf),
For he said, "Though there may be both monster and gale,
I'd like to find out for myself."

And he sailed and he sailed and he *sailed* and he SAILED,
Though his crew would have gladly turned round
And, morning and evening, distressfully wailed
"This is running things into the ground!"

The Grammatical Stage: Poetry Selections

But he paid no attention to protest or squall,
This obstinate son of the mast,
And so, in the end, he discovered us all,
Remarking, "Here's India, at last!"

He didn't intend it, he meant to heave to
At Calcutta, Rangoon, or Shanghai,
There are many queer things that discoverers do.
But his was the queerest. Oh my!

Pocahontas

by Rosemary Carr Benét

Princess Pocahontas,
Powhatan's daughter,
Stared at the white men
Come across the water.

She was like a wild deer
Or a bright, plumed bird,
Ready then to flash away
At one harsh word.

When the faces answered hers,
Paler yet, but smiling,
Pocahontas looked and looked,
Found them quite beguiling.

Liked the whites and trusted them,
Spite of kin and kith,
Fed and protected
Captain John Smith.

Pocahontas was revered
By each and every one.
She married John Rolfe
She had a Rolfe son.

She crossed the sea to London Town.
And must have found it queer,
To be Lady Rebecca
And the toast of the year.

"La Belle Sauvage! La Belle Sauvage!
Our nonpareil is she!"
But Princess Pocahontas
Gazed sadly toward the sea.

They gave her silks and furbelows.
She pined, as wild things do
And, when she died at Gravesend
She was only twenty-two.

Poor wild bird—
No one can be blamed.
But gentle Pocahontas
Was a wild thing tamed.

And everywhere the lesson runs,
All through the ages:
Wild things die
In the very finest cages.

George Washington
by Stephen Vincent Benét

Sing hey! for bold George Washington,
That jolly British tar,
King George's famous admiral
From Hull to Zanzibar!
No—wait a minute—something's wrong—
George *wished* to sail the foam.
But, when his mother thought, aghast,
Of Georgie shinning up a mast,
Her tears and protests flowed so fast
That George remained at home.

Sing ho! for grave George Washington,
The staid Virginia squire,
Who farms his fields and hunts his hounds
And aims at nothing higher!
Stop, stop, it's going wrong again!
George *liked* to live on farms,
But, when the Colonies agreed
They could and should and would be freed,
They called on George to do the deed
And George cried "Shoulder arms!"

Sing ha! for Emperor Washington,
That hero of renown,
Who freed his land from Britain's rule
To win a golden crown!
No, no, that's what George *might* have won
But didn't, for he said,
"There's not much point about a king,
They're pretty but they're apt to sting
And, as for crowns—the heavy thing
Would only hurt my head."

Sing ho! for our George Washington!
(At last I've got it straight.)
The first in war, the first in peace,
The goodly and the great.
But, when you think about him now,
From here to Valley Forge,
Remember this—he might have been
A highly different specimen,
And, where on earth would we be, then?
I'm glad that George was George.

The Grammatical Stage: Poetry Selections

Benjamin Franklin
by Stephen Vincent Benét

Ben Franklin munched a loaf of bread while walking down
    the street
And all the Philadelphia girls tee-heed to see him eat,
A country boy come up to town with eyes as big as saucers
At the ladies in their furbelows, the gempmun on their horses.

Ben Franklin wrote an almanac, a smile upon his lip,
It told you when to plant your corn and how to cure the pip,
But he salted it and seasoned it with proverbs sly and sage,
And the people read "Poor Richard" till Poor Richard was
    the rage.

Ben Franklin made a pretty kite and flew it in the air
To call upon a thunderstorm that happened to be there,

—And all our humming dynamos and our electric light
Go back to what Ben Franklin found, the day he flew his kite.

Ben Franklin was the sort of man that people like to see,
For he was very clever but as human as could be.
He had an eye for pretty girls, a palate for good wine,
And all the court of France were glad to ask him in to dine.

But it didn't make him stuffy and he wasn't spoiled by fame
But stayed Ben Franklin to the end, as Yankee as his name.
"He wrenched their might from tyrants and its lightning from
    the sky."
And oh, when he saw pretty girls, he had a taking eye!

The Ballad of William Sycamore
(1790–1871)
by Stephen Vincent Benét

My father, he was a mountaineer,
His fist was a knotty hammer;
He was quick on his feet as a running deer,
And he spoke with a Yankee stammer.

My mother, she was merry and brave,
And so she came to her labor,
With a tall green fir for her doctor grave
And a stream for her comforting neighbor.

And some are wrapped in the linen fine,
And some like a godling's scion;
But I was cradled on twigs of pine
In the skin of a mountain lion.

The Grammatical Stage: Poetry Selections

And some remember a white, starched lap
And a ewer with silver handles;
But I remember a coonskin cap
And the smell of bayberry candles.

The cabin logs, with the bark still rough,
And my mother who laughed at trifles,
And the tall, lank visitors, brown as snuff,
With their long, straight squirrel-rifles.

I can hear them dance, like a foggy song,
Through the deepest one of my slumbers,
The fiddle squeaking the boots along
And my father calling the numbers.

The quick feet shaking the puncheon-floor,
And the fiddle squealing and squealing,
Till the dried herbs rattled above the door
And the dust went up to the ceiling.

There are children lucky from dawn till dusk,
But never a child so lucky!
For I cut my teeth on "Money Musk"
In the Bloody Ground of Kentucky!

When I grew tall as the Indian corn,
My father had little to lend me,
But he gave me his great, old powder-horn
And his woodsman's skill to befriend me.

With a leather shirt to cover my back,
And a redskin nose to unravel
Each forest sign, I carried my pack
As far as a scout could travel.

Till I lost my boyhood and found my wife,
A girl like a Salem clipper!
A woman straight as a hunting-knife
With eyes as bright as the Dipper!

We cleared our camp where the buffalo feed,
Unheard-of streams were our flagons;
And I sowed my sons like the apple-seed
On the trail of the Western wagons.

They were right, tight boys, never sulky or slow,
A fruitful, a goodly muster.
The eldest died at the Alamo.
The youngest fell with Custer.

The letter that told it burned my hand.
Yet we smiled and said, "So be it!"
But I could not live when they fenced the land,
For it broke my heart to see it.

I saddled a red, unbroken colt
And rode him into the day there;
And he threw me down like a thunderbolt
And rolled on me as I lay there.

The hunter's whistle hummed in my ear
As the city-men tried to move me,
And I died in my boots like a pioneer
With the whole wide sky above me.

Now I lie in the heart of the fat, black soil,
Like the seed of a prairie-thistle;
It has washed my bones with honey and oil
And picked them clean as a whistle.

And my youth returns, like the rains of Spring,
And my sons, like the wild-geese flying;
And I lie and hear the meadow-lark sing
And have much content in my dying.

Go play with the towns you have built of blocks,
The towns where you would have bound me!
I sleep in my earth like a tired fox,
And my buffalo have found me.

Concord Hymn
by Ralph Waldo Emerson

By the rude bridge that arched the flood,
   Their flag to April's breeze unfurled,
Here once the embattled farmers stood
   And fired the shot heard round the world.

The foe long since in silence slept;
   Alike the conqueror silent sleeps;
And Time the ruined bridge has swept
   Down the dark stream which seaward creeps.

On this green bank, by this soft stream,
   We set to-day a votive stone;
That memory may their deed redeem,
   When, like our sires, our sons are gone.

Spirit, that made those heroes dare
   To die, and leave their children free,
Bid Time and Nature gently spare
   The shaft we raise to them and thee.

Paul Revere's Ride

by Henry Wadsworth Longfellow

Listen, my children, and you shall hear
Of the midnight ride of Paul Revere,
On the eighteenth of April, in Seventy-five;
Hardly a man is now alive
Who remembers that famous day and year.

He said to his friend, "If the British march
By land or sea from the town to-night,
Hang a lantern aloft in the belfry arch
Of the North Church tower as a signal light,—
One if by land, and two if by sea;
And I on the opposite shore will be,
Ready to ride and spread the alarm
Through every Middlesex village and farm,
For the country folk to be up and to arm."

Then he said, "Good-night!" and with muffled oar
Silently rowed to the Charlestown shore,
Just as the moon rose over the bay,
Where swinging wide at her moorings lay
The *Somerset*, British man-of-war;
A phantom ship, with each mast and spar
Across the moon like a prison bar,
And a huge black hulk, that was magnified
By its own reflection in the tide.

Meanwhile, his friend through alley and street
Wanders and watches, with eager ears,
Till in the silence around him he hears
The muster of men at the barrack door,
The sound of arms, and the tramp of feet,

And the measured tread of the grenadiers,
Marching down to their boats on the shore.

Then he climbed the tower of the Old North Church,
By the wooden stairs, with stealthy tread,
To the belfry chamber overhead,
And startled the pigeons from their perch
On the somber rafters, that round him made
Masses and moving shapes of shade,—
By the trembling ladder, steep and tall,
To the highest window in the wall,
Where he paused to listen and look down
A moment on the roofs of the town
And the moonlight flowing over all.

Beneath, in the churchyard, lay the dead,
In their night encampment on the hill,
Wrapped in silence so deep and still
That he could hear, like a sentinel's tread,
The watchful night-wind, as it went
Creeping along from tent to tent,
And seeming to whisper, "All is well!"
A moment only he feels the spell
Of the place and the hour, and the secret dread
Of the lonely belfry and the dead;
For suddenly all his thoughts are bent
On a shadowy something far away,
Where the river widens to meet the bay,—
A line of black that bends and floats
On the rising tide like a bridge of boats.

Meanwhile, impatient to mount and ride,
Booted and spurred, with a heavy stride
On the opposite shore walked Paul Revere.

The Grammatical Stage: Poetry Selections

Now he patted his horse's side,
Now he gazed at the landscape far and near,
Then, impetuous, stamped the earth,
And turned and tightened his saddle girth;
But mostly he watched with eager search
The belfry tower of the Old North Church,
As it rose above the graves on the hill,
Lonely and spectral and somber and still.
And lo! as he looks, on the belfry's height
A glimmer, and then a gleam of light!
He springs to the saddle, the bridle he turns,
But lingers and gazes, till full on his sight
A second lamp in the belfry burns.

A hurry of hoofs in a village street,
A shape in the moonlight, a bulk in the dark,
And beneath, from the pebbles, in passing, a spark
Struck out by a steed flying fearless and fleet;
That was all! And yet, through the gloom and the light,
The fate of a nation was riding that night;
And the spark struck out by that steed, in his flight,
Kindled the land into flame with its heat.
He has left the village and mounted the steep,
And beneath him, tranquil and broad and deep,
Is the Mystic, meeting the ocean tides;
And under the alders that skirt its edge,
Now soft on the sand, now loud on the ledge,
Is heard the tramp of his steed as he rides.

It was twelve by the village clock
When he crossed the bridge into Medford town.
He heard the crowing of the cock,
And the barking of the farmer's dog,

And felt the damp of the river fog,
That rises after the sun goes down.

It was one by the village clock,
When he galloped into Lexington.
He saw the gilded weathercock
Swim in the moonlight as he passed,
And the meeting-house windows, black and bare,
Gaze at him with a spectral glare,
As if they already stood aghast
At the bloody work they would look upon.

It was two by the village clock,
When he came to the bridge in Concord town.
He heard the bleating of the flock,
And the twitter of birds among the trees,
And felt the breath of the morning breeze
Blowing over the meadow brown.
And one was safe and asleep in his bed
Who at the bridge would be first to fall,
Who that day would be lying dead,
Pierced by a British musket ball.

You know the rest. In the books you have read
How the British Regulars fired and fled,—
How the farmers gave them ball for ball,
From behind each fence and farmyard wall,
Chasing the redcoats down the lane,
Then crossing the fields to emerge again
Under the trees at the turn of the road,
And only pausing to fire and load.

So through the night rode Paul Revere;
And so through the night went his cry of alarm

To every Middlesex village and farm,—
A cry of defiance, and not of fear,
A voice in the darkness, a knock at the door,
And a word that shall echo for evermore!
For, borne on the night-wind of the Past,
Through all our history, to the last,
In the hour of darkness and peril and need,
The people will waken and listen to hear
The hurrying hoof-beats of that steed,
And the midnight message of Paul Revere.

O Captain! My Captain!
by Walt Whitman

O Captain! my Captain! our fearful trip is done;
The ship has weather'd every rack, the prize we sought is won;
The port is near, the bells I hear, the people all exulting,
While follow eyes the steady keel, the vessel grim and daring:

    But O heart! heart! heart!
     O the bleeding drops of red,
       Where on the deck my Captain lies,
        Fallen cold and dead.

O Captain! my Captain! rise up and hear the bells;
Rise up—for you the flag is flung—for you the bugle trills;
For you bouquets and ribbon'd wreaths—for you the shores
    a-crowding;
For you they call, the swaying mass, their eager faces turning:

    Here Captain! dear father!
      This arm beneath your head;
        It is some dream that on the deck
        You've fallen cold and dead.

My Captain does not answer, his lips are pale and still;
My father does not feel my arm, he has no pulse or will;
The ship is anchor'd safe and sound, its voyage closed and done;
From the fearful trip the victor ship comes in with object won:

    Exult, O shores, and ring, O bells!
      But I, with mournful tread,
        Walk the deck my Captain lies,
        Fallen cold and dead.

Sheridan's Ride

by Thomas Buchanan Read

Up from the South at break of day,
Bringing to Winchester fresh dismay,
The affrighted air with a shudder bore,
Like a herald in haste, to the chieftain's door,
The terrible grumble, and rumble, and roar,
Telling the battle was on once more,
    And Sheridan twenty miles away.

And wider still those billows of war
Thundered along the horizon's bar;
And louder yet into Winchester rolled
The roar of that red sea uncontrolled,
Making the blood of the listener cold,
As he thought of the stake in that fiery fray,
     With Sheridan twenty miles away.

But there is a road from Winchester town,
A good, broad highway leading down;
And there, through the flush of the morning light,
A steed as black as the steeds of night
Was seen to pass, as with eagle flight;
As if he knew the terrible need,
He stretched away with his utmost speed;
Hills rose and fell; but his heart was gay,
     With Sheridan fifteen miles away.

Still sprung from those swift hoofs, thundering South,
The dust, like smoke from the cannon's mouth;
Or the trail of a comet, sweeping faster and faster.
Foreboding to traitors the doom of disaster,
The heart of the steed and the heart of the master
Were beating like prisoners assaulting their walls,
Impatient to be where the battlefield calls;
Every nerve of the charger was strained to full play,
     With Sheridan only ten miles away.

Under his spurning feet the road
Like an arrowy Alpine river flowed,
And the landscape sped away behind
Like an ocean flying before the wind,
And the steed, like a barque fed with furnace ire,
Swept on, with his wild eye full of fire.

But lo! he is nearing his heart's desire;
He is snuffling the smoke of the roaring fray,
　　With Sheridan only five miles away.

The first that the general saw were the groups
Of stragglers, and then the retreating troops;
What was done? What to do? A glance told him both,
Then, striking his spurs, with a terrible oath,
He dashed down the line 'mid a storm of huzzas,
And the wave of retreat checked its course there, because
The sight of the master compelled it to pause.
With foam and with dust the black charger was gray;
By the flash of his eye, and the red nostril's play,
He seemed to the whole great army to say,
"I have brought you Sheridan all the way
　　From Winchester down to save the day!"

Hurrah! Hurrah for Sheridan!
Hurrah! Hurrah for horse and man!
And when their statues are placed on high,
Under the dome of the Union sky,
The American soldier's Temple of Fame;
There with the glorious general's name,
Be it said, in letters both bold and bright,
　"Here is the steed that saved the day,
By carrying Sheridan into the fight,
　　From Winchester, twenty miles away!"

The Star-Spangled Banner

by Francis Scott Key

O say, can you see, by the dawn's early light,
   What so proudly we hailed at the twilight's last gleaming,
Whose broad stripes and bright stars through the perilous fight,
   O'er the ramparts we watched were so gallantly streaming?
And the rockets' red glare, the bombs bursting in air,
Gave proof through the night that our flag was still there.
O say, does that star-spangled banner yet wave
O'er the land of the free, and the home of the brave!

On that shore, dimly seen through the mists of the deep,
   Where the foe's haughty host in dread silence reposes,
What is that which the breeze, o'er the towering steep,
   As it fitfully blows, now conceals, now discloses?
Now it catches the gleam of the morning's first beam,
In full glory reflected, now shines on the stream.
'Tis the star-spangled banner; O long may it wave
O'er the land of the free, and the home of the brave!

And where is that band who so vauntingly swore
   That the havoc of war and the battle's confusion
A home and a country should leave us no more?
   Their blood has washed out their foul footsteps' pollution.
No refuge could save the hireling and the slave
From the terror of flight, or the gloom of the grave:
And the star-spangled banner in triumph doth wave
O'er the land of the free, and the home of the brave!

O thus be it ever, when freemen shall stand
   Between their loved homes and the war's desolation!
Blest with victory and peace, may the heaven-rescued land
   Praise the power that hath made and preserved us a nation.

Then conquer we must, when our cause it is just,
And this be our motto: "In God is our trust!"
And the star-spangled banner in triumph doth wave,
O'er the land of the free, and the home of the brave!

Solitude

by Ella Wheeler Wilcox

Laugh, and the world laughs with you;
    Weep, and you weep alone.
For the sad old earth must borrow its mirth,
    But has trouble enough of its own.
Sing, and the hills will answer;
    Sigh, it is lost on the air.
The echoes bound to a joyful sound,
    But shrink from voicing care.

Rejoice, and men will seek you;
    Grieve, and they turn and go.
They want full measure of all your pleasure,
    But they do not need your woe.
Be glad, and your friends are many;
    Be sad, and you lose them all.
There are none to decline your nectared wine,
    But alone you must drink life's gall.

Feast, and your halls are crowded;
    Fast, and the world goes by.
Succeed and give, and it helps you live,
    But no man can help you die.
There is room in the halls of pleasure
    For a long and lordly train,
But one by one we must all file on
    Through the narrow aisles of pain.

The Destruction of Sennacherib

by George Gordon Byron

The Assyrian came down like the wolf on the fold,
And his cohorts were gleaming in purple and gold;
And the sheen of their spears was like stars on the sea,
When the blue wave rolls nightly on deep Galilee.

Like the leaves of the forest when Summer is green,
That host with their banners at sunset were seen;
Like the leaves of the forest when Autumn hath blown,
That host on the morrow lay withered and strown.

For the Angel of Death spread his wings on the blast,
And breathed in the face of the foe as he passed;
And the eyes of the sleepers waxed deadly and chill,
And their hearts but once heaved, and forever grew still!

And there lay the steed with his nostril all wide,
But through it there rolled not the breath of his pride;
And the foam of his gasping lay white on the turf,
And cold as the spray of the rock-beating surf.

And there lay the rider distorted and pale,
With the dew on his brow, and the rust on his mail;
And the tents were all silent, the banners alone,
The lances unlifted, the trumpet unblown.

And the widows of Ashur are loud in their wail,
And the idols are broke in the temple of Baal;
And the might of the Gentile, unsmote by the sword,
Hath melted like snow in the glance of the Lord!

A Child's Wish

by Abram J. Ryan

I wish I were the little key
   That locks Love's Captive in,
And lets Him out to go and free
   A sinful heart from sin.

I wish I were the little bell
   That tinkles for the Host
When God comes down each day to dwell
   With hearts He loves the most.

I wish I were the chalice fair
   That holds the Blood of Love,
When every flash lights holy prayer
   Upon its way above.

I wish I were the little flower
   So near the Host's sweet face,
Or like the light that half an hour
   Burned on the shrine of grace.

I wish I were the altar where
   As on His mother's breast
Christ nestles, like a child, fore'er
   In Eucharistic rest.

But oh, my God, I wish the most
   That my poor heart may be
A home all holy for each Host
   That comes in love to me.

The Spider and the Fly

by Mary Howitt

"Will you walk into my parlor?" said the Spider to the Fly,
" 'Tis the prettiest little parlor that ever you did spy;
The way into my parlor is up a winding stair,
And I've many curious things to show when you are there."
"O no, no," said the little Fly, "to ask me is in vain,
For who goes up your winding stair can ne'er come down
    again."

"I'm sure you must be weary, dear, with soaring up so high;
Will you rest upon my little bed?" said the Spider to the Fly.
"There are pretty curtains drawn around; the sheets are fine
    and thin,
And if you like to rest a while, I'll snugly tuck you in!"
"O no, no," said the little Fly, "for I've often heard it said,
They *never, never wake* again, who sleep upon *your* bed!"

Said the cunning Spider to the Fly, "Dear Friend, what can
    I do,
To prove the warm affection I've always felt for you?
I have within my pantry good store of all that's nice;
I'm sure you're very welcome—will you please to take a
    slice?"
"O no, no," said the little Fly, "kind sir, that cannot be;
I've heard what's in your pantry, and I do not wish to see!"

"Sweet creature!"said the Spider, "you're witty and you're
    wise,
How handsome are your gauzy wings, how brilliant are your
    eyes!
I have a little looking–glass upon my parlor shelf,
If you'll step in one moment, dear, you shall behold yourself."

"I thank you, gentle sir," she said, "for what you're pleased
    to say,
And bidding you good-morning *now*, I'll call *another* day."

The Spider turned him round about, and went into his den,
For well he knew the silly Fly would soon come back again:
So he wove a subtle web, in a little corner sly,
And he set his table ready to dine upon the Fly.
Then he came out to his door again, and merrily did sing,
"Come, hither, hither, pretty Fly, with the pearl and silver
    wing:
Your robes are green and purple; there's a crest upon your
    head;
Your eyes are like the diamond bright, but mine are dull as
    lead."

Alas, alas! how very soon this silly little Fly,
Hearing his wily flattering words, came slowly flitting by.
With buzzing wings she hung aloft, then near and nearer
    drew,
Thinking only of her brilliant eyes, and green and purple hue;
Thinking only of her crested head—*poor foolish thing!* At last,
Up jumped the cunning Spider, and fiercely held her fast.
He dragged her up his winding stair, into his dismal den,
Within his little parlor; but she ne'er came out again!

And now, dear little children, who may this story read,
To idle, silly, flattering words, I pray you ne'er give heed;
Unto an evil counselor close heart, and ear, and eye,
And take a lesson from this tale of the Spider and the Fly.

The Ride of Collins Graves

(May 16, 1874)

by John Boyle O'Reilly

No song of a soldier riding down
To the raging fight from Winchester town;
No song of a time that shook the earth
With the nations' throe at a nation's birth;
But the song of a brave man, free from fear
As Sheridan's self or Paul Revere;
Who risked what they risked, free from strife
And its promise of glorious pay,—his life!

The peaceful valley has waked and stirred,
And the answering echoes of life are heard;
The dew still clings to the trees and grass,
And the early toilers smiling pass,
As they glance aside at the white-walled homes,
Or up the valley, where merrily comes
The brook that sparkles in diamond rills
As the sun comes over the Hampshire hills.

What was it passed like an ominous breath—
Like a shiver of fear, or a touch of death?
What was it? The valley is peaceful still,
And the leaves are afire on top of the hill;
It was a sound, nor a thing of sense,—
But a pain, like the pang of the short suspense
That thrills the being of those who see
At their feet the gulf of Eternity.

The air of the valley has felt the chill;
The workers pause at the door of the mill;

The housewife, keen to the shivering air,
Arrests her foot on the cottage stair,
Instinctive taught by the mother-love,
And thinks of the sleeping ones above.

Why start the listeners? Why does the course
Of the mill-stream widen? Is it a horse—
"Hark to the sound of the hoofs!" they say—
That gallops so wildly Williamsburg way?

Oh! what was that, like a human shriek
From the winding valley? Will nobody speak?
Will nobody answer those women who cry
As the awful warnings thunder by?

Whence come they? Listen! And now they hear
The sound of the galloping horse-hoofs near;
They watch the trend of the vale, and see
The rider who thunders so menacingly,
With waving arms and warning scream
To the home-filled banks of the valley stream.
He draws no rein, but he shakes the street
With a shout and the ring of the galloping feet,
And this the cry he flings to the wind,—
"To the hills for your lives! The flood is behind!"

He cries and is gone, but they know the worst,—
The breast of the Williamsburg dam has burst!
The basin that nourished their happy homes
Is changed to a demon. It comes! it comes!

A monster in aspect, with shaggy front
Of shattered dwellings to take the brunt
Of the homes they shatter;—white-maned and hoarse,

The Grammatical Stage: Poetry Selections

The merciless Terror fills the course
Of the narrow valley, and rushing raves,
With death on the first of its hissing waves,
Till cottage and street and crowded mill
Are crumbled and crushed.

                        But onward still,
In front of the roaring flood, is heard
The galloping horse and the warning word.
Thank God! The brave man's life is spared!
From Williamsburg town he nobly dared
To race with the flood, and take the road
In front of the terrible swath it mowed.

For miles it thundered and crashed behind,
But he looked ahead with a steadfast mind:
"They must be warned!" was all he said,
As away on his terrible ride he sped.

When heroes are called for, bring the crown
To this Yankee rider; send him down
On the stream of time with the Curtius old;
His deed, as the Roman's, was brave and bold;
And the tale can as noble a thrill awake,
For he offered his life for the people's sake!

How They Brought the Good News from Ghent to Aix
by Robert Browning

I sprang to the stirrup, and Joris, and he;
I galloped, Dirck galloped, we galloped all three;
"Good speed!" cried the watch, as the gatebolts undrew;
"Speed!" echoed the wall to us galloping through;
Behind shut the postern, the lights sank to rest,
And into the midnight we galloped abreast.

Not a word to each other; we kept the great pace
Neck by neck, stride by stride, never changing our place;
I turned in my saddle and made its girths tight,
Then shortened each stirrup, and set the pique right,
Rebuckled the cheek-strap, chained slacker the bit,
Nor galloped less steadily Roland a whit.

'Twas moonset at starting; but while we drew near
Lokeren, the cocks crew, and twilight dawned clear;
At Boom, a great yellow star came out to see;
At Düffeld, 'twas morning as plain as could be;
And from Mecheln church-steeple we heard the half-chime,
So Joris broke silence with, "Yet there is time!"

At Aerschot, up leaped of a sudden the sun,
And against him the cattle stood black every one,
To stare through the mist at us galloping past,

And I saw my stout galloper Roland at last,
With resolute shoulders, each butting away
The haze, as some bluff river headland its spray;

And his low head and crest, just one sharp ear bent back
For my voice, and the other pricked out on his track;
And one eye's black intelligence—ever that glance
O'er its white edge at me, his own master, askance!
And the thick heavy spume-flakes which aye and anon
His fierce lips shook upwards in galloping on.

By Hasselt, Dirck groaned; and cried Joris, "Stay spur!
Your Roos galloped bravely, and fault's not in her;
We'll remember at Aix"—for one heard the quick wheeze
Of her chest, saw the stretched neck and staggering knees,
And sunk tail, and horrible heave of the flank,
As down on her haunches she shuddered and sank.

So we were left galloping, Joris and I,
Past Looz and past Tongres, no cloud in the sky;
The broad sun above laughed a pitiless laugh,
'Neath our feet broke the brittle bright stubble like chaff;
Till over by Dalhem a dome-spire sprang white,
And "Gallop," gasped Joris, "for Aix is in sight!"

"How they'll greet us!"—and all in a moment his roan
Rolled neck and crop over; lay dead as a stone;
And there was my Roland to bear the whole weight
Of the news which alone could save Aix from her fate,
With his nostrils like pits full of blood to the brim,
And with circles of red for his eye-socket's rim.

Then I cast loose my buffcoat, each holster let fall,
Shook off both my jack-boots, let go belt and all,
Stood up in the stirrup, leaned, patted his ear,

Called my Roland his pet-name, my horse without peer;
Clapped my hands, laughed and sang, any noise, bad or good,
Till at length into Aix Roland galloped and stood.

And all I remember is—friends flocking round
As I sat with his head 'twixt my knees on the ground;
And no voice but was praising this Roland of mine,
As I poured down his throat our last measure of wine,
Which (the burgesses voted by common consent)
Was no more than his due who brought good news from
    Ghent.

Opportunity

by Edward Rowland Sill

This I beheld, or dreamed it in a dream:—
There spread a cloud of dust along a plain;
And underneath the cloud, or in it, raged
A furious battle, and men yelled, and swords
Shocked upon swords and shields. A prince's banner
Wavered, then staggered backward, hemmed by foes.

A craven hung along the battle's edge,
And thought, "Had I a sword of keener steel—
That blue blade that the king's son bears—but this
Blunt thing!—" he snapped and flung it from his hand.
And lowering crept away and left the field.

Then came the king's son, wounded, sore bestead,
And weaponless, and saw the broken sword,
Hilt-buried in the dry and trodden sand,
And ran and snatched it, and with battle-shout
Lifted afresh he hewed his enemy down,
And saved a great cause that heroic day.

The Charge of the Light Brigade
by Alfred Lord Tennyson

Half a league, half a league,
  Half a league onward,
All in the valley of Death
  Rode the six hundred.
"Forward, the Light Brigade!
Charge for the guns," he said:
Into the valley of Death
  Rode the six hundred.
"Forward, the Light Brigade!"
Was there a man dismay'd?
Not tho' the soldier knew
  Someone had blunder'd:
Theirs not to make reply,
Theirs not to reason why,
Theirs but to do and die:
Into the valley of Death
  Rode the six hundred.

Cannon to right of them,
Cannon to left of them,
Cannon in front of them
  Volley'd and thunder'd;
Storm'd at with shot and shell,
Boldly they rode and well,
Into the jaws of Death,
Into the mouth of Hell
  Rode the six hundred.

Flash'd all their sabers bare,
Flash'd as they turn'd in air.
Sabring the gunners there,

Charging an army, while
    All the world wonder'd:
Plunged in the battery-smoke
Right thro' the line they broke;
Cossack and Russian
Reel'd from the saber-stroke
    Shatter'd and sunder'd.
Then they rode back, but not,
    Not the six hundred.

Cannon to right of them,
Cannon to left of them,
Cannon behind them
    Volley'd and thunder'd;
Storm'd at with shot and shell,
While horse and hero fell,
They that had fought so well
Came thro' the jaws of Death,
Back from the mouth of Hell,
All that was left of them,
    Left of six hundred.

When can their glory fade?
O the wild charge they made!
    All the world wonder'd.
Honor the charge they made!
Honor the Light Brigade,
    Noble six hundred!

The Grammatical Stage: Poetry Selections

Father William

by Robert Southey

"You are old, Father William," the young man cried;
  "The few locks that are left you are gray:
You are hale, Father William, a hearty old man;
  Now tell me the reason, I pray."

"In the days of my youth," Father William replied,
  "I remembered that youth would fly fast;
And abused not my health and my vigor at first,
  That I never might need them at last."

"You are old, Father William," the young man cried,
  "And pleasures with youth pass away;
And yet you lament not the days that are gone;
  Now tell me the reason, I pray."

"In the days of my youth," Father William replied,
  "I remembered that youth could not last;
I thought of the future, whatever I did,
  That I never might grieve for the past."

"You are old, Father William," the young man cried,
  "And life must be hastening away;
You are cheerful, and love to converse upon death;
  Now tell me the reason, I pray."

"I am cheerful, young man," Father William replied;
  "Let the cause thy attention engage;
In the days of my youth I remembered my God,
  And He hath not forgotten my age!"

The Lake Isle of Innisfree
by William Butler Yeats

I will arise and go now, and go to Innisfree,
And a small cabin build there, of clay and wattles made:
Nine bean-rows will I have there, a hive for the honey-bee,
And live alone in the bee-loud glade.

And I shall have some peace there, for peace comes dropping
    slow,
Dropping from the veils of the morning to where the cricket
    sings;
There midnight's all a glimmer, and noon a purple glow,
And evening full of the linnet's wings.

I will arise and go now, for always night and day
I hear lake water lapping with low sounds by the shore;
While I stand on the roadway, or on the pavements grey,
I hear it in the deep heart's core.

The Night Has a Thousand Eyes
by Francis William Bourdillon

The night has a thousand eyes,
    And the day but one;
Yet the light of the bright world dies
    With the dying sun.

The mind has a thousand eyes,
    And the heart but one;
Yet the light of a whole life dies
    When love is done.

An Old Woman of the Roads

by Padraic Colum

O to have a little house!
To own the hearth and stool and all!
The heaped up sods upon the fire,
The pile of turf against the wall!

To have a clock with weights and chains
And pendulum swinging up and down!
A dresser filled with shining delph,
Speckled with white and blue and brown!

I could be busy all the day
Cleaning and sweeping hearth and floor,
And fixing on their shelf again
My white and blue and speckled store!

I could be quiet there at night
Beside the fire and by myself,
Sure of a bed, and loth to leave
The ticking clock and the shining delph!

Och! but I'm weary of mist and dark,
And roads where there's never a house or bush,
And tired I am of bog and road
And the crying wind and the lonesome hush!

And I am praying to God on high,
And I am praying Him night and day,
For a little house—a house of my own—
Out of the wind's and the rain's way.

The Violet

by Jane Taylor

Down in a green and shady bed
    A modest violet grew,
Its stalk was bent, it hung its head,
    As if to hide from view.

And yet it was a lovely flower,
    Its color bright and fair;
It might have graced a rosy bower,
    Instead of hiding there.

Yet there it was content to bloom,
    In modest tints arrayed;
And there diffused its sweet perfume,
    Within the silent shade.

Then let me to the valley go,
    This pretty flower to see;
That I may also learn to grow
    In sweet humility.

The Grammatical Stage: Poetry Selections

The Builders

by Henry Wadsworth Longfellow

All are architects of Fate,
  Working in these walls of Time;
Some with massive deeds and great,
  Some with ornaments of rhyme.

Nothing useless is, or low;
  Each thing in its place is best;
And what seems but idle show
  Strengthens and supports the rest.

For the structure that we raise,
  Time is with materials filled;
Our to-days and yesterdays
  Are the blocks with which we build.

Truly shape and fashion these;
  Leave no yawning gaps between;
Think not, because no man sees,
  Such things will remain unseen.

In the elder days of Art,
  Builders wrought with greatest care
Each minute and unseen part;
  For the gods see everywhere.

Let us do our work as well,
  Both the unseen and the seen;
Make the house where gods may dwell
  Beautiful, entire, and clean.

Else our lives are incomplete,
    Standing in these walls of Time,
Broken stairways, where the feet
    Stumble, as they seek to climb.

Build to-day, then, strong and sure,
    With a firm and ample base;
And ascending and secure
    Shall to-morrow find its place.

Thus alone can we attain
    To those turrets, where the eye
Sees the world as one vast plain,
    And one boundless reach of sky.

Be Strong!

by Maltbie Davenport Babcock

Be strong!
We are not here to play, to dream, to drift;
We have hard work to do and loads to lift;
Shun not the struggle—face it; 'tis God's gift.

Be strong!
Say not, "The days are evil. Who's to blame?"
And fold the hands and acquiesce—oh, shame!
Stand up, speak out, and bravely, in God's name.

Be strong!
It matters not how deep intrenched the wrong,
How hard the battle goes, the day how long;
Faint not—fight on! Tomorrow comes the song.

Jabberwocky

by Lewis Carroll

'Twas brillig, and the slithy toves
   Did gyre and gimble in the wabe;
All mimsy were the borogoves,
   And the mome raths outgrabe.

"Beware the Jabberwock, my son!
   The jaws that bite, the claws that catch!
Beware the Jubjub bird, and shun
   The frumious Bandersnatch!"

He took his vorpal sword in hand:
   Long time the manxome foe he sought—
So rested he by the Tumtum tree,
   And stood awhile in thought.

And, as in uffish thought he stood,
   The Jabberwock, with eyes of flame,
Came whiffling through the tulgey wood,
   And burbled as it came!

One, two! One, two! And through and through
   The vorpal blade went snicker-snack!
He left it dead, and with its head
   He went galumphing back.

"And hast thou slain the Jabberwock?
   Come to my arms, my beamish boy!
O frabjous day! Callooh! Callay!"
   He chortled in his joy.

'Twas brillig, and the slithy toves
   Did gyre and gimble in the wabe;
All mimsy were the borogoves,
   And the mome raths outgrabe.

The Eagle

(From *The Princess*)

by Alfred Lord Tennyson

He clasps the crag with crooked hands;
Close to the sun on lonely lands,
Ringed with the azure world, he stands.

The wrinkled sea beneath him crawls;
He watches from his mountain walls,
And like a thunderbolt he falls.

The Light of Bethlehem

by Father John Banister Tabb

'Tis Christmas Night! the snow
   A flock unnumbered lies;
The old Judean stars aglow
   Keep watch within the skies.

An icy stillness holds
   The pulses of the night;
A deeper mystery enfolds
   The wondering Hosts of Light.

Till lo, with reverence pale
   That dims each diadem,
The lordliest, earthward bending, hail
   The Light of Bethlehem!

The Grammatical Stage: Poetry Selections

Hymn

by Saint Thomas Aquinas

Sing, my tongue, the Saviour's glory,
    Of His flesh the mystery sing;
Of the blood, all price excelling,
    Shed by our Immortal King.
Destined for the world's redemption
    From a noble womb to spring.

Of a pure and spotless Virgin
    Born for us on earth below,
He, as Man with man conversing,
    Stayed the seeds of truth to sow;
Then He closed in solemn order
    Wondrously His life of woe.

On the night of that Last Supper
    Seated with His chosen band,
He the paschal victim eating,
    First fulfils the Law's command;
Then as food to all His brethren
    Gives Himself with His own Hand.

Word made flesh, the bread of nature
    By His word to Flesh He turns;
Wine into His blood He changes:—
    What though sense no change discerns,
Only be the heart in earnest,
    Faith her lesson quickly learns.

Down in adoration falling,
    Lo! the Sacred Host we hail;

Lo! o'er ancient forms departing,
  Newer rites of grace prevail;
Faith for all defects supplying,
  Where the feeble senses fail.

To the Everlasting Father; ᐟ
  And the Son who reigns on high,
With the Holy Ghost proceeding
  Forth from each eternally,
Be salvation, honor, blessing,
  Might and endless majesty!

—translated from the Latin by Edward Caswall

OTHER SELECTIONS TO MEMORIZE

Jesu Dulcis Memoria

Jesu dulcis memoria,
Dans vera cordis gaudia:
Sed super mel et omnia,
Ejus dulcis praesentia.

Nil canitur suavius,
Nil auditur jucundius,
Nil cogitatur dulcius,
Quam Jesus Dei Filius.

Jesu spes paenitentibus,
Quam pius es
    petentibus!
Quam bonus
    te quaerentibus!
Sed quid invenientibus?

Nec lingua valet dicere,
Nec littera exprimere:
Expertus
    potest credere,
Quid sit Jesum diligere.

Sis Jesu nostrum gaudium,
Qui es futurus praemium:
Sit nostra in te gloria,
Per cuncta semper saecula.
    Amen.

Sweet the Memory of Jesus

Sweet the memory of Jesus,
Giving true joys of heart:
But above honey and all else
Is his presence sweet.

Nothing more pleasant is sung,
Nothing more delightful is heard,
Nothing sweeter is thought,
Than Jesus, the Son of God.

Jesus, hope of penitents,
How kind Thou art
    to those who ask!
How good to those
    who seek Thee!
But what to those who find Thee?

Tongue hath no strength to say,
Nor letter to express,
Yet having sensed,
    one can believe,
What it is to love Jesus.

Jesus, be our joy,
Who will be our reward.
May our glory be in Thee,
Through all ages, forever.
    Amen.

Anima Christi	Soul of Christ
Anima Christi, sanctifica me.	Soul of Christ, sanctify me.
Corpus Christi, salva me.	Body of Christ, save me.
Sanguis Christi, inebria me.	Blood of Christ, inebriate me.
Aqua lateris Christi,	Water from the side of Christ,
lava me.	wash me.
Passio Christi,	Passion of Christ,
conforta me.	strengthen me.
O bone Jesu, exaudi me.	O good Jesus, hear me.
Intra tua vulnera,	Within Thy wounds,
absconde me.	hide me.
Ne permittas me	Never permit me to be
separari a te.	separated from Thee.
Ab hoste maligno,	From the evil enemy,
defende me.	defend me.
In hora mortis meae,	In the hour of my death,
voca me.	call me.
Et jube me venire ad te.	And bid me come to Thee.
Ut cum sanctis tuis	So that with Thy saints
laudem te,	I may praise Thee,
In saecula saeculorum.	Forever and ever.
Amen.	Amen.

The Preamble to the Constitution
of the United States of America

We, the people of the United States, in order to form a more perfect union, establish justice, insure domestic tranquility, provide for the common defence, promote the general welfare, and secure the blessings of liberty to ourselves and our posterity, do ordain and establish this Constitution for the United States of America.

The War Inevitable
March 1775

They tell us, Sir, that we are weak—unable to cope with so formidable an adversary. But when shall we be stronger? Will it be the next week, or the next year? Will it be when we are totally disarmed, and when a British guard shall be stationed in every house? Shall we gather strength by irresolution and inaction? Shall we acquire the means of effectual resistance by lying supinely on our backs, and hugging the delusive phantom of hope, until our enemies shall have bound us hand and foot? Sir, we are not weak, if we make proper use of those means which the God of nature hath placed in our power.

Three millions of People, armed in the holy cause of liberty, and in such a country as that which we possess, are invincible by any force which our enemy can send against us. Besides, Sir, we shall not fight our battles alone. There is a just God who presides over the destinies of Nations, and who will raise up friends to fight our battles for us. The battle, Sir, is not to the strong alone; it is to the vigilant, the active, the brave. Besides, Sir, we have no election. If we were base enough to desire it, it is now too late to retire from the contest. There is no retreat but in submission and slavery! Our chains are forged! Their clanking may be heard on the plains of Boston! The war is inevitable; and let it come! I repeat, Sir, let it come!

It is in vain, Sir, to extenuate the matter. Gentlemen may cry, Peace, Peace!—but there is no peace. The war is actually begun! The next gale that sweeps from the North will bring to our ears the clash of resounding arms! Our brethren are already in the field! Why stand we here idle? What is it that Gentlemen wish? What would they have? Is life so dear, or peace so sweet, as to be purchased at the price of chains and slavery? Forbid it, Almighty God! I know not what course others may take; but as for me, give me liberty or give me death!   — *Patrick Henry*

Washington on His Appointment
as Commander-in-Chief

Mr. President: Though I am truly sensible of the high honor done me in this appointment, yet I feel great distress, from a consciousness that my abilities and military experience may not be equal to the extensive and important trust. However, as the Congress desire it, I will enter upon the momentous duty, and exert every power I possess in their service, and for the support of the glorious cause. I beg they will accept my most cordial thanks for this distinguished testimony of their approbation.

But lest some unlucky event should happen, unfavorable to my reputation, I beg it may be remembered by every gentleman in the room, that I, this day, declare with the utmost sincerity, I do not think myself equal to the command I am honored with.

As to pay, Sir, I beg leave to assure the Congress, that, as no pecuniary consideration could have tempted me to accept this arduous employment, at the expense of my domestic ease and happiness, I do not wish to make any profit from it. I will keep an exact account of my expenses. Those, I doubt not, they will discharge, and that is all I desire.

—George Washington

Washington's Address to His Troops

The time is near at hand which must probably determine whether Americans are to be freemen or slaves; whether they are to have any property they can call their own; whether their houses are to be pillaged and destroyed and themselves consigned to a state of wretchedness from which no human efforts will deliver them. The fate of unborn millions will now depend, under God, on the courage and conduct of this army. Our enemy leaves us only the choice of a brave resistance or the most abject submission. We have, therefore, to resolve to conquer or die. Our own, our country's honor, calls upon us for a vigorous and manly exertion; and, if we now shamefully fail, we shall become infamous before the whole world. Let us, then, rely on the goodness of our cause, and the aid of the Supreme Being, in whose hands victory is, to animate and encourage us to great and noble actions. The eyes of all our countrymen are now upon us, and we shall have their blessings and praises if happily we are the instruments of saving them from the tyranny meditated against them.

Let us, therefore, animate and encourage each other, and show the whole world that a freeman contending for liberty on his own ground is superior to any slavish mercenary on earth. Liberty, property, life and honor are all at stake. Upon your courage and conduct rest the hopes of our bleeding and insulted country. Our wives, children and parents expect safety from us only; and they have every reason to believe that heaven will crown with success so just a cause.

The enemy will endeavor to intimidate us by show and appearance; but, remember, they have been repulsed on various occasions by a few brave Americans. Their cause is bad—their men are conscious of it; and, if opposed with firmness and coolness on their first onset, with our advantages of works and knowledge of the ground, the victory is most assuredly ours. Every good soldier will be silent and attentive, wait for orders and reserve his fire until he is sure of doing execution.

—*George Washington*

DICTATION SELECTIONS

From *Once upon a Time Saints*, by *Ethel Pochocki*

1. All Alice could hear was the scurrying of hard-shelled black bugs, up and down the walls, to and fro, hither and thither, across the floor and under the door.

2. But above this came the sound of tap-tap-tapping. It came from the grate of the window set high above her.

3. Ambrose went to the election and tried to calm down the shouting crowd. For a moment it became very quiet, and then from the mob came a child's voice, sharp and clear: "Ambrose for Bishop."

4. But he laughed at such foolishness. First of all, he said, he wasn't even baptized, although he considered himself a Christian in his heart. And furthermore, he wasn't a priest, so how could he be a bishop?

5. Barbara had heard about these people who said the love of God and their neighbors was the most important thing in life. Why did her father hate them so?

6. The prior grew curious as to what the little monk was doing there, so he and another monk quietly followed Barnaby in the shadows of the hallway. Who knew what this crazy fellow might be doing? After all, Barnaby had been just a juggler before he came to the monastery to live.

7. Each day he gave away every bit of bread stored in the pantry only to find the shelves filled with more than in the beginning.

8. Christopher had a very special gift. He could not write poetry or split an atom or tap dance. All he could do was use his strength to help Christ carry the world and lighten His load. And he did!

9. While they were praying, trying to think about God's grace coming down like rain, a small white lamb came out from under the puckerbrush and nuzzled Clement's arm.

10. Hundreds and thousands of mice crawled into the barn and ate one kernel apiece and carried one back with them. The younger ones ate more so they would have enough energy for the return trip. When they scurried out of the barn, there was not one stray, loose, neglected, stomped-on, hidden-under-a-bit-of-hay grain to be found.

11. Dorothy was also a Christian, which in those days took courage.

12. "No, my friend, I come before you because I now believe in Dorothy's Christ and I want to join her in paradise."
    And so he did.

13. Edward was determined to be a father to his people and show how good a Christian king could be. He even looked like a father, with snow white hair and rosy cheeks. He walked among his people, fished and hunted with them.

From *A Day on Skates,* by *Hilda van Stockum*

14. Suddenly he stumbled on a rough bit of ice and fell, slithering along straight toward a fishing-hole. Simon, who

had also been skating by himself not far away, too shy to join in the others' fun, saw his danger and gave a scream, but it was too late. There was a tremendous cracking of ice, a splashing of water, and Evert fell right into the dangerous spot.

15. What if her dear twin brother had been drowned? "Oh!" she exclaimed, clasping her hands, "I'm *glad* he's saved! Thank you, Simon, oh, thank you!"

16. But Evert and his two friends walked away from the others. "It's a great chance. Surely we must do some exploring here," he whispered.
    "Will we have time?" Okke asked, anxiously glancing at Teacher.
    "It won't take long, and think! we might find a secret passage."

17. Simon nodded and promised and waved and went home happier than he had ever thought he could be. His loneliness was over. He had friends, and especially one friend, of whom he felt proud.

From *The Mitchells: Five for Victory*, by Hilda van Stockum

18. "Oh I *do* wish I had a birthday too, sometimes."
    The children looked at her in amazement. One's birthday was the foundation of one's life, so to speak. Every self-respecting child had one. Sometimes parents might not go so far as to give a party, but the birthday was there just the same.

19. "We regret to inform you that your husband, Lieutenant John Ruysdaal Mitchell, is missing in action," she read. The paper shook between her fingers.

20. But the children were sure that God would hear their prayers, and it was their confidence which somehow kept hope alive in Mother's and Grannie's hearts.

From *Canadian Summer, by Hilda van Stockum*

21. They did not need to say that twice. They had not suspected that the doctor could run so fast. Even on their sneakers it was hard to keep up with him. However, all was well in the end.

22. "If it hadn't been for you and your children, I'd have lost my son," she said. Mother told her that she hadn't done anything. It was all Peter's work.

From *Friendly Gables, by Hilda van Stockum*

23. Joan listened in stunned surprise to this outburst of Miss Thorpe's. She realized that her wish to see Pierre's shop had blinded her to the situation. Of course she could not leave. She told Miss Thorpe so. "But the others can go, can't they?" She asked anxiously. "I wouldn't like to have Pierre disappointed." She couldn't, of course, mention the serious reason behind this trip.

24. Patsy went to Mother's room. "I've sent Miss Thorpe to bed," she told her. "Do you know what? She was *crying* because she has to leave us! *Imagine!*"
    Mother smiled. "Yes, Miss Thorpe is a dear," she said. "I'll miss her, too."

25. Then he said in English, "That is a beautiful little poem. I shall keep this always, in memory of a little girl whose eyes don't see far, but verree deep."

26. "Oh, you have, you *have!*"said Miss Thorpe, and to his disgust she kissed him. But he remembered that it was her party, so he didn't protest.

From *Augustine Came to Kent, by Barbara Willard*

27. The story Wolfstan had to tell his young son and daughter was so wild and strange that it seemed to come from another world. It was indeed a true tale, and certainly it had been told many times. But as she urged her father on, Ana's eyes were already round with anticipation.

28. Wolfstan had been working in the fields when the raiders—fierce marauding bands from across the seas—swooped on the village. They rounded up every soul in sight except the old people and drove them to the coast twenty miles to the south. As he was dragged off, only half conscious, Wolfstan had been aware of his young wife, Ea, screaming to him.

29. Both men were plainly dressed. Since he knew nothing of the country's customs, Wolfstan had no idea who or what they might be. Merchants or scholars, men of influence— he could not tell. All he knew was that here were two who might be prospective buyers.

30. That had all been a long time ago. The name of the tall stranger who had saved Wolfstan and Eobald was Gregory. The son of a Roman patrician who had hoped to see him high in the government of the country, Gregory had abandoned all wealth and comfort to become a monk of the Order of St. Benedict. Now nearly ten years after that day in the market place, he was Pope Gregory the First.

31. "Yes, it is Augustine. And he is to be my active self. He is to fulfill my dearest ambition while I must remain behind in Rome. He is going to take you home, Wolfstan, my friend."

32. The monks gathered about him. One thing was certain; today they would be either rejected or accepted. If rejected, what would become of them? Would they be allowed to depart peacefully, or would they face martyrdom?

33. He raised up the Cross, and the sun caught it and turned it to fire. He moved forward, standing so that the Cross was like a great golden weapon upraised to protect those below and behind it.

    This time the King dropped the reins on his horse's neck and held up both hands firmly and commandingly.

    The impulsive movement forward of the men at arms, the chieftains, and the crowd of peasants was checked into a jostle that at last died away into stillness.

34. Cyneog paused when he heard her voice. He looked at Wolf and gave him a quick, friendly nod.

    "How are things with you and the brothers, Wolf? You have been missed. Is your father well?"

From *Madeleine Takes Command, by Ethel C. Brill*

35. Madame de Vercheres put both arms around her daughter and held her close. "You are brave, my Madeleine. We must be brave in this dangerous country of New France."

36. "Gatchet!" she cried. "What are you doing?"

    "I am going to blow the place up," he replied huskily. "It's better to die that way than by torture."

    "You miserable coward," blazed the girl. "Take that

thing out of here and stamp on it. Then go back to your post on the north bastion. Go!"

37. "There is another thing," Madeleine went on. "Fires should be made in the manor house and some of the cabins. If no smoke rises from our chimneys, the enemy will notice it."

38. To the leader of the relief party the greatest surprise of all was the occupant of the fourth bastion. Like his elder brother, Alexandre drew himself up and saluted in a soldierly manner. Had the candle lantern given a stronger light, it might have shown a moistness in La Monnerie's eyes as he gazed at the gallant little lad with the big musket.

From *Archimedes and the Door of Science*, by Jeanne Bendick

39. Euclid was a good mathematician, but what is even more important, he had a scholarly, brilliantly orderly mind. He had collected, slowly, carefully, and painstakingly, all the bits and pieces of geometrical learning that were known in the world of his day. He had arranged and rearranged them, in the way you would start putting together a giant jigsaw puzzle, until they began to form a picture.

40. A wooden screw, like a long corkscrew, was fitted into a cylinder-shaped case. The bottom of the screw was placed in the water, and the top rested over land. At the top of the screw there was a handle.

41. When Archimedes turned the handle, the screw turned, too. As long as the screw was placed in the water at the right angle, when the screw turned it raised the water from one spiral up to the next. Up came the water out of the Nile, until it flowed out over the land into the fields.

42. "You always seem able to answer any problem, Archimedes," Hiero said, "so I shall give you this one. Find out for me whether my crown is solid gold, or if that scoundrel of a goldsmith has mixed the gold with silver."

43. Aristotle, the tutor of Alexander the Great, pointed out that since the shadow of the earth on the moon was curved, the earth itself must be curved and have the form of a sphere.

44. "See how we are situated," he said. "Here on this peninsula we can be cut off so completely that no help can come to us from our allies. Syracuse has been taken by siege before. I beg of you, Archimedes, help me make plans for defending the city."

44. Some people's minds are like that. The things they think and the ideas they have and the discoveries they make never stop triggering other people's minds and other ideas, until the world is filled with them.

From *The Cottage at Bantry Bay*, *by Hilda van Stockum*

45. Mother sighed a little, but she smiled bravely and said: "No harm, we'll manage." By the way her needles clicked the children could tell she did mind. There was always a lot to be bought and never much money to do it with.

46. "Heaven help us," said Michael, watching the road wind itself down into the valley. "If it's all that way we still have to go, how will we ever get home at all?"

47. "Thanks be to God! Ye had a hard time of it! I don't know how ye escaped him," said Brigid. "Yes, me bold Bran, look at that for ye! Ye've all but kilt us both. Will ye behave

better now in the future?" Bran promised faithfully with limpid brown eyes, so the children forgave him.

48. "There must have been an accident!" cried Mother, wringing her hands. Bran barked and ran to the door and back, pulling Michael's coat, as though asking him to follow.

49. "They say you've told them a plan you have and they say it's a secret!" began Michael indignantly, pointing to Liam. Liam blushed, but Paddy kept a grave face.

From *Francie on the Run*, *by Hilda van Stockum*

50. Francie thought his foot must be better by now. It didn't hurt anymore, and with the stout shoes the doctor had given him he could walk well, so well that he could almost—yes, he could almost—walk home! The idea struck Francie with light. Why not? He looked around the ward.

51. He struggled with the lock of the door for a moment, opened it and stood on the street. The heavy door slid shut behind him with a sigh and a click. Francie was outside for the first time in seven months!

52. "Francie, what are you doing here? It's not dreaming I am, am I? An' I thinking ye were tucked in your bed in the hospital!"

    "It's a long story," said Father Kelly. "Perhaps we'd better have tea somewhere an' tell ye all about it."

From *Pegeen, by Hilda van Stockum*

53. "Is it five o'clock yet, Mother? Don't we have to be meeting the bus?" asked Francie for the hundredth time.

54. "What do ye think of her now, Mother? Isn't she grand?" asked Francie breathlessly, leaving Liam to struggle with the suitcase.

55. Pegeen took the doll and pressed it against her cotton nightdress. "Oh, Brigid, I'll never forget it," she whispered. "Never. An' I'll try to be a good mother to Patricia, indeed I will."

The Dialectical Stage

POETRY SELECTIONS

From *The Tempest* (Act V, i, 34–58)
by William Shakespeare

PROSPERO:
Ye elves of hills, brooks, standing lakes, and groves:
And ye that on the sands with printless foot
Do chase the ebbing Neptune, and do fly him
When he comes back; you demi-puppets that
By moonshine do the green sour ringlets make,
Whereof the ewe not bites; and you whose pastime
Is to make midnight mushrooms, that rejoice
To hear the solemn curfew; by whose aid—
Weak masters though ye be—I have bedimm'd
The noontide sun, call'd forth the mutinous winds,
And 'twixt the green sea and the azured vault
Set roaring war: to the dread rattling thunder
Have I given fire, and rifted Jove's stout oak
With his own bolt; the strong-based promontory
Have I made shake, and by the spurs pluck'd up
The pine and cedar: graves at my command
have waked their sleepers, oped, and let 'em forth
By my so potent art. But this rough magic
I here abjure; and, when I have required
Some heavenly music,—which even now I do—
To work mine end upon their senses, that
This airy charm is for, I'll break my staff,
Bury it certain fathoms in the earth,
And deeper than did ever plummet sound
I'll drown my book.

From *Julius Caesar* (Act III, ii, 76–109)

by William Shakespeare

ANTONY:

Friends, Romans, countrymen, lend me your ears;
I come to bury Caesar, not to praise him.
The evil that men do lives after them;
The good is oft interred with their bones;
So let it be with Caesar. The noble Brutus
Hath told you Caesar was ambitious:
If it were so, it was a grievous fault,
And grievously hath Caesar answer'd it.
Here, under leave of Brutus and the rest,—
For Brutus is an honorable man;
So are they all, all honorable men,—
Come I to speak in Caesar's funeral.
He was my friend, faithful and just to me:
But Brutus says he was ambitious;
And Brutus is an honorable man.
He hath brought many captives home to Rome,
Whose ransoms did the general coffers fill:
Did this in Caesar seem ambitious?
When that the poor have cried, Caesar hath wept:
Ambition should be made of sterner stuff:
Yet Brutus says he was ambitious;
And Brutus is an honorable man.
You all did see that on the Lupercal
I thrice presented him a kingly crown,
Which he did thrice refuse: was this ambition?
Yet Brutus says he was ambitious;
And, sure, he is an honorable man.
I speak not to disprove what Brutus spoke,
But here I am to speak what I do know.
You all did love him once, not without cause:

What cause withholds you then to mourn for him?
O judgment! Thou art fled to brutish beasts,
And men have lost their reason. Bear with me;
My heart is in the coffin there with Caesar,
And I must pause till it come back to me.

From *Hamlet* (Act I, iii, 55–81)

by William Shakespeare

POLONIUS:
Yet here, Laertes! Aboard, aboard, for shame!
The wind sits in the shoulder of your sail,
And you are stay'd for. There; my blessing with thee!
And these few precepts in thy memory
Look thou character. Give thy thoughts no tongue,
Nor any unproportion'd thought his act.
Be thou familiar, but by no means vulgar.
Those friends thou hast, and their adoption tried,
Grapple them unto thy soul with hoops of steel,
But do not dull thy palm with entertainment
Of each new-hatch'd unfledged comrade. Beware
Of entrance to a quarrel; but being in,
Bear't, that the opposed may beware of thee.
Give every man thy ear, but few thy voice.
Take each man's censure, but reserve thy judgment.
Costly thy habit as thy purse can buy,
But not express'd in fancy; rich, not gaudy:
For the apparel oft proclaims the man;
And they in France of the best rank and station
Are of a most select and generous chief in that.
Neither a borrower nor a lender be:
For loan oft loses both itself and friend,
And borrowing dulls the edge of husbandry.

This above all: to thine own self be true,
And it must follow as the night the day,
Thou cans't not then be false to any man.
Farewell: my blessing season this in thee!

From *Henry V* (Act IV, iii, 17–67)

by William Shakespeare

WESTMORELAND:
                     O that we now had here
But one ten thousand of those men in England
That do no work to-day!
KING:
                          What's he that wishes so?
My cousin Westmoreland? No, my fair cousin:
If we are mark'd to die, we are enow
To do our country loss; and if to live,
The fewer men, the greater share of honor.
God's will! I pray thee, wish not one man more.
By Jove, I am not covetous for gold,
Nor care I who doth feed upon my cost;
It yearns me not if men my garments wear;
Such outward things dwell not in my desires:
But if it be a sin to covet honor,
I am the most offending soul alive.
No, faith, my coz, wish not a man from England:
God's peace! I would not lose so great an honor
As one man more, methinks, would share from me
For the best hope I have. Oh, do not wish one more!
Rather proclaim it, Westmoreland, through my host,
That he which hath no stomach to this fight,
Let him depart; his passport shall be made
And crowns for convoy put into his purse:

We would not die in that man's company
That fears his fellowship to die with us.
This day is call'd the feast of Crispian:
He that outlives this day, and comes safe home,
Will stand a tip-toe when this day is named,
And rouse him at the name of Crispian.
He that shall live this day, and see old age,
Will yearly on the vigil feast his neighbors,
And say 'Tomorrow is Saint Crispian:'
Then will he strip his sleeve and show his scars,
And say, 'These wounds I had on Crispin's day.'
Old men forget; yet all shall be forgot,
But he'll remember with advantages
What feats he did that day: then shall our names,
Familiar in his mouth as household words,
Harry the King, Bedford and Exeter,
Warwick and Talbot, Salisbury and Gloucester,
Be in their flowing cups freshly remember'd.
This story shall the good man teach his son;
And Crispin Crispian shall ne'er go by,
From this day to the ending of the world,
But we in it shall be remembered;
We few, we happy few, we band of brothers;
For he to-day that sheds his blood with me
Shall be my brother; be he ne'er so vile,
This day shall gentle his condition:
And gentlemen in England now a-bed
Shall think themselves accursed they were not here,
And hold their manhoods cheap whiles any speaks
That fought with us upon Saint Crispin's day.

From *Henry V* (Act IV, i, 230–84)

by William Shakespeare

KING:

Upon the king! let us our lives, our souls,
Our debts, our careful wives,
Our children and our sins lay on the king!
We must bear all. O hard condition,
Twin-born with greatness, subject to the breath
Of every fool, whose sense no more can feel
But his own wringing! What infinite heart's-ease
Must kings neglect, that private men enjoy!
And what have kings, that privates have not too,
Save ceremony, save general ceremony?
And what art thou, thou idol ceremony?
What kind of god art thou, that suffer'st more
Of mortal griefs than do thy worshippers?
What are thy rents? What are thy comings in?
O ceremony, show me but thy worth!
What is thy soul of adoration?
Art thou aught else but place, degree and form,
Creating awe and fear in other men?
Wherin thou art less happy being fear'd
Than they in fearing.
What drink'st thou oft, instead of homage sweet,
But poison'd flattery? O, be sick, great greatness,
And bid thy ceremony give thee cure!
Think'st thou the fiery fever will go out
With titles blown from adulation?
Will it give place to flexure and low bending?
Can'st thou, when thou command'st the beggar's knee,
Command the health of it? No, thou proud dream,
That play'st so subtly with a king's repose;
I am a king that find thee, and I know

'Tis not the balm, the sceptre and the ball,
The sword, the mace, the crown imperial,
The intertissued robe of gold and pearl,
The farced title running 'fore the king,
The throne he sits on, nor the tide of pomp
That beats upon the high shore of this world,
No, not all these, thrice-gorgeous ceremony,
Not all these, laid in bed majestical,
Can sleep so soundly, as the wretched slave,
Who with a body fill'd and vacant mind
Gets him to rest, cramm'd with distressful bread;
Never sees horrid night, the child of hell,
But, like a lackey, from the rise to set
Sweats in the eye of Phoebus and all night
Sleeps in Elysium; next day after dawn,
Doth rise and help Hyperion to his horse,
And follows so the ever-running year,
With profitable labor, to his grave:
And, but for ceremony, such a wretch,
Winding up days with toil and nights with sleep,
Had the fore-hand and vantage of a king.
The slave, a member of the country's peace,
Enjoys it; but in gross brain little wots
What watch the king keeps to maintain the peace,
Whose hours the peasant best advantages.

From *Macbeth* (Act V, v, 19–27)

by William Shakespeare

MACBETH:
She should have died hereafter;
There would have been a time for such a word.
To-morrow, and to-morrow, and to-morrow,
Creeps in this petty pace from day to day,
To the last syllable of recorded time;
And all our yesterdays have lighted fools
The way to dusty death. Out, out, brief candle!
Life's but a walking shadow, a poor player
That struts and frets his hour upon the stage
And then is heard no more: it is a tale
Told by an idiot, full of sound and fury,
Signifying nothing.

From *The Merchant of Venice* (Act IV, i, 183–204)

by William Shakespeare

PORTIA:
The quality of mercy is not strain'd,
It droppeth as the gentle rain from heaven
Upon the place beneath: it is twice blest;
It blesseth him that gives, and him that takes:
'Tis mightiest in the mightiest: it becomes
The throned monarch better than his crown;
His sceptre shows the force of temporal power,
The attribute to awe and majesty,
Wherein doth sit the dread and fear of kings;
But mercy is above this sceptred sway;
It is enthroned in the heart of kings,
It is an attribute to God Himself;

And earthly power doth then show likest God's
When mercy seasons justice. Therefore, Jew,
Though justice be thy plea, consider this,
That, in the course of justice, none of us
Should see salvation: we do pray for mercy;
And that same prayer doth teach us all to render
The deeds of mercy. I have spoke thus much
To mitigate the justice of thy plea;
Which if thou follow, this strict court of Venice
Must needs give sentence 'gainst the merchant there.

From *The Merchant of Venice* (Act V, i, 54–88)
by William Shakespeare

LORENZO:
How sweet the moonlight sleeps upon this bank!
Here will we sit, and let the sounds of music
Creep in our ears: soft stillness and the night
Become the touches of sweet harmony.
Sit, Jessica. Look how the floor of heaven
Is thick inlaid with patines of bright gold:
There's not the smallest orb which thou behold'st
But in his motion like an angel sings,
Still quiring to the young-eyed cherubins;
Such harmony is in immortal souls;
But whilst this muddy vesture of decay
Doth grossly close it in, we cannot hear it.

[*Enter* MUSICIANS]

Come, ho, and wake Diana with a hymn!
With sweetest touches pierce your mistress' ear,
And draw her home with music.

JESSICA:
I am never merry when I hear sweet music.
LORENZO:
The reason is, your spirits are attentive:
For do but note a wild and wanton herd,
Or race of youthful and unhandled colts,
Fetching mad bounds, bellowing and neighing loud,
Which is the hot condition of their blood;
If they but hear perchance a trumpet sound,
Or any air of music touch their ears,
You shall perceive them make a mutual stand,
Their savage eyes turn'd to a modest gaze
By the sweet power of music: therefore the poet
Did feign that Orpheus drew trees, stones and floods;
Since nought so stockish, hard and full of rage,
But music for the time doth change his nature.
The man that hath no music in himself,
Nor is not moved with concord of sweet sounds,
Is fit for treasons, stratagems and spoils;
The motions of his spirit are dull as night,
And his affections dark as Erebus:
Let no such man be trusted.

Sonnets

by William Shakespeare

XVIII

Shall I compare thee to a summer's day?
Thou art more lovely and more temperate:
Rough winds do shake the darling buds of May,
And summer's lease hath all too short a date:
Sometime too hot the eye of heaven shines,
And often is his gold complexion dimm'd;
And every fair from fair sometime declines,
By chance or nature's changing course untrimm'd;
But thy eternal summer shall not fade,
Nor lose possession of that fair thou owest;
Nor shall Death brag thou wander'st in his shade,
When in eternal lines to time thou grow'st:
    So long as men can breathe, or eyes can see,
    So long lives this, and this gives life to thee.

XIX

Devouring Time, blunt thou the lion's paws,
And make the earth devour her own sweet brood;
Pluck the keen teeth from the fierce tiger's jaws,
And burn the long-lived phoenix in her blood;
Make glad and sorry seasons as thou fleet'st,
And do whate'er thou wilt, swift-footed Time,
To the wide world and all her fading sweets;
But I forbid thee one most heinous crime:
O, carve not with thy hours my love's fair brow,
Nor draw no lines there with thine antique pen;
Him in thy course untainted do allow
For beauty's pattern to succeeding men.
    Yet do thy worst, old Time: despite thy wrong,
    My love shall in my verse ever live young.

XXX

When to the sessions of sweet silent thought
I summon up remembrance of things past,
I sigh the lack of many a thing I sought,
And with old woes new wail my dear time's waste:
Then can I drown an eye, unused to flow,
For precious friends hid in death's dateless night,
And weep afresh love's long since cancell'd woe,
And moan the expense of many a vanish'd sight:
Then can I grieve at grievances foregone,
And heavily from woe to woe tell o'er
The sad account of fore-bemoaned moan,
Which I new pay as if not paid before.
    But if the while I think on thee, dear friend,
    All losses are restored and sorrows end.

XXXVI

Let me confess that we two must be twain,
Although our undivided loves are one:
So shall those blots that do with me remain,
Without thy help, by me be borne alone.
In our two loves there is but one respect,
Though in our lives a separable spite,
Which though it alter not love's sole effect,
Yet doth it steal sweet hours from love's delight.
I may not evermore acknowledge thee,
Lest my bewailed guilt should do thee shame,
Nor thou with public kindness honor me,
Unless thou take that honor from thy name:
    But do not so; I love thee in such sort,
    As thou being mine, mine is thy good report.

CXVI

Let me not to the marriage of true minds
Admit impediments. Love is not love
Which alters when it alteration finds,
Or bends with the remover to remove:
O, no! it is an ever-fixed mark,
That looks on tempests and is never shaken;
It is the star to every wandering bark,
Whose worth's unknown, although his height be taken.
Love's not Time's fool, though rosy lips and cheeks
Within his bending sickle's compass come;
Love alters not with his brief hours and weeks,
But bears it out even to the edge of doom.
    If this be error and upon me proved,
    I never writ, nor no man ever loved.

CXXXVIII

When my love swears that she is made of truth,
I do believe her, though I know she lies,
That she might think me some untutor'd youth,
Unlearned in the world's false subtleties.
Thus vainly thinking that she thinks me young,
Although she knows my days are past the best,
Simply I credit her false-speaking tongue:
On both sides thus is simple truth suppress'd.
But wherefore says she not she is unjust?
And wherefore say not I that I am old?
O, love's best habit is in seeming trust,
And age in love loves not to have years told:
    Therefore I lie with her and she with me,
    And in our faults by lies we flatter'd be.

Horatius

by Thomas Babington Macaulay

Lars Porsena of Clusium,
　By the nine gods he swore
That the great house of Tarquin
　Should suffer wrong no more.
By the nine gods he swore it,
　And named a trysting day,
And bade his messengers ride forth,
East and west and south and north,
　To summon his array.

East and west and south and north
　The messengers ride fast,
And tower and town and cottage
　Have heard the trumpet's blast.
The horseman and the footmen
　Are pouring in amain
From many stately market-place,
　From many a fruitful plain;

* * *

And now hath every city
 Sent up her tale of men;
The foot are fourscore thousand
 The horse are thousands ten.
Before the gates of Sutrium
 Is met the great array,
A proud man was Lars Porsena
 Upon the trysting day.

* * *

But by the yellow Tiber
 Was tumult and affright:
From all the spacious champaign
 To Rome men took their flight.
A mile around the city,
 The throng stopped up the ways;
A fearful sight it was to see
 Through two long nights and days.

* * *

Now, from the rock Tarpeian,
 Could the wan burghers spy
The line of blazing villages
 Red in the midnight sky.
The Fathers of the City,
 They sat all night and day
For every hour some horseman came
 With tidings of dismay.

They held a council standing
    Before the river-gate;
Short time was there, ye well may guess,
    For musing or debate.
Outspake the Consul roundly:
    "The bridge must go straight down;
For since Janiculum is lost
    Naught else can save the town."

Just then a scout came flying,
    All wild with haste and fear:
"To arms! to arms! Sir Consul;
    Lars Porsena is here."
On the low hills to westward
    The Consul fixed his eye,
And saw the swarthy storm of dust
    Rise fast along the sky.

And nearer, fast and nearer,
    Doth the red whirlwind come;
And louder still and still more loud,
From underneath that rolling cloud,
Is heard the trumpet's war-note proud,
    The trampling and the hum.
And plainly and more plainly
    Now through the gloom appears,
Far to left and far to right,
In broken gleams of dark-blue light,
The long array of helmets bright,
    The long array of spears.

But the Consul's brow was sad,
　And the Consul's speech was low,
And darkly looked he at the wall,
　And darkly at the foe:
"Their van will be upon us
　Before the bridge goes down;
And if they once may win the bridge
　What hope to save the town?"

Then outspake brave Horatius.
　The captain of the gate:
"To every man upon this earth
　Death cometh soon or late.
And how can man die better
　Than facing fearful odds
For the ashes of his fathers
　And the temples of his gods?

"Hew down the bridge, Sir Consul,
　With all the speed ye may;
I, with two more to help me,
　Will hold the foe in play,—
In yon strait path a thousand
　May well be stopped by three.
Now who will stand on either hand,
　And keep the bridge with me?"

Then outspake Spurius Lartius,—
　A Ramnian proud was he:
"Lo, I will stand at thy right hand,
　And keep the bridge with thee."
And outspake strong Herminius,—
　Of Titan blood was he:
"I will abide on thy left side,
And keep the bridge with thee."

"Horatius," quoth the Consul,
  "As thou sayest, so let it be."
And straight against that great array,
  Forth went the dauntless Three.
Now, while the Three were tightening
  Their harness on their backs,
The Consul was the foremost man
  To take in hand an axe;
And Fathers mixed with Commons
  Seized hatchet, bar, and crow,
And smote upon the planks above,
  And loosed the props below.

* * *

Meanwhile the Tuscan army,
  Right glorious to behold,
Came flashing back the noonday light,
Rank behind rank, like surges bright
  Of a broad sea of gold.
Four hundred trumpets sounded
  A peal of warlike glee,
As that great host, with measured tread,
And spears advanced, the ensigns spread,
Rolled slowly toward the bridge's head,
  Where stood the dauntless Three.

The Three stood calm and silent,
  And looked upon the foes,
And a great shout of laughter
  From all the vanguard rose;
And forth three chiefs came spurring
  Before the mighty mass;
To earth they sprang, their swords they drew,

And lifted high their shields, and flew
    To win the narrow pass.

Aunus, from green Tifernum,
    Lord of the hill of vines;
And Seius, whose eight hundred slaves
    Sicken in Ilva's mines;
And Picus, long to Clusium
    Vassal in peace and war,

Who led to fight his Umbrian powers
From that grey crag where, girt with towers,
The fortress of Nequinum towers
    O'er the pale waves of Nar.

Stout Lartius hurled down Aunus
    Into the stream beneath;
Herminius struck at Seius,
    And clove him to the teeth;
At Picus brave Horatius
    Darted one fiery thrust,
And the proud Umbrian's gilded arms
    Clashed in the bloody dust.

Then Ocnus of Falerii
    Rushed on the Roman three;
And Lausulus of Urgo,
    The rover of the sea;
And Aruns of Volsinium,
    Who slew the great wild boar,—
The great wild boar that had his den
Amidst the reeds of Cosa's fen,
And wasted fields, and slaughtered men,
    Along Albinia's shore.

Herminius smote down Aruns;
    Lartius laid Ocnus low;
Right to the heart of Lausulus
    Horatius sent a blow:
"Lie there," he cried, "fell pirate!
    No more, aghast and pale,
From Ostia's walls the crowd shall mark
The track of thy destroying bark;
No more Campania's hinds shall fly
To woods and caverns, when they spy
    Thy thrice-accursed sail!"

But now no sound of laughter
    Was heard amongst the foes.
A wild and wrathful clamor
    From all the vanguard rose.
Six spears' length from the entrance
    Halted that mighty mass,
And for a space no man came forth
    To win the narrow pass.

But, hark! the cry is Astur:
    And lo! the ranks divide;
And the great lord of Luna
    Comes with his stately stride.
Upon his ample shoulders
    Clangs loud the fourfold shield,
And in his hand he shakes the brand
    Which none but he can wield.

He smiled on those bold Romans,
    A smile serene and high;
He eyed the flinching Tuscans,
    And scorn was in his eye.

Quoth he, "The she-wolf's litter
    Stands savagely at bay;
But will ye dare to follow,
    If Astur clears the way?"

Then, whirling up his broadsword
    With both hands to the height,
He rushed against Horatius,
    And smote with all his might,
With shield and blade Horatius
    Right deftly turned the blow,
The blow, though turned, came yet too nigh;
    It missed his helm, but gashed his thigh.
The Tuscans raised a joyful cry
    To see the red blood flow.

He reeled, and on Herminius
    He leaned one breathing-space,
Then, like a wild-cat mad with wounds,
    Sprang right at Astur's face.
Through teeth and skull and helmet
    So fierce a thrust he sped,
The good sword stood a handbreadth out
    Behind the Tuscan's head.

And the great lord of Luna
    Fell at that deadly stroke,
As falls on Mount Avernus
    A thunder-smitten oak.
Far o'er the crashing forest
    The giant arms lie spread;
And the pale augurs, muttering low,
    Gaze on the blasted head.

On Astur's throat Horatius
   Right firmly pressed his heel,
And thrice and four times tugged amain,
Ere he wrenched out the steel.
"And see," he cried, "the welcome,
   Fair guests, that waits you here!
What noble Lucumo comes next
   To taste our Roman cheer?

But meanwhile axe and lever
   Have manfully been plied,
And now the bridge hangs tottering
   Above the boiling tide.
"Come back, come back, Horatius!"
   Loud cried the Fathers all;
"Back Lartius! back Herminius!
   Back, ere the ruin fall!"

Back darted Spurius Lartius;
   Herminius darted back;
And, as they passed, beneath their feet
   They felt the timbers crack;
But when they turned their faces,
   And on the further shore
   Saw brave Horatius stand alone,
   They would have crossed once more.

But, with a crash like thunder,
   Fell every loosened beam,
And, like a dam, the mighty wreck
   Lay right athwart the stream;
And a long shout of triumph
   Rose from the walls of Rome,
As to the highest turret-tops
   Was splashed the yellow foam.

Alone stood brave Horatius,
　　But constant still in mind,—
Thrice thirty thousand foes before,
　　And the broad flood behind.
"Down with him!" cried false Sextus,
　　With a smile on his pale face;
"Now yield thee," cried Lars Porsena,
　　"Now yield thee to our grace!"

Round turned he, as not deigning
　　Those craven ranks to see;
Naught spake he to Lars Porsena,
　　To Sextus naught spake he;
But he saw on Palatinus
　　The white porch of his home;
And he spake to the noble river
　　That rolls by the towers of Rome:

"O Tiber! Father Tiber!
　　To whom the Romans pray
A Roman's life, a Roman's arms,
　　Take thou in charge this day!"
So he spake, and speaking, sheathed
　　The good sword by his side,
And, with his harness on his back,
　　Plunged headlong in the tide.

No sound of joy or sorrow
　　Was heard from either bank,
But friends and foes in dumb surprise,
With parted lips and straining eyes,
　　Stood gazing where he sank;

And when above the surges
   They saw his crest appear,
All Rome sent forth a rapturous cry,
And even the ranks of Tuscany
   Could scarce forbear to cheer.

But fiercely ran the current,
   Swollen high by months of rain,
And fast his blood was flowing;
   And he was sore in pain,
And heavy with his armor,
   And spent with changing blows;
And oft they thought him sinking,
   But still again he rose.

* * *

And now he feels the bottom;—
   Now on dry earth he stands;
Now round him throng the Fathers
   To press his gory hands.
And, now, with shouts and clapping,
   And noise of weeping loud,
He enters through the River Gate,
   Borne by the joyous crowd.

On First Looking into Chapman's Homer

by John Keats

Much have I travell'd in the realms of gold,
    And many goodly states and kingdoms seen;
    Round many western islands have I been
Which bards in fealty to Apollo hold.
Oft of one wide expanse had I been told
    That deep-brow'd Homer ruled as his demesne:
    Yet did I never breathe its pure serene
Till I heard Chapman speak out loud and bold:
Then felt I like some watcher of the skies
    When a new planet swims into his ken;
Or like stout Cortez when with eagle eyes
    He stared at the Pacific—and all his men
Look'd at each other with a wild surmise—
    Silent, on a peak in Darien.

From *The Princess*

by Alfred Lord Tennyson

The splendor falls on castle walls
   And snowy summits old in story;
The long light shakes across the lakes,
   And the wild cataract leaps in glory.
Blow, bugle, blow, set the wild echoes flying,
Blow, bugle; answer, echoes, dying, dying, dying.

O, hark, O, hear! how thin and clear,
   And thinner, clearer, farther going!
O, sweet and far from cliff and scar
   The horns of Elfland faintly blowing!
Blow, let us hear the purple glens replying,
Blow, bugle; answer, echoes, dying, dying, dying.

O love, they die in yon rich sky,
   They faint on hill or field or river;
Our echoes roll from soul to soul,
   And grow for ever and for ever.
Blow, bugle, blow, set the wild echoes flying,
And answer, echoes, answer, dying, dying, dying.

The Lady of Shalott

by Alfred Lord Tennyson

PART I

On either side the river lie
Long fields of barley and of rye,
That clothe the world and meet the sky;
And thro' the field the road runs by
    To many tower'd Camelot;
And up and down the people go,
Gazing where the lilies blow
Round an island there below,
    The island of Shalott.

Willows whiten, aspens quiver,
Little breezes dusk and shiver
Thro' the wave that runs for ever
By the island in the river
    Flowing down to Camelot.
Four gray walls, and four gray towers,
Overlook a space of flowers,
And the silent isle embowers
    The Lady of Shalott.

By the margin, willow-veil'd
Slide the heavy barges trail'd
By slow horses; and unhail'd
The shallop flitteth silken-sail'd
    Skimming down to Camelot:
But who hath seen her wave her hand?
Or at the casement seen her stand?
Or is she known in all the land,
    The Lady of Shalott?

Only reapers, reaping early
In among the bearded barley,
Hear a song that echoes cheerily
From the river winding clearly,
    Down to tower'd Camelot;
And by the moon the reaper weary,
Piling sheaves in uplands airy,
Listening, whispers ' 'Tis the fairy
    Lady of Shalott.'

PART II

There she weaves by night and day
A magic web with colors gay.
She has heard a whisper say,
A curse is on her if she stay
    To look down to Camelot.
She knows not what the curse may be,
And so she weaveth steadily,
And little other care hath she,
    The Lady of Shalott.

And moving thro' a mirror clear
That hangs before her all the year,
Shadows of the world appear.
There she sees the highway near
    Winding down to Camelot;
There the river eddy whirls,
And there the surly village-churls,
And the red cloaks of market-girls,
    Pass onward from Shalott.

Sometimes a troop of damsels glad,
An abbot on an ambling pad,
Sometimes a curly shepherd-lad,

Or long-hair'd page in crimson clad,
   Goes by to tower'd Camelot;
And sometime thro' the mirror blue
The knights come riding two and two:
She hath no loyal knight and true,
   The Lady of Shalott.

But in her web she still delights
To weave the mirror's magic sights,
For often thro' the silent nights
A funeral, with plumes and lights
   And music, went to Camelot:
Or when the moon was overhead,
Came two young lovers lately wed:
'I am half sick of shadows,' said
   The Lady of Shalott.

PART III
A bow-shot from her bower-eaves,
He rode between the barley-sheaves,
The sun came dazzling thro' the leaves,
And flamed upon the brazen greaves
   Of bold Sir Lancelot.
A red-cross knight for ever kneel'd
To a lady in his shield,
That sparkled on the yellow field,
   Beside remote Shalott.

The gemmy bridle glitter'd free,
Like to some branch of stars we see
Hung in the golden Galaxy.
The bridle bells rang merrily
   As he rode down to Camelot:

And from his blazon'd baldric slung
A mighty silver bugle hung,
And as he rode his armor rung,
    Beside remote Shalott.

All in the blue unclouded weather
Thick-jewell'd shone the saddle-leather,
The helmet and the helmet-feather
Burn'd like one burning flame together,
    As he rode down to Camelot;
As often thro' the purple night,
Below the starry clusters bright,
Some bearded meteor, trailing light,
    Moves over still Shalott.

His broad clear brow in sunlight glow'd;
On burnish'd hooves his war-horse trode;
From underneath his helmet flow'd
His coal black curls as he rode,
    As he rode down to Camelot
From the bank and from the river
He flashed into the crystal mirror,
'Tirra lirra,' by the river
    Sang Sir Lancelot.

She left the web, she left the loom,
She made three paces thro' the room,
She saw the water-lily bloom,
She saw the helmet and the plume,
    She look'd down to Camelot.
Out flew the web and floated wide;
The mirror cracked from side to side
'The curse is come upon me,' cried
    The Lady of Shalott.

PART IV

In the stormy east-wind straining,
The pale yellow woods were waning,
The broad stream in his banks complaining,
Heavily the low sky raining
   Over tower'd Camelot;
Down she came and found a boat
Beneath a willow left afloat,
And round about the prow she wrote
   The Lady of Shalott.

And down the river's dim expanse
Like some bold seer in a trance,
Seeing all his own mischance—
With a glassy countenance
   Did she look to Camelot.
And at the closing of the day
She loosed the chain, and down she lay;
The broad stream bore her far away,
   The Lady of Shalott.

Lying, robed in snowy white
That loosely flew to left and right—
The leaves upon her falling light—
Thro' the noises of the night
   She floated down to Camelot;
And as the boat-head wound along
The willowy hills and fields among,
They heard her singing her last song,
   The Lady of Shalott.

Heard a carol, mournful, holy,
Chanted loudly, chanted lowly,
Till her blood was frozen slowly,

The Dialectical Stage: Poetry Selections

And her eyes were darken'd wholly,
    Turn'd to tower'd Camelot.
For ere she reach'd upon the tide
The first house by the water-side,
Singing in her song she died,
    The Lady of Shalott.

Under tower and balcony,
By garden-wall and gallery,
A gleaming shape she floated by,
Dead-pale between the houses high,
    Silent into Camelot.
Out upon the wharfs they came,
Knight and burgher, lord and dame,
And round the prow they read her name,
    The Lady of Shalott.

Who is this? and what is here?
And in the lighted palace near
Died the sound of royal cheer;
And they cross'd themselves for fear,
    All the knights at Camelot;
But Lancelot mused a little space;
He said, 'She has a lovely face;
God in His mercy lend her grace,
    The Lady of Shalott.'

The Dialectical Stage: Poetry Selections

Lochinvar

by Sir Walter Scott

Oh! young Lochinvar is come out of the west,
Through all the wide Border his steed was the best,
And save his good broadsword he weapons had none,
He rode all unarmed and he rode all alone.
So faithful in love and so dauntless in war,
There never was knight like the young Lochinvar.

He stayed not for brake and he stopped not for stone,
He swam the Eske river where ford there was none;
But ere he alighted at Netherby gate,
The bride had consented, the gallant came late:
For a laggard in love and a dastard in war
Was to wed the fair Ellen of brave Lochinvar.

So boldly he entered the Netherby Hall,
Among bridesmen and kinsmen, and brothers and all:
Then spoke the bride's father, his hand on his sword,—
For the poor craven bridegroom said never a word,—
"Oh! come ye in peace here, or come ye in war,
Or to dance at our bridal, young Lord Lochinvar?"—

"I long wooed your daughter, my suit you denied;
Love swells like the Solway, but ebbs like its tide—
And now I am come, with this lost love of mine,
To lead but one measure, drink one cup of wine.
There are maidens in Scotland more lovely by far,
That would gladly be bride to the young Lochinvar."

The bride kissed the goblet; the knight took it up,
He quaffed off the wine, and he threw down the cup.
She looked down to blush, and she looked up to sigh,

With a smile on her lips and a tear in her eye.
He took her soft hand ere her mother could bar,—
"Now tread we a measure!" said young Lochinvar.

So stately his form, and so lovely her face,
That never a hall such a galliard did grace;
While her mother did fret, and her father did fume,
And the bridegroom stood dangling his bonnet and plume;
And the bride-maidens whispered, " 'Twere better by far
To have matched our fair cousin with young Lochinvar."

One touch to her hand and one word in her ear,
When they reached the hall-door, and the charger stood near;
So light to the croupe the fair lady he swung,
So light to the saddle before her he sprung!
"She is won! we are gone, over bank, bush, and scaur;
They'll have fleet steeds that follow," quoth young Lochinvar.

There was mounting 'mong Graemes of the Netherby clan;
Forsters, Fenwicks, and Musgraves, they rode and they ran:
There was racing and chasing on Cannobie Lee,
But the lost bride of Netherby ne'er did they see.
So daring in love and so dauntless in war,
Have ye e'er heard of gallant like young Lochinvar?

The Soul

by Richard Henry Dana

Come, Brother, turn with me from pining thought
And all the inward ills that sin has wrought;
Come, send abroad a love for all who live,
And feel the deep content in turn they give.
Kind wishes and good deeds,—they make not poor;
They'll home again, full laden, to thy door;
The streams of love flow back where they begin,
For springs of outward joys lie deep within,
Even let them flow, and make the places glad
Where dwell thy fellow-men. Shouldst thou be sad,
And earth seem bare, and hours, once happy press
Upon thy thoughts, and make thy loneliness
More lonely for the past, thou then shalt hear
The music of those waters running near;
And thy faint spirit drink the cooling stream,
And thine eye gladden with the playing beam
That now upon the water dances, now
Leaps up and dances in the hanging bough.
Is it not lovely? Tell me, where doth dwell
The power that wrought so beautiful a spell?
In thine own bosom, Brother? Then as thine
Guard with a reverent fear this power divine.
And it, indeed, 't is not the outward state,
But temper of the soul by which we rate
Sadness or joy, even let thy bosom move
With noble thoughts and wake thee into love,
And let each feeling in thy breast be given
An honest aim, which, sanctified by Heaven,
And springing into act, new life imparts,
Till beats thy frame as with a thousand hearts.

Sin clouds the mind's clear vision,
Around the self-starved soul has spread a dearth.
The earth is full of life; the living Hand
Touched it with life; and all its forms expand
With principles of being made to suit
Man's varied powers and raise him from the brute.
And shall the earth of higher ends be full,—
Earth which thou tread'st,—and thy poor mind be dull?
Thou talk of life, with half thy soul asleep?
Thou "living dead man," let thy spirit leap
Forth to the day, and let the fresh air blow
Through thy soul's shut-up mansion. Would'st thou know
Something of what is life, shake off this death;
Have thy soul feel the universal breath
With which all nature's quick, and learn to be
Sharer in all that thou dost touch or see;
Break from thy body's grasp, thy spirit's trance;
Give thy soul air, thy faculties expanse;
Love, joy, even sorrow,—yield thyself to all!
They make thy freedom, groveler, not thy thrall.
Knock off the shackles which thy spirit bind
To dust and sense, and set at large the mind!
Then move in sympathy with God's great whole,
And be like man at first, *a living soul.*

Woodman, Spare That Tree!

by George Pope Morris

Woodman, spare that tree!
    Touch not a single bough!
In youth it sheltered me,
    And I'll protect it now.

'Twas my forefather's hand
    That placed it near his cot;
There, woodman, let it stand,
    Thy axe shall harm it not.

That old familiar tree,
    Whose glory and renown
Are spread o'er land and sea,
    And wouldst thou hew it down?
Woodman, forbear thy stroke!
    Cut not its earth-bound ties;
O, spare that aged oak
    Now towering to the skies!

When but an idle boy,
    I sought its grateful shade;
In all their gushing joy
    Here too my sisters played.
My mother kissed me here;
    My father pressed my hand—
Forgive this foolish tear,
    But let that old oak stand!

My heart-strings round thee cling,
    Close as thy bark, old friend!
Here shall the wild-bird sing,
    And still thy branches bend.
Old tree! the storm still brave!
    And, woodman, leave the spot;
While I've a hand to save,
    Thy axe shall harm it not.

A Psalm of Life
What the Heart of the Young Man Said to the Psalmist
by Henry Wadsworth Longfellow

Tell me not, in mournful numbers,
   "Life is but an empty dream!"
For the soul is dead that slumbers,
   And things are not what they seem.

Life is real! Life is earnest!
   And the grave is not its goal;
"Dust thou art, to dust returnest,"
   Was not spoken of the soul.

Not enjoyment, and not sorrow,
   Is our destined end or way;
But to act, that each to-morrow
   Finds us farther than to-day.

Art is long, and Time is fleeting,
   And our hearts, though stout and brave,
Still, like muffled drums, are beating
   Funeral marches to the grave.

In the world's broad field of battle,
   In the bivouac of Life,
Be not like dumb, driven cattle!
   Be a hero in the strife!

Trust no Future, howe'er pleasant!
   Let the dead Past bury its dead!
Act,—act in the living Present!
   Heart within, and God o'erhead!

Lives of great men all remind us
    We can make our lives sublime,
And, departing, leave behind us
    Footprints on the sands of time;

Footprints, that perhaps another,
    Sailing o'er life's solemn main,
A forlorn and shipwrecked brother,
    Seeing, shall take heart again.

Let us, then be up and doing,
    With a heart for any fate;
Still achieving, still pursuing,
    Learn to labor and to wait.

The Arrow and the Song

by Henry Wadsworth Longfellow

I shot an arrow into the air,
It fell to earth, I knew not where;
For, so swiftly it flew, the sight
Could not follow it in its flight.

I breathed a song into the air,
It fell to earth, I knew not where;
For who has sight so keen and strong,
That it can follow the flight of song?

Long, long afterward, in an oak
I found the arrow, still unbroke;
And the song, from the beginning to end,
I found again in the heart of a friend.

The Builders

by Henry Wadsworth Longfellow

All are architects of Fate,
   Working in these walls of Time;
Some with massive deeds and great,
   Some with ornaments of rhyme.

Nothing useless is, or low;
   Each thing in its place is best;
And what seems but idle show
   Strengthens and supports the rest.

For the structure that we raise,
   Time is with materials filled;
Our to-days and yesterdays
   Are the blocks with which we build.

Truly shape and fashion these;
   Leave no yawning gaps between;
Think not, because no man sees,
   Such things will remain unseen.

In the elder days of Art,
   Builders wrought with greatest care
Each minute and unseen part;
   For the gods see everywhere.

Let us do our work as well,
   Both the unseen and the seen;
Make the house where gods may dwell
   Beautiful, entire, and clean.

Else our lives are incomplete,
　　Standing in these walls of Time,
Broken stairways, where the feet
　　Stumble, as they seek to climb.

Build to-day, then, strong and sure,
　　With a firm and ample base;
And ascending and secure
　　Shall to-morrow find its place.

Thus alone can we attain
　　To those turrets, where the eye
Sees the world as one vast plain,
　　And one boundless reach of sky.

The Barefoot Boy

by John Greenleaf Whittier

　　Blessings on thee, little man,
Barefoot boy, with cheek of tan!
With thy turned-up pantaloons,
And thy merry whistled tunes;
With thy red lip, redder still
Kissed by strawberries on the hill;
With the sunshine on thy face,
Through thy torn brim's jaunty grace;
From my heart I give thee joy,—
I was once a barefoot boy!
Prince thou art,—the grown-up man
Only is republican.
Let the million-dollared ride!
Barefoot, trudging at his side,
Thou hast more than he can buy

In the reach of ear and eye,—
Outward sunshine, inward joy:
Blessings on thee, barefoot boy!

O for boyhood's painless play,
Sleep that wakes in laughing day,
Health that mocks the doctor's rules,
Knowledge never learned of schools,
Of the wild bee's morning chase,
Of the wild-flower's time and place,
Flight of fowl and habitude
Of the tenants of the wood;
How the tortoise bears his shell,
How the woodchuck digs his cell,
And the ground-mole sinks his well;
How the robin feeds her young,
How the oriole's nest is hung;
Where the whitest lilies blow,
Where the freshest berries grow,
Where the ground-nut trails its vine,
Where the wood-grape's clusters shine;
Of the black wasp's cunning way,
Mason of his walls of clay,
And the architectural plans
Of gray hornet artisans!—
For, eschewing books and tasks,
Nature answers all he asks;
Hand in hand with her he walks,
Face to face with her he talks,
Part and parcel of her joy,—
Blessings on the barefoot boy!

O for boyhood's time of June,
Crowding years in one brief moon,

When all things I heard or saw,
Me, their master, waited for.
I was rich in flowers and trees,
Humming-birds and honey-bees;
For my sport the squirrel played,
Plied the snouted mole his spade;
For my taste the blackberry cone
Purpled over hedge and stone;
Laughed the brook for my delight
Through the day and through the night,
Whispering at the garden wall,
Talked with me from fall to fall;
Mine the sand-rimmed pickerel pond,
Mine the walnut slopes beyond,
Mine, on bending orchard trees,
Apples of Hesperides!
Still as my horizon grew,
Larger grew my riches too;
All the world I saw or knew
Seemed a complex Chinese toy,
Fashioned for a barefoot boy!

    O for festal dainties spread,
Like my bowl of milk and bread,—
Pewter spoon and bowl of wood,
On the door-stone, gray and rude!
O'er me, like a regal tent,
Cloudy-ribbed, the sunset bent,
Purple-curtained, fringed with gold,
Looped in many a wind-swung fold;
While for music came the play
Of the pied frogs' orchestra;
And, to light the noisy choir,
Lit the fly his lamp of fire.

I was monarch: pomp and joy
Waited on the barefoot boy!

Cheerily, then, my little man,
Live and laugh, as boyhood can!
Though the flinty slopes be hard,
Stubble-speared the new-mown sward,
Every morn shall lead thee through
Fresh baptisms of the dew;
Every evening from thy feet
Shall the cool wind kiss the heat:
All too soon these feet must hide
In the prison cells of pride,
Lose the freedom of the sod,
Like a colt's for work be shod,
Made to tread the mills of toil,
Up and down in ceaseless moil:
Happy if their track be found
Never on forbidden ground;
Happy if they sink not in
Quick and treacherous sands of sin.
Ah! that thou couldst know thy joy,
Ere it passes, barefoot boy!

The Dialectical Stage: Poetry Selections

In School-Days

by John Greenleaf Whittier

Still sits the school-house by the road,
    A ragged beggar sleeping;
Around it still the sumachs grow
    And blackberry-vines are creeping.

Within, the master's desk is seen,
    Deep scarred by raps official;
The warping floor, the battered seats,
    The jack-knife's carved initial;

The charcoal frescoes on its wall;
    Its door's worn sill, betraying
The feet that, creeping slow to school,
    Went storming out to playing!

Long years ago a winter sun
    Shone over it at setting;
Lit up its western window-panes,
    And low eaves' icy fretting.

It touched the tangled golden curls,
    And brown eyes full of grieving,
Of one who still her steps delayed
    When all the school were leaving.

For near her stood the little boy
    Her childish favor singled;
His cap pulled low upon a face
    Where pride and shame were mingled.

Pushing with restless feet the snow
    To right and left, he lingered;—
As restlessly her tiny hands
    The blue-checked apron fingered.

He saw her lift her eyes; he felt
    The soft hand's light caressing,
And heard the tremble of her voice,
    As if a fault confessing.

"I'm sorry that I spelt the word:
    I hate to go above you,
Because,"—the brown eyes lower fell,—
    "Because, you see, I love you!"

Still memory to a gray-haired man
    That sweet child-face is showing.
Dear girl! the grasses on her grave
    Have forty years been growing!

He lives to learn, in life's hard school,
    How few who pass above him
Lament their triumph and his loss,
    Like her,—because they love him.

Winter Memories

by Henry David Thoreau

Within the circuit of this plodding life
There enter moments of an azure hue,
Untarnished fair as is the violet
Or anemone, when the spring strews them
By some meandering rivulet, which make
The best philosophy untrue that aims
But to console man for his grievances.
I have remembered when the winter came,
High in my chamber in the frosty nights,
When in the still light of the cheerful moon,
On every twig and rail and jutting spout,
The icy spears were adding to their length
Against the arrows of the coming sun,
How in the shimmering noon of summer past
Some unrecorded beam slanted across
The upland pastures where the Johnswort grew;
Or heard, amid the verdure of my mind,
The bee's long smothered hum, on the blue flag
Loitering amidst the mead: or busy rill,
Which now through all its course stands still and dumb
Its own memorial,—purling at its play
Along the slopes, and through the meadows next,
Until its youthful sound was hushed at last
In the staid current of the lowland stream;
Or seen the furrows shine but late upturned,
And where the fieldfare followed in the rear,
When all the fields around lay bound and hoar
Beneath a thick integument of snow.
So by God's cheap economy made rich
To go upon my winter's task again.

Dickens in Camp

by Bret Harte

Above the pines the moon was slowly drifting,
    The river sang below;
The dim Sierras, far beyond, uplifting
    Their minarets of snow.

The roaring camp-fire, with rude humor, painted
    The ruddy tints of health
On haggard face and form that drooped and fainted
    In the fierce race for wealth;

Till one arose, and from his pack's scant treasure
    A hoarded volume drew,
And cards were dropped from hands of listless leisure
    To hear the tale anew.

And then, while round them shadows gathered faster,
    And as the firelight fell,
He read aloud the book wherein the Master
    Had writ of "Little Nell".

Perhaps 't was boyish fancy,—for the reader
    Was youngest of them all,—
But, as he read, from clustering pine and cedar
    A silence seemed to fall;

The fir-trees, gathering closer in the shadows,
    Listened in every spray,
While the whole camp with "Nell" on English meadows
    Wandered and lost their way.

And so in mountain solitudes—o'ertaken
　　As by some spell divine—
Their cares dropped from them like the needles shaken
　　From out the gusty pine.

Lost is that camp and wasted all its fire;
　　And he who wrought that spell?
Ah! towering pine and stately Kentish spire,
　　Ye have one tale to tell!

Lost is that camp, but let its fragrant story
　　Blend with the breath that thrills
With hop-vine's incense all the pensive glory
　　That fills the Kentish hills.

And on that grave where English oak and holly
　　And laurel wreaths entwine,
Deem it not all a too presumptuous folly,
　　This spray of Western pine!

The Maldive Shark
by Herman Melville

About the Shark, phlegmatical one,
Pale sot of the Maldive sea,
The sleek little pilot-fish, azure and slim,
How alert in attendance be.
From his saw-pit of mouth, from his charnel of maw,
They have nothing of harm to dread,
But liquidly glide on his ghastly flank
Or before his Gorgonian head;
Or lurk in the port of serrated teeth
In white triple tiers of glittering gates,

And there find a haven when peril's abroad,
An asylum in jaws of the Fates!
They are friends; and friendly they guide him to prey,
Yet never partake of the treat—
Eyes and brains to the dotard lethargic and dull,
Pale ravener of horrible meat.

There Are Gains for All Our Losses

by Richard Henry Stoddard

There are gains for all our losses,
    There are balms for all our pain:
But when youth, the dream, departs,
It takes something from our hearts,
    And it never comes again.

We are stronger, and are better,
    Under manhood's sterner reign:
Still we feel that something sweet
Followed youth, with flying feet,
    And will never come again.

Something beautiful is vanished,
    And we sigh for it in vain:
We behold it everywhere,
On the earth, and in the air,
    But it never comes again.

The Things That Will Not Die

by Edward Rowland Sill

What am I glad will stay when I have passed
    From this dear valley of the world, and stand
On yon snow-glimmering peaks, and lingering cast
    From that dim land
  A backward look, and haply stretch my hand,
Regretful, now the wish comes true at last?

Sweet strains of music I am glad will be
    Still wandering down the wind, for men will hear
And think themselves from all their care set free,
    And heaven near
  When summer stars burn very still and clear,
And waves of sound are swelling like the sea.

And it is good to know that overhead
    Blue skies will brighten, and the sun will shine,
And flowers be sweet in many a garden bed,
    And all divine,
  (For are they not, O Father, thoughts of thine?)
Earth's warmth and fragrance shall on men be shed.

And I am glad that Night will always come,
    Hushing all sounds, even the soft-voiced birds,
Putting away all light from her deep dome,
    Until are heard
  In the wide starlight's stillness, unknown words,
That make the heart ache till it finds its home.

And I am glad that neither golden sky,
    Nor violet lights that linger on the hill,

Nor ocean's wistful blue shall satisfy,
  But they shall fill
With wild unrest and endless longing still,
The soul whose hope beyond them all must lie.

And I rejoice that love shall never seem
  So perfect as it ever was to be,
But endlessly that inner haunting dream
  Each heart shall see
  Hinted in every dawn's fresh purity,
Hopelessly shadowed in each sunset's gleam.

And though warm mouths will kiss and hands will cling,
  And thought by silent thought be understood,
I do rejoice that the next hour will bring
  That far off mood,
  That drives one like a lonely child to God,
Who only sees and measures everything.

And it is well that when these feet have pressed
  The outward path from earth, 't will not seem sad
To them that stay; but they who love me best
  Will be most glad
  That such a long unquiet now has had,
At last, a gift of perfect peace and rest.

When the Frost Is on the Punkin

by James Whitcomb Riley

When the frost is on the punkin and the fodder's in the shock,
And you hear the kyouck and gobble of the struttin' turkey-
    cock,
And the clackin' of the guineys, and the cluckin' of the hens,
And the rooster's hallylooyer as he tiptoes on the fence;
O it's then's the times a feller is a-feelin' at his best,
With the risin' sun to greet him from a night of peaceful rest,
As he leaves the house, bare-headed, and goes out to feed the
    stock,
When the frost is on the punkin and the fodder's in the shock.

They's something kindo' hearty-like about the atmosphere,
When the heat of summer's over and the coolin' fall is here—
Of course we miss the flowers, and the blossoms on the trees,
And the mumble of the hummin'-birds and buzzin' of the
    bees;
But the air's so appetisn'; and the landscape through the haze
Of a crisp and sunny morning of the airly autumn days
Is a pictur' that no painter has the colorin' to mock—
When the frost is on the punkin and the fodder's in the shock.

The husky, rusty rustle of the tossels of the corn,
And the raspin' of the tangled leaves, as golden as the morn;
The stubble in the furries—kindo' lonesome-like, but still
A-preachin' sermons to us of the barns they growed to fill;
The strawstack in the medder, and the reaper in the shed;
The hosses in theyr stalls below—the clover overhead!—
O, it sets my heart a-clickin' like the tickin' of a clock,
When the frost is on the punkin and the fodder's in the shock!

The Dilettante

by Paul Laurence Dunbar

He scribbles some in prose and verse,
    And now and then he prints it;
He paints a little,—gathers some
    Of Nature's gold and mints it.

He plays a little, sings a song,
    Acts tragic roles, or funny;
He does, because his love is strong,
    But not, oh, not for money!

He studies almost everything
    From social art to science;
A thirsty mind, a flowing spring,
    Demand and swift compliance.

He looms above the sordid crowd—
    At least through friendly lenses;
While his mamma looks pleased and proud,
    And kindly pays expenses.

Conscience and Remorse

by Paul Laurence Dunbar

"Good-bye," I said to my conscience—
    "Good-bye for aye and aye,"
And I put her hands off harshly,
    And turned my face away;
And conscience smitten sorely
    Returned not from that day.

But a time came when my spirit
    Grew weary of its pace;
And I cried: "Come back, my conscience;
    I long to see thy face."
But conscience cried: "I cannot;
    Remorse sits in my place."

Fog

by Carl Sandburg

The fog comes
on little cat feet.

It sits looking
over harbor and city
on silent haunches
and then moves on.

OTHER SELECTIONS TO MEMORIZE

The Second Inaugural Address of Abraham Lincoln
March 4, 1865

1. At this second appearing to take the oath of the presidential office, there is less occasion for an extended address than there was at first. Then a statement, somewhat in detail, of a course to be pursued, seemed fitting and proper. Now, at the expiration of four years, during which public declarations have been constantly called forth on every point and phase of the great contest which still absorbs the attention and engrosses the energies of the nation, little that is new could be presented. The progress of our arms, upon which all else chiefly depends, is as well known to the public as to myself; and it is, I trust, reasonably satisfactory and encouraging to all. With high hope for the future, no prediction in regard to it is ventured.

2. On the occasion corresponding to this four years ago, all thoughts were anxiously directed to an impending civil war. All dreaded it—all sought to avert it. While the inaugural address was being delivered from this place, devoted altogether to *saving* the Union without war, insurgent agents were in the city seeking to *destroy* it without war—seeking to dissolve the Union and divide effects by negotiation. Both parties deprecated war; but one of them would *make* war rather than let the nation survive; and the other would *accept* war rather than let it perish. And the war came.

3. One eighth of the whole population were colored slaves, not distributed generally over the Union, but localized in the

Southern part of it. These slaves constituted a peculiar and powerful interest. All knew that this interest was, somehow, the cause of the war. To strengthen, perpetuate, and extend this interest was the object for which the insurgents would rend the Union, even by war; while the government claimed no right to do more than to restrict the territorial enlargement of it. Neither party expected for the war the magnitude or the duration which it has already attained. Neither anticipated that the *cause* of the conflict might cease when, or even before, the conflict itself should cease. Each looked for an easier triumph, and a result less fundamental and astounding. Both read the same Bible, and pray to the same God; and each invokes His aid against the other. It may seem strange that any men should dare to ask a just God's assistance in wringing their bread from the sweat of other men's faces; but let us judge not that we be not judged. The prayers of both could not be answered; that of neither has been answered fully. The Almighty has His own purposes. "Woe unto the world because of offences! for it must needs be that offences come; but woe to that man by whom the offence cometh!" If we shall suppose that American slavery is one of those offences which, in the providence of God, must needs come, but which, having continued through His appointed time, He now wills to remove, and that He gives to both North and South, this terrible war, as the woe due to those by whom the offence came, shall we discern therein any departure from those divine attributes which the believers in a Living God always ascribe to Him? Fondly do we hope—fervently do we pray—that this mighty scourge of war may speedily pass away. Yet, if God wills that it continue, until all the wealth piled by the bondman's two hundred and fifty years of unrequited toil shall be sunk, and until every drop of blood drawn with the lash, shall be paid by another drawn with the sword, as was said three thousand years ago, so still it must be said "the judgments of the Lord are true and righteous altogether."

4. With malice toward none, with charity for all, with firmness in the right as God gives us to see the right, let us strive on to finish the work we are in, to bind up the nation's wounds, to care for him who shall have borne the battle, and for his widow and his orphan—to do all which may achieve and cherish a just and lasting peace among ourselves and with all nations.

DICTATION SELECTIONS

From *The Winged Watchman, by Hilda van Stockum*

1. Joris Verhagen was six years old when the Germans invaded Holland. At ten he could remember little of what it had been like before the war. Dirk Jan, his brother, who was four years older, could tell him more about it, but Joris suspected that he made things up. Surely there never could have been a time when people threw away potato parings and apple cores and fed their precious sugar beets to the pigs!

2. "Whatever happened?" she cried. "Don't tell me you've been fighting!"

   "I had to rescue this pup," said Joris, putting it on the floor, where it started to sniff around curiously.

   "Merciful St. Joseph!" cried Mother. "And what about my message?"

3. Then the aviator slowly lowered his weapon and grinned. It was a wide, infectious grin that gave a sunny look to his face. It was too absurd to be frightened of a thin, ten-year-old boy in a faded red jersey, with sun-burnt legs stuck in rough clogs and arms tightly clasped around a huge gray cat!

   Joris' smile answered his, beginning tremulously at the corners of his mouth and then spreading over his whole face, so that his freckled nose wrinkled up and the gap between his front teeth showed.

The two shook hands. They had established a bond over a gulf of different ages and nationalities. Some instinct told them that they could trust each other.

4. "Whatever happens," she said, "at least we'll have *something* to eat. It's going to be a hard winter. People may prattle about liberation, but the Germans have taken away so much of our food that even the Allies won't be able to help us right away. And we are *not* liberated. . . ."

There was so much real fear in her voice that Joris wandered off. It didn't seem right to tell her about Charles King. She had enough on her mind. But how was he going to get the food he'd promised to bring?

5. "Never, never," said Mother, and she was half choking, "was there such a sin since Adam fell." Then it was that Joris saw her angry with the terrible anger of an avenging angel. Her blue eyes flashed and her voice trembled as she said, "I would not blame God if he destroyed us for it." The words seemed to hover in the air like a menacing cloud.

Joris trotted on silently for a while. Then he asked: "Do you think God is going to destroy us?"

Some of Mother's anger seemed to melt away as she looked at him. "No," she said in a gentler voice. "God isn't like that. He returns good for evil."

6. "The Germans are dangerous," he said seriously. "They can do terrible things to you and to all of us, because they have all the weapons. We have nothing."

Charles stopped pacing and looked down at Dirk Jan.

"Yes, you have," he said quietly. "You have right on your side. That's the biggest weapon."

7. "Religion is not just a matter of going to church. We must love God with our whole strength and all our mind, and

our neighbor as ourselves. It is upon what we do to our neighbor that we shall be judged, a solemn thought. Now let us pray that we may receive the strength to do the loving thing in these perilous times."

Joris was thinking, as he knelt down, that Uncle Cor and Father and Mother need not worry. They were helping their neighbors with all their strength. After Mass people chatted in the churchyard. As Joris joined his family he saw Leendert Schenderhans sauntering toward them.

8. Uncle Cor had arranged to send word of his safe arrival by windmill "telegraph," for windmills have always had their own language. In the old days, when Catholics were persecuted in Holland, a white rag tied to the wing of a windmill showed that a priest had come to say Mass. When a mill is at rest, its wings form a St. Andrew's cross, the position least likely to attract lightning. Traveling millwrights know that a mill needs repair when this cross is crooked. On a feast day, or when there is a birth or wedding in a family, the wings of its mill form an upright cross, leaning slightly to the right, the "joy" position. A leaning of the wings to the left indicates sorrow.

9. Father would sometimes say: "Oh, be quiet, you're too young to understand this," but Hildebrand always took them seriously.

"No, let them think," he'd say. "That's good for them. They're going to have their part to play in building a new Holland. The more they think and argue, the better."

10. "Your brother was quite ready to go," he said. "He talked to me the last time he was here. He went to confession and to Communion. He spoke beautifully of his love for you and your family. He said that whenever he felt discouraged, his visits here renewed and refreshed him. He spoke

of your firm faith, of your affection . . . and remember, he is happy now. There is a great crown in heaven for such as he! 'Greater love than this hath no man, that he lay down his life for his friends.' "

11. But Mrs. Groen shook her head. "Oh no," she said. "I'm sorry for them. To suffer yourself, that is nothing. God will wipe all tears from our eyes. But to hear God ask, 'Where is your brother?'—that must be dreadful. The hardest to bear are the wrongs we do to others. It was not only the Germans, either. Some Germans were kind, at great risk to themselves. In the camp we saw our own people kill each other over a crust of bread. In the old days I used to think that religion did not matter much, that people could be good without it. That was not true in the camps. If you had no hope or faith to keep you human, you sank to the lowest depths. I'll practice my religion more faithfully now."

From *The Story of Rolf and the Viking Bow*, *by Allen French*

12. Then Rolf was silent, and thought of what had been said: how the old woman had prophesied trouble at the law, and by what man that trouble should come. And as he thought upon the words she and his father had spoken, he thought that they had spoken with knowledge, though of different kinds: for while the woman prophesied vaguely, his father had seemed to know who the man should be.

"Father," asked Rolf, "knowest thou who the man is that came upon the ship?"

"I know," answered Hiarandi.

13. Then the vikings despoiled the ship of the chapmen and set her adrift, but the captives were set to row the war-ship. Rolf and Frodi toiled at one oar together, and sore was the labor, but not for long. For on the third day, as they rowed under a bright sky with no wind, they heard a clamor among the vikings, who cried that a long ship was bearing down on them—an Orkney ship, great in size.

14. So they stayed only long enough to see that the fisher fleet, leaving nets and lines, was hurrying to the shore. Those three left the headland and ran to Hawksness; there they told the tidings and gathered men, arming all those who came to the hall. The women were sent into the church with the children, but the men went down to the beach. There the fishermen first made a landing, and hurried for their arms; but when all were gathered together they were very few against what must be the might of the Scots.

15. But she looked at it carefully from end to end, and over-looked the string, and after that she raised it and shook it aloft. Then first men saw any part of her, namely her arm, which was not withered, but firm and large, like a man's. When she spoke her voice was no longer cracked.

    "Water hath not harmed thee, oh my bow! Thou art the same as when thou slewest the baresark. Now shalt thou do a greater deed!"

    And in a moment she set the end of the bow to her foot, and bent the bow, and slipped the string along, and the bow was strung! There stood the homefolk gazing, but the crone cast off the cloak. No woman was she at all, but Rolf in his weapons!

16. Grani answered: "It is true that I might take Rolf un-awares, and slay him. But I remember when he was my thrall in the Orkneys, going with me everywhere, and my

life was daily in his hands. For when we were on the cliffs he might have cast me down, and no man would have known he did it. Or when we were fishing he might have drowned me, and have sailed away in the boat. But he never did evil for evil, and I remember it now."

From *Flint's Island, by Leonard Wibberly*

17. " 'Tis the worst coast in all the world, Mr. Arrow," he said just before the island appeared. "Not a light nor a town in a thousand miles, and reefs as soon as you've made soundings. I'd choose Africa in a hurricane to the American main on a thick night and an onshore wind."

    "What can't be changed must be borne, sir," said Mr. Arrow and, turning to me at the wheel, asked, "What's her head now?"

    "South by east, sir," I replied, though in the rolling and pitching of the brig, the compass was swinging three points on either side of that mark.

18. Captain Samuels and Mr. Arrow now left the rigging and went below to consult the charts with Mr. Hogan. They all returned in a little while with several charts, the better to compare the appearance of the peak with the view, from various approaches, of the islands shown on the charts. None of these views, however, answered to the peak ahead, and the problem was all the harder to solve in that, having run so long on dead reckoning, we did not know our position within a hundred or maybe a hundred and fifty miles.

19. The shock of so terrible a turnabout—to lose ship and treasure and face the prospect of being marooned on a desert island for the rest of my days (if indeed I were not

The Dialectical Stage: Dictation Selections

killed)—deprived me of all reason for a moment. I could only stare at the *Jane*, struggling to accept the truth of what I saw. It was Hodge who first recovered. He touched me on the shoulder and, stooping, motioned that we should get back out of sight among the trees, and this we did without being seen from the brig.

20. On the fourth day, I think, in the evening, when Captain Samuels had led us in prayer, we heard a great deal of fluttering in the bow of the yawl and found a flying fish there, weighing about a pound and a half. It was divided among the six of us—the first nourishment we had had since leaving the *Jane*—and it was eaten entrails and all. Nothing before or since ever tasted so delicious, and although it is the fashion these days to mock the Providence of God, yet it seemed to me then, and does now that our earnest prayers for help (should we be thought deserving of it) had been heard by our Heavenly Father.

From **The Rose Round**, *by Meriol Trevor*

21. The first time Matt went to Woodhall it was June, it was midsummer and the sun shone all day long in the middle of the blue sky. All the fields were green with corn as he went through them, the meadows with long grass waving till the hay-cutter came, or short and emerald where the cows were grazing, for there had been days of rain, but now the rain was gone, cleared off as if it had never been and all the middle country of England lay bright around as he went through, going in the train.

22. Turning away from the tree he saw a decrepit wall, all grown over with ivy and plants, but tall, seven foot tall at

least, and still strong enough to stand. In the wall was a very old door, that had once been painted blue, but now the faded paint had peeled and scaled away almost to the wood. There was a keyhole in the door.

23. Through the hole he saw, bright and small, a blaze of colors, flowers growing. Then the door creaked and leant inwards, rather than opened. The lock was out, but the metal had all rusted away, and Matt's weight had broken it through. He stood up and took hold of the door and lifted it on its complaining hinges and shifted it ajar. Then he squeezed through sideways, and there he was on the other side of the wall.

24. He went into the house, which was very still. Slatted blinds were drawn down over the south and west windows, thin bars of light lay across the old carpets, on the polished floors. Alix went on ahead, light-footed, careless, confident, at home. Matt followed her, anxious, uncertain, curious, the intruder.

25. Alix suddenly shut her eyes, listening, and Matt watched that listening face, drawn away from earth by the strange sound. For it was somehow a stranger sound than the sea: the murmur of the trees lulled in their ears, whispering of remoter shores, infinite regions, another world, a world without people.

26. "Of course they did. Think of Newton," said Alix. "Bertrand met him. He knew all those people, Fellows of the Royal Society and so on. He was a scientist himself in his way, a Natural Philosopher, they called it then. But the funny thing is, that although he was so clever and Theo is so stupid, he looks like Theo, only not so ugly, and he has two proper hands, of course."

27. "Don't you preach to me, Theodore," his mother said, in-
dignantly, rising to her feet and speaking in a sharp quiver-
ing voice. "Let this good God look after those he has
allowed to come into the world so twisted and deformed!
He took from me my perfect child, my innocent: let Him
take these, whom nobody wants. What has God suffered
that I should do anything for Him?"

Theo stood facing her. He said, "You know He suffered
it all, both as Father and as Child."

Madame was absolutely silent, her face white and still.

28. He walked a little way towards the western arch; the
yellow roses were pale in the shadowy air. A small wind
was blowing out of the west against his face, a wet wind
that he felt might grow to a great gale and roar through
the forests outside the garden. The wind came over the
mountains of Wales and the mountains of Ireland, those
ancient countries, homes of harp and song and sad tales
of loss and wandering; the wind came from the sea, the
great grey Atlantic, the huge tides, thousands of miles
across where no land was, only the waste of water, the
mystery of chaos and the deep. And what then? America,
the fabulous continent, once the new lands, always the
strange lands, full of marvels. And miles and miles fur-
ther, the other ocean, deepest, widest on earth, the vast
Pacific.

29. Alix giggled. "He said, 'Louise, you are a very obstinate
woman, but if you imagine you can outlast Almighty God,
you are just a fool.' "

"Goodness gracious!" said Caro.

"He's known her for years," said Theo. "Since before
she was married and before he became a monk. That's why
I wrote and asked if he could come."

30. Caro did not answer this directly. She said thoughtfully, "You know, Matt, when I first met Theo I thought he was rather a weak person, a passive character, because he let people say what they liked about him and didn't seem to have any authority in his own house. It was awfully stupid of me."

"You don't think that now, then?" said Matt.

"I should say not!" said Caro.

31. "I don't like the word eternal," said Alix. "It's so huge and hollow-sounding, and unreal."

"But there was nothing unreal about Christ when he rose from the grave," said Theo. "It was time and space, walls and moments that were unreal: he just walked through them."

From *They Loved to Laugh, by Kathryn Worth*

32. And suddenly all the air over the gig was full of flying apples. From everywhere and from nowhere they seemed to come in their hurtling flight. Martitia huddled against Dr. David in the bottom of the cart. The apples plopped and sang and zoomed above their heads. Once a big, soft globe struck Dr. David's arm where he had thrown it protectingly over Martitia's bent body.

33. Martitia ran into the hall and knocked at Grandfather Daniel's door. The old voice answered her dimly. She went in. It was the first time that she had ever been there. It struck the girl immediately as resembling the pictures she had seen of ship's cabins. The two windows were small and round, shaped like portholes. The bed was built into the wall of the room like the bunk on a ship. A

The Dialectical Stage: Dictation Selections

whaler's chest stood in one corner. The floor was bare and shipshape.

34. Madame brought forth first from a cellar a little box which she unsealed carefully. She displayed some infinitesimal yellow-brown dots. "These are my French silkworm eggs. Out of these eggs come the silkworms themselves each spring. In six weeks the magic worms convert my mulberry leaves into rich cocoons."

35. One question alone consumed her brain: "Will Uncle James' lawyer convince the court of Guilford that Uncle James instead of Doctor David is my true guardian? Or will Jonathan convince the court of Guilford through Lawyer Peesley that Doctor David and not Uncle James is fittest man to make me his ward?"

36. Jonathan shook his shoulders. "They don't come any finer than Clarkson. He deserves the best in all of this world. And if I have anything to do with it, he shall have it."

   The girl looked at him curiously. "You sound as though you were signing away your rights to a future fortune."

   "Maybe I am."

37. "You and Doctor David and Ruth and Aunt Eunice are keeping something from me, Addison. I feel it in the air. Something very wrong is the matter with Doctor David and the rest of you lately. Do tell me what it is."

38. Martitia stiffened. She stared into Ruth's eyes across the table. That old antagonism of the strong for the weak was still working like yeast in Ruth's independent ego! During the long hard months of effort at the loom and in the kitchen Martitia had grown to believe that Ruth was beginning to respect her. Yet here was the old contempt still alive.

Martitia spoke clearly: "I may be small, and I may have small hands, but I can tote a thousand pounds of leaves easily. I can tote *ten* thousand pounds of leaves if necessary. I can tote *twenty* thousand pounds of leaves. I can . . ."

39. Dusk came, bringing with it showers of rain. Three figures still worked madly under the mulberry trees. Before the great rain squall broke over the grove Addison, Martitia, and Ruth ran wildly into the hay barn. There they stood, watching the downpour outside, and surveyed the great mounds of green mulberry leaves heaped up in the dry hay barn.

The Rhetorical Stage

POETRY SELECTIONS

with Study Questions and Answers

SECTION I

Terms to Know for the Study of Poetry

The following terms will be helpful in the analysis of poetry. A useful exercise would be to read these definitions and talk about them before beginning a study of the poems in this section. Then go through the poems, using the study questions. When that is completed, come back to these terms, find an example of each, and discuss them again in the light of the poems in which they are used. Some of the terms will be used in each of the poems that follows, *meter* and *rhythm*, for example. But it is still worthwhile to talk about the ideas as concretized in specific poems.

Alliteration: usually the repetition of a beginning stressed sound, often, though not always, a consonant sound. "I must go down to the **s**eas again, to the lonely **s**ea and the **s**ky,/ All I ask is a tall ship and a **s**tar to **s**teer her by . . ." is an example of consonantal alliteration. Vowel alliteration is seen in the following selection: "**A**pt **a**lliteration's **a**rtful **ai**d is often an occasional ornament in prose." There can also be alliteration of sounds within words, as appears in the poem "To a Waterfowl": "And **s**oon that toil **sh**all end;/ **S**oon **sh**alt thou find a **s**ummer home, and re**s**t,/ And **s**cream among thy fellow**s**; reed**s sh**all bend/ **S**oon, o'er thy **sh**eltered ne**s**t."

Assonance: the repetition of vowel sounds in stressed syllables that end in different consonant sounds, as in *holy* and *story*. The words *lake* and *fake* are rhymes; the words *lake* and *fate* have assonance.

Connotation: the associations caused by a particular word. The difference between *denotation* and *connotation* is clearly seen by thinking about the different effects of the words *childish* and *childlike*. Both mean "like a child", or "befitting a child", but *childlike* is a positive adjective, and *childish* is negative. It has a different *connotation*.

Couplet: two successive verses rhyming with each other. See "Why Tigers Can't Climb" for an example of couplets.

Denotation: the simple meaning of a term.

Figure of speech: a use of the language that achieves a special effect or meaning by using special constructions, order, or significance. Common figures of speech are hyperbole, imagery, irony, metaphor, personification, repetition, and simile.

Hyperbole: an extravagant exaggeration, done for effect. Much of "The Cremation of Sam Magee" is hyperbole.

Imagery: the use of language to call to mind the likeness of something perceived by the senses.

Irony: an expression of humor, ridicule, or light sarcasm in which the intended implication of what is said is the opposite of the literal sense of the words. An example would be "Strictly Germ-Proof".

Lyric poetry: poetry marked by imagination, melody, emotion, and the creation of a single, unified impression on the reader. It is expressive of the poet's feeling rather than of outward incident or events. It is usually fairly short.

Metaphor: a figure of speech in which one thing is likened to another, otherwise dissimilar, thing. It does not employ the words *like* or *as*, but rather says that the object compared to another *is* that other. "Rumor is a flute" is an example of a metaphor.

Narrative poetry: poetry that tells a story rather than express-
ing a feeling and often is longer than lyric poetry.

Onomatopoeia: the formation of words in imitation of natural
sounds, like *buzz* or *hiss*. The poem "The Bells", by Edgar
Allen Poe, is a good example of onomatopoeia.

Paradox: an apparent contradiction that is yet true in fact, e.g.,
Christ died to give life; it is only by losing your life that you
can gain it.

Personification: a figure of speech in which human character-
istics are attributed to something nonhuman.

Refrain: a group of words repeated at regular intervals, usually
the end of a stanza, which sums up or calls attention to a
particularly important point of the poem. The poem "Ed-
ward, Edward", found in the section on types of poetry,
uses a refrain.

Rhyme: the repetition of ending sounds that are identical,
similar, or related. The pattern of sounds must include an
accented vowel with identical sounds or syllables after it
and a different immediately preceding consonant (e.g., *rise*
and *size* or *ending* and *lending*). Words of such a sort are usu-
ally placed at the end of lines of poetry, but there may be
repeated sounds within a line of poetry. This is called inter-
nal rhyme. The pattern of ending rhymes in the lines of a
poem is called the rhyme scheme. A typical rhyme scheme
would be *abab*. See the poem "In Coventry" for an example
of this rhyme scheme. The first line rhymes with the third
line and the second line rhymes with the fourth. Each
stanza, or section, of this poem has the same rhyme
scheme.

Rhythm: the basically regular rise and fall of sounds according
to pitch, stress, or speed. Read a verse from any of the po-
ems in this section. You will notice that some of the words
are more accented than others and that within a word some
of the syllables receive more emphasis than others. This is

one of the features of the language with which the poet works to create something beautiful. The beautiful in any of the fine arts comes, at least in some measure, from a right ordering of the parts. In language, one of the elements that must be rightly ordered is the sound of words according to quantity or stress, that is, how long the sound is held and what kind of emphasis it receives.

Simile: a figure of speech wherein one thing is compared explicitly to another, usually (though not always) using the words *like* or *as*. ("Shall I compare thee to a summer's day" is a simile, but "How like a winter hath my absence been/ From thee, the pleasure of the fleeting year!" is more typical.)

Stanza: a recurrent grouping of two or more lines of a poem in terms of length, metrical form, and, usually, rhyme scheme. Technically speaking, *verse* and *stanza* are not interchangeable, because, properly, *verse* means only a single line of poetry.

Symbolism: the use of one thing to suggest, or represent, another by reason of relationship or association, especially the use of the visible to suggest the invisible, as "The lion is a symbol of courage."

Tone: the style or manner of expression, the emotional content of a piece of writing. The connotations of various words can have a profound effect upon the tone of a poem.

Understatement: deliberately to represent something less strongly than might be truthfully done, for rhetorical effect.

In Coventry

by James J. Daly, S.J.

My friends, the leaves, who used to entertain me
   On summer afternoons with idle chatter,
Are dropping off in ways that shock and pain me.
   I wonder what's the matter.

My friends, the birds, are quietly withdrawing;
   The meadow-larks are gone from fence and stubble;
Even the crows are gone; I liked their cawing.
   I wonder what's the trouble.

My friend, the sun, is here, but altered slightly;
   He acts more coolly than he has been doing;
He seems more distant, and he smiles less brightly.
   I wonder what is brewing.

Study Questions

1. "In Coventry" means to be excluded from the society to which one belongs. How is this phrase appropriate to the theme of the poem?
2. Personification is a figure of speech wherein something non-human is spoken of as if it were human. Point out the uses of personification in this poem.

The Vulture

by Hilaire Belloc

The vulture eats between his meals,
    And that's the reason why
He very, very rarely feels
    As well as you or I.

His eye is dull, his head is bald,
    His neck is growing thinner,
Oh, what a lesson for us all,
    To only eat at dinner!

Study Questions

1. What is the central idea of the poem? Which is a more memorable way to put it, in bald prose or as Mr. Belloc does it here?

The Height of the Ridiculous

by Oliver Wendell Holmes

I wrote some lines once on a time
   In wondrous merry mood,
And thought, as usual, men would say
   They were exceeding good.

They were so queer, so very queer,
   I laughed as I would die;
Albeit, in the general way,
   A sober man am I.

I called my servant, and he came;
   How kind it was of him
To mind a slender man like me,
   He of the mighty limb.

"These to the printer," I exclaimed,
   And, in my humorous way,
I added (as a trifling jest),
   "There'll be the devil to pay."

He took the paper, and I watched,
   And saw him peep within;
At the first line he read, his face
   Was all upon the grin.

He read the next; the grin grew broad,
   And shot from ear to ear;
He read the third; a chuckling noise
   I now began to hear.

The fourth: he broke into a roar;
　　The fifth: his waistband split;
The sixth: he burst five buttons off,
　　And tumbled in a fit.

Ten days and nights, with sleepless eye,
　　I watched that wretched man,
And since, I never dare to write
　　As funny as I can.

Study Questions

1. Is this a serious story? Or a humorous story with an underlying point? Or is it just plain fun? How is the humor achieved?
2. What kind of a man is speaking? Is he telling the truth? Or is this poem an excuse?
3. What is the rhyme scheme here?

How Cyrus Laid the Cable

A Ballad

by *John Godfrey Saxe*

Come, listen all unto my song;
　　It is no silly fable;
'Tis all about the mighty cord
　　They call the Atlantic Cable.

Bold Cyrus Field he said, says he,
　　I have a pretty notion
That I can run a telegraph
　　Across the Atlantic Ocean.

Then all the people laughed, and said,
    They'd like to see him do it;
He might get half-seas-over, but
    He never could go through it.

To carry out his foolish plan
    He never would be able;
He might as well go hang himself
    With his Atlantic Cable.

But Cyrus was a valiant man,
    A fellow of decision;
And heeded not their mocking words,
    Their laughter and derision.

Twice did his bravest efforts fail,
    And yet his mind was stable;
He wa'n't the man to break his heart
    Because he broke his cable.

"Once more, my gallant boys!" he cried:
    Three times!—you know the fable,—
(I'll make it *thirty*," muttered he,
    "But I will lay the cable!")

Once more they tried,—hurrah! hurrah!
    What means this great commotion?
The Lord be praised! the cable's laid
    Across the Atlantic Ocean!

Loud ring the bells,—for, flashing through
    Six hundred leagues of water,
Old Mother England's benison
    Salutes her eldest daughter!

O'er all the land the tidings speed,
    And soon, in every nation,
They'll hear about the cable with
    Profoundest admiration!

Now, long live President and Queen;
    And long live gallant Cyrus;
And may his courage, faith, and zeal
    With emulation fire us;

And may we honor evermore
    The manly, bold, and stable;
And tell our sons, to make them brave,
    How Cyrus laid the cable!

Study Questions

1. Is there a moral or point to this retelling? Or is it a simple retelling?
2. What is the rhyme scheme?
3. Is this narrative or lyric poetry?
4. Is there an instance of alliteration in the poem?

Why Tigers Can't Climb

by Arthur Guiterman

This tale is of the Tiger and his Aunt, who is the Cat;
They dwelt among the jungles in the shade of Ararat,
The Cat was very clever, but the Tiger, he was slow;
He couldn't catch the Nilghau nor the heavy Buffalo;
His claws were long and pointed, but his wit was short and
    blunt;
He begged his Wise Relation to instruct him how to hunt.

The Rhetorical Stage: Poetry Selections: Section I

The Cat on velvet pattens stole along the quiet hill:
"Now this," she whispered, "Nephew, is the way to stalk your
    Kill."
The Cat drew up her haunches on the mossy forest couch:
"And this," she said, "my Nephew, is the proper way to
    crouch."
She hurtled through the shadows like a missile from a sling:
"And that, my loving Nephew, is the only way to spring!"

Oh, hungry was the Nephew, and the Aunt was sleek and
    plump;
The Tiger at his Teacher made his first apprentice Jump;
He did it very ably, but the Cat, more quick than he,
Escaped his clutching talons and ran up a cedar tree,
And purred upon the Snarler from the bough on which she
    sat,
"How glad I am, my Nephew, that I didn't teach you that!"

And, since that Curtailed Lesson in the Rudiments of Crime,
The most ambitious Tiger hasn't learned to climb.

Study Questions

1. What is the story in this poem? According to this poem, why
   can't tigers climb trees? What is the Aunt glad that she didn't
   teach her Nephew?
2. What is the rhyme scheme in this poem?
3. What figure of speech is used here?

My Familiar

by John Godfrey Saxe

Ecce iterum crispinus!

I

Again I hear that creaking step!—
　　He's rapping at the door!—
Too well I know the boding sound
　　That ushers in a bore.
I do not tremble when I meet
　　The stoutest of my foes,
But Heaven defend me from the friend
　　Who comes—but never goes!

II

He drops into my easy-chair,
　　And asks about the news;
He peers into my manuscript,
　　And gives his candid views;
He tells me where he likes the line,
　　And where he's forced to grieve;
He takes the strangest liberties,—
　　But never takes his leave!

III

He reads my daily paper through
　　Before I've seen a word;
He scans the lyric (that I wrote)
　　And thinks it quite absurd;
He calmly smokes my last cigar,
　　And coolly asks for more;
He opens everything he sees—
　　Except the entry door!

IV

He talks about his fragile health,
    And tells me of the pains
He suffers from a score of ills
    Of which he ne'er complains;
And how he struggled once with death
    To keep the fiend at bay;
On themes like those away he goes,—
    But never goes away!

V

He tells me of the carping words
    Some shallow critic wrote;
And every precious paragraph
    Familiarly can quote;
He thinks the writer did me wrong;
    He'd like to run him through!
He says a thousand pleasant things,—
    But never says, "Adieu!"

VI

Whene'er he comes,—that dreadful man,—
    Disguise it as I may,
I know that, like an Autumn rain,
    He'll last throughout the day.
In vain I speak of urgent tasks;
    In vain I scowl and pout;
A frown is no extinguisher,—
    It does not put him out!

VII

I mean to take the knocker off,
    Put crape upon the door,
Or hint to John that I am gone

To stay a month or more.
I do not tremble when I meet
The stoutest of my foes,
But Heaven defend me from the friend
Who never, never goes!

Study Questions

1. Again, is this lyric or narrative poetry?
2. What is the rhyme scheme?
3. Why is this funny? Does it suggest any behaviors you might want to avoid?

When I Was in Love

by A. E. Houseman

Oh, when I was in love with you,
Then I was clean and brave,
And miles around the wonder grew
How well did I behave.

And now the fancy passes by,
And nothing will remain,
And miles around they'll say that I
Am quite myself again.

Study Questions

1. What was the great wonder spoken of in the poem? What does the fact that it was a great wonder suggest to you?
2. What is the tone of this poem?

Portrait by a Neighbor

by Edna St. Vincent Millay

Before she has her floor swept
  Or her dishes done,
Any day you'll find her
  A-sunning in the sun!

It's long after midnight
  Her key's in the lock,
And you never see her chimney smoke
  Till past ten o'clock!

She digs in her garden
  With a shovel and a spoon,
She weeds her lazy lettuce
  By the light of the moon.

She walks up the walk
  Like a woman in a dream,
She forgets she borrowed butter
  And pays you back cream!

Her lawn looks like a meadow,
And if she mows the place
She leaves the clover standing
And the Queen Anne's lace!

Study Questions

1. What is the rhyme scheme?
2. What figure of speech is employed?
3. What kind of a person is being described?

The Ticket Agent

by Edmund Leamy

Like any merchant in a store
Who sells things by the pound or score,

He deals with scarce perfunctory glance
Small pass-keys to the world's Romance.

He takes dull money, turns and hands
The roadways to far distant lands.

Bright shining rail and fenceless sea
Are partners of his wizardry.

He calls off names as if they were
Just names to cause no heart to stir.

For listening you'll hear him say
". . . and then to Aden and Bombay . . ."

Or ". . . 'Frisco first and then to Nome.
Across the Rocky Mountains—Home . . ."

And never catch of voice to tell
He knows the lure or feels the spell.

Like any salesman in a store,
He sells but tickets—nothing more.

And casual as any clerk
He deals in dreams, and calls it—work!

Study Questions

1 How does the ticket agent look upon his job? How does the author feel? What is the phrase Mr. Leamy uses to describe the ticket agent's job?
2. Where is the theme of the poem first revealed? And what do you think is the most memorable line?

The Feast of Padre Chala

by Thomas Walsh

There are solemn figures walking up the Tocaima roadway;
There are gestures and loud talking 'neath sombreros and
   umbrellas;
For the sun is shining brightly through the palms along the
   valley,
And the bells are tinkling lightly for the feast-day of Saint
   Thomas.
Padre Chala, with bandanna stands and greets them from the
   doorway—

And the belfry rings Hosanna as they mount unto the chapel;
Padre Gomez de Camilla, on his easy-pacing mula,
And the Padre Carrasquilla, reining in his restive stallion.
While on foot come Fray Ansado, rector of the Recoletos,
Padre Ramon de Tejado, preacher from the Jesuitas,
And the portly Fray Rosildo, from the house of San
    Domingo.
And lean Fray Hermenegildo, from Our Lady de la Pena.
Carmelites and Augustinians, Escolapians and Marists,
All are airing their opinions, as they tread the dusty highway;
And their steps become the faster near the belfry of Tocaima,
Where the Padre Chala, pastor, is awaiting with his dinner.
In the early morn the squawking from the barnyard of the
    Cura,
Set the neighborhood a-talking of the chickens old Jesusa
was preparing for the dinner of the feast-day of the parish.
What a spread for saint and sinner!—cool papayas, aguacates;
Juicy yuccas and melones, with the platanos and pinas,
And the maizes and rinones, from the sopa to the dulces!
As the cura asked the blessing, and his guests were bowed in
    silence,
One could hear the parrot calling from the garden a
    petition—
"Pray for us!" (it was the loro) "Pray for us, O great Saint
    Thomas!"
As it learned it from the coro and had chanted and repeated,
Years without a variation—"Pray for us, O great Saint
    Thomas!"
And from this demure oration, it had never deigned to vary,
Though the brightest minds had striven, with most
    implicating questions
To have explanations given for devotion so exclusive;
But the Cura their endeavor answered—"Ask not what Saint
    Thomas—

'Tis our patron-saint, however, our Saint Thomas of
    Tocaima!"
Padre Ramon, forward leaning, with his finger made
    objection;
"Yet the customary meaning of the Church in such
    connections,
With no other term appended, is to indicate Apostles—
So 'twould seem to us intended, that this sole ejaculation
Of the loro, is the Doubter—Thomas Didymus, Apostle!"
Fray Rosildo, red and stouter, choking down a piece of
    chicken,
Gave it out as his opinion, where there was a greater figure
In theology's dominion, such as Thomas the Aquinas,
That his claims should be admitted in the naming of the
    patron.
Padre Carrasquilla twitted Padre Ramon's orthodoxy,
Blinking through his glasses merry: "Should we seek
    distinguished patrons,
There is Thomas Canterbury, if we won't accept Apostles!"
While an Augustinian friar: "He, of Spanish Villanova,
Our Saint Thomas," he'd inquire—"how about him as a
    patron?"
While they argued, there came swooping o'er the patio a
    falcon,
Which dropped down upon the parrot, scooping it amid its
    talons,
While the priests and servants hurried, as it rose above the
    garden,
Where poor Padre Chala worried, and bemoaned his ravished
    loro,
Sudden in the upper reaches of the noontides blazing
    splendor,
Woke the startled loro's screeches: "Pray for us, O great Saint
    Thomas!"

And the frightened falcon, hearing, loosed its prey and soared
    defeated—
While the loro reappearing, took his perch and sat unruffled.
Then the Padre Chala kneeling, with his pious guests around
    him,
Raised his broken voice, appealing: " 'Tis a miracle of
    Heaven!
Let us cease our disputations, raise no further points about
    him—
Praise Saint Thomas of Tocaima—none can question now or
    doubt him!"

Study Questions

1. This is a little story in verse, a narrative poem. State the story in your own words.
2. Does this story end with a little unexpected surprise? What is it?
3. Where are the rhyming words in this poem?
4. In the fourth line there is an example of onomatopoeia. What is it?
5. What different religious orders are represented in this poem?
6. In lines 36–46 there are four different Saint Thomases mentioned. Identify them.

Robinson Crusoe's Story

by Charles Edward Carryl

The night was thick and hazy
    When the *Piccadilly Daisy*
Carried down the crew and captain in the sea;
    And I think the water drowned 'em
    For they never, never found 'em
And I know they didn't come ashore with me.

Oh! 'twas very sad and lonely
    When I found myself the only
Population on this cultivated shore;
    But I've made a little tavern
    In a rocky little cavern,
And I sit and watch for people at the door.

I spent no time in looking
    For a girl to do my cooking,
As I'm quite a clever hand at making stews;
    But I had that fellow Friday,
    Just to keep the tavern tidy,
And to put a Sunday polish on my shoes.

I have a little garden
    That I'm cultivating lard in,
As the things I eat are rather tough and dry;
    For I live on toasted lizards.
    Prickly pears and parrot gizzards.
And I'm really very fond of beetle-pie.

The clothes I had were furry,
    And it made me fret and worry
When I found the moths were eating off the hair;

And I had to scrape and sand 'em
And I boiled 'em and I tanned 'em
Till I got the fine morocco suit I wear.

I sometimes seek diversion
In a family excursion
With a few domestic animals you see;
And we take along a carrot
As refreshment for the parrot
And a little can of jungleberry tea.

Then we gather as we travel,
Bits of moss and dirty gravel,
And we chip off little specimens of stone;
And we carry home as prizes
Funny bugs, of handy sizes,
Just to give the day a scientific tone.

If the roads are wet and muddy
   We remain at home and study,—
For the Goat is very clever at the sum,—
   And the Dog, instead of fighting,
   Studies ornamental writing,
While the Cat is taking lessons on the drum.

   We retire at eleven,
   And we arise again at seven;
And I wish to call attention, as I close,
   To the fact that all the scholars
   Are correct about their collars,
And particular in turning out their toes.

Study Questions

1. Tell in prose the story of this poem. What happened to Robinson Crusoe's ship? How did he establish himself? Who are his companions, and what do they all do for entertainment?
2. What is the rhyme scheme of this poem?
3. What would you say is the purpose of this poem?

The Cremation of Sam McGee

by Robert W. Service

There are strange things done in the midnight sun
   By the men who moil for gold;
The Arctic trails have their secret tales
   That would make your blood run cold;
The Northern Lights have seen queer sights.
   But the queerest they ever did see
Was that night on the marge of Lake Lebarge
   I cremated Sam McGee.

Now Sam McGee was from Tennessee, where the cotton
blooms and blows.
Why he left his home in the South to roam 'round the Pole,
God only knows.
He was always cold, but the land of gold seemed to hold him
like a spell;
Though he'd often say in his homely way that "he'd sooner
live in hell."

On a Christmas Day we were mushing our way over the
Dawson trail.
Talk of your cold! through the parka's fold it stabbed like a
driven nail.
If our eyes we'd close, then the lashes froze till sometimes we
couldn't see;
It wasn't much fun, but the only one to whimper was Sam
McGee.

And that very night, as we lay packed tight in our robes
beneath the snow,
And the dogs were fed, and the stars o'erhead were dancing
heel and toe,
He turned to me, and "Cap," says he, "I'll cash in this trip, I
guess;
And if I do, I'm asking that you won't refuse my last request."

Well, he seemed so low that I couldn't say no; then he says
with a sort of moan:
"It's the cursed cold, and it's got right hold till I'm chilled
clean through to the bone.
Yet 'tain't being dead—it's my awful dread of the icy grave
that pains;
So I want you to swear that, foul or fair, you'll cremate my last
remains."

A pal's last need is a thing to heed, so I swore I would not fail;
And we started on at the streak of dawn; but ah! he looked
    ghastly pale.
He crouched on the sleigh, and he raved all day of his home in
    Tennessee;
And before nightfall a corpse was all that was left of Sam
    McGee.

There wasn't a breath in that land of death, and I hurried,
    horror-driven,
With a corpse half hid that I couldn't get rid, because of a
    promise given;
It was lashed to the sleigh, and it seemed to say: "You may tax
    your brawn and brains,
But you promised true, and it's up to you to cremate those last
    remains."

Now a promise made is a debt unpaid, and the trail has its
    own stern code.
In the days to come, though my lips were dumb, in my heart
    how I cursed that load.
In the long, long night, by the lone firelight, while the
    huskies, round in a ring,
Howled out their woes to the homeless snows—O man! how
    I loathed the thing.

And every day that quiet clay seemed to heavy and heavier
    grow;
And on I went, though the dogs were spent and the grub was
    getting low;
The trail was bad, and I felt half mad, but I swore I would not
    give in;
And I'd often sing to the hateful thing, and it hearkened with
    a grin.

Till I came to the marge of Lake Lebarge, and a derelict there
 lay;
It was jammed in the ice, but I saw in a trice it was called the
 "Alice May".
And I looked at it, and I thought a bit, and I looked at my
 frozen chum;
Then "Here," said I, with a sudden cry, "is my cre-ma-tor-e-
 um."

Some planks I tore from the cabin floor, and I lit the boiler
 fire;
Some coal I found that was lying around, and I heaped the
 fuel higher;
The flames just soared, and the furnace roared—such a blaze
 you seldom see;
And I burrowed a hole in the glowing coal, and I stuffed in
 Sam McGee.

Then I made a hike, for I didn't like to hear him sizzle so;
And the heavens scowled, and the huskies howled, and the
 wind began to blow.
It was icy cold, but the hot sweat rolled down my cheeks, and
 I don't know why;
And the greasy smoke in an inky cloak went streaking down
 the sky.

I do not know how long in the snow I wrestled with grisly
 fear;
But the stars came out and they danced about ere again I
 ventured near;
I was sick with dread, but I bravely said: "I'll just take a peep
 inside.
I guess he's cooked and it's time I looked"; . . . then the door I
 opened wide.

And there sat Sam, looking cold and calm, in the heart of the
  furnace roar;
And he wore a smile you could see a mile, and he said: "Please
  close that door!
It's fine in here, but I greatly fear you'll let in the cold and
  storm—
Since I left Plumtree, down in Tennessee, it's the first time
  I've been warm."

> There are strange things done in the midnight sun
>   By the men who moil for gold;
> The Arctic trails have their secret tales
>   That would make your blood run cold;
> The Northern Lights have seen queer sights,
>   But the queerest they ever did see
> Was that night on the marge of Lake Lebarge
>   I cremated Sam McGee.

Study Questions

1. What is the rhyme scheme of this poem? What other kind of
   rhyming is involved in the verses?
2. Can you find some examples of personification?
3. Can you find an example of alliteration?
4. How about a simile? A metaphor?
5. Briefly recount the story of Sam McGee.

Matilda

Who Told Lies, and Was Burned to Death

by Hilaire Belloc

Matilda told such Dreadful Lies,
It made one Gasp and Stretch one's Eyes;
Her Aunt, who, from her Earliest Youth,
Had kept a Strict Regard for Truth,
Attempted to Believe Matilda:
The effort very nearly killed her,
And would have done so, had not She
Discovered this Infirmity.
For once, towards the Close of Day,
Matilda, growing tired of play,
And finding she was left alone,
Went tiptoe to the Telephone
And summoned the Immediate Aid
Of London's Noble Fire-Brigade.
Within an hour the Gallant Band
Were pouring in on every hand,
From Putney, Hackney Downs and Bow,
With Courage high and Hearts a-glow
They galloped, roaring through the Town,
"Matilda's House is Burning Down!"
Inspired by British Cheers and Loud
Proceeding from the Frenzied Crowd,
They ran their ladders through a score
Of windows on the Ball Room Floor;
And took Peculiar Pains to souse
The Pictures up and down the House,
Until Matilda's Aunt succeeded
In showing them they were not needed

And even then she had to pay
To get the Men to go away!

It happened that a few Weeks later
Her Aunt was off to the Theatre
To see that Interesting Play
The Second Mrs. Tanqueray.
She had refused to take her Niece
To hear this Entertaining Piece:
A deprivation Just and Wise
To Punish her for Telling Lies.
That Night a Fire *did* break out—
You should have heard Matilda Shout!
You should have heard her Scream and Bawl,
And throw the window up and call
To People passing in the Street—
(The rapidly increasing Heat
Encouraging her to obtain
Their confidence)—but all in vain!
For every time She shouted "Fire!"
They only answered "Little Liar!"
And therefore when her Aunt returned,
Matilda, and the House, were Burned.

Study Questions

1. From which of Aesop's fables is this poem taken?
2. What is the rhyme scheme?
3. Why do you think Mr. Belloc chose to capitalize the words he did?

Strictly Germ-Proof

by Arthur Guiterman

The Antiseptic Baby and the Prophylactic Pup
Were playing in the garden when the Bunny gamboled up;
They looked upon the Creature with a loathing undis-
   guised;—
It wasn't Disinfected and it wasn't Sterilized.

They said it was a Microbe and a Hotbed of Disease;
They steamed it in a vapor of a thousand-odd degrees;
They froze it in a freezer that was cold as Banished Hope
And washed it in permanganate with carbolated soap.

In sulphurated hydrogen they steeped its wiggly ears;
They trimmed its frisky whiskers with a pair of hard-boiled
   shears;
They donned their rubber mittens and they took it by the
   hand
And 'lected it a member of the Fumigated Band.

There's not a Micrococcus in the garden where they play;
They bathe in pure iodoform a dozen times a day;
And each imbibes his rations from a Hygienic Cup—
The Bunny and the Baby and the Prophylactic Pup.

Study Questions

1. Find an example of assonance in this poem.
2. Find a simile.
3. Find an example of alliteration.
4. Look up the following words: antiseptic, prophylactic, perman-
   ganate, carbolated, sulphurated, fumigated, micrococcus, iodo-
   form, and hygenic.
5. What kind of humor is this?

The Sycophantic Fox and the Gullible Raven

by Guy Wetmore Carryl

A raven sat upon a tree,
   And not a word he spoke, for
His beak contained a piece of Brie,
   Or, maybe, it was Roquefort:
     We'll make it any kind you please—
     At all events, it was a cheese.

Beneath the tree's umbrageous limb
   A hungry fox sat smiling;
He saw the raven watching him,
   And spoke in words beguiling:
     "J'admire," said he, "ton beau plumage."
     (The which was simply persiflage.)

Two things there are, no doubt you know,
   To which a fox is used:
A rooster that is bound to crow,
   A crow that's bound to roost;
     And whichsoever he espies,
     He tells the most unblushing lies.

"Sweet fowl," he said, "I understand
   You're more than merely natty,
I hear you sing to beat the band
   And Adelina Patti.
     Pray render with your liquid tongue
     A bit from *Götterdämmerung*!"

This subtle speech was aimed to please
   The crow, and it succeeded;
He thought no bird in all the trees

Could sing as well as he did.
   In flattery completely doused,
He gave the "Jewel Song" from *Faust*.

But gravitation's law, of course,
   As Isaac Newton showed it,
Exerted on the cheese its force,
   And elsewhere soon bestowed it.
      In fact, there is no need to tell
      What happened when to earth it fell.

I blush to add that when the bird
   Took in the situation,
He said one brief, emphatic word,
   Unfit for publication.
      The fox was greatly startled, but
      He only sighed and answered "Tut."

The Moral is: A fox is bound
   To be a shameless sinner.
And also: When the cheese comes round
   You know it's after dinner.
      But (what is only known to few)
      The fox is after dinner, too.

Study Questions

1. Which fable is the source of this story?
2. What is the rhyme scheme?
3. Find an example of alliteration.
4. Can you find an example of a pun?

The Purple Cow
Reflections on a Mythic Beast,
Who's Quite Remarkable, at Least
by Gelett Burgess

I never saw a Purple Cow;
I never Hope to See One;
But I can Tell you, Anyhow,
I'd rather See than Be One.

Cinq Ans Après
Confession: and a Portrait, Too,
Upon a Background That I Rue!
by Gelett Burgess

Ah, yes, I wrote the "Purple Cow"—
I'm sorry, now, I Wrote it!
But I can Tell you, Anyhow,
I'll Kill you if you Quote it!

Study Questions

1. Why do you think Mr. Burgess wrote "Cinq Ans Après" (Five Years Later)?
2. What is the rhyme scheme in each poem?
3. What is the reason for the capitalizations in the poems?

The Embarrassing Episode of Little Miss Muffet

by Guy Wetmore Carryl

Little Miss Muffet discovered a tuffet,
    (Which never occurred to the rest of us)
And, as 'twas a June day, and just about noonday,
    She wanted to eat—like the best of us:
Her diet was whey, and I hasten to say
    It is wholesome and people grow fat on it.
The spot being lonely, the lady not only
    Discovered the tuffet, but sat on it.

A rivulet gabbled beside her and babbled,
    As rivulets always are thought to do,
And dragon flies sported around and cavorted,
    As poets say dragon flies ought to do;
When, glancing aside for a moment, she spied
    A horrible sight that brought fear to her,
A hideous spider was sitting beside her,
    And most unavoidably near to her!

Albeit unsightly, this creature politely
    Said: "Madam, I earnestly vow to you,
I'm penitent that I did not bring my hat. I
    Should otherwise certainly bow to you."
Though anxious to please, he was so ill at ease
    That he lost all sense of propriety,
And grew so inept that he clumsily stept
    In her plate—which is barred in Society.

This curious error completed her terror;
    She shuddered, and growing much paler, not
Only left tuffet, but dealt him a buffet
    Which doubled him up in a sailor knot.

It should be explained that at this he was pained:
   He cried, "I have vexed you, no doubt of it!
Your fist's like a truncheon." "You're still in my luncheon,"
   Was all that she answered. "Get out of it!"

And the *Moral* is this: Be it madam or miss
   To whom you have something to say,
You are only absurd when you get in the curd
   But you're rude when you get in the whey!

Study Questions

1. What is the rhyme scheme?
2. What is the pun in the poem?
3. Is this lyric or narrative poetry?

Jabberwocky

by Lewis Carroll

'Twas brillig, and the slithy toves
   Did gyre and gimble in the wabe:
All mimsy were the borogoves,
   And the mome raths outgrabe.

"Beware the Jabberwock, my son!
   The jaws that bite, the claws that catch!
Beware the Jubjub bird, and shun
   The frumious Bandersnatch!"

He took his vorpal sword in hand:
   Long time the manxome foe he sought—
So rested he by the Tumtum tree,
   And stood awhile in thought.

And, as in uffish thought he stood,
   The Jabberwock, with eyes of flame,
Came whiffling through the tulgey wood,
   And burbled as it came!

One, two! One, two! And through and through
   The vorpal blade went snicker-snack!
He left it dead, and with its head
   He went galumphing back.

"And hast thou slain the Jabberwock?
   Come to my arms, my beamish boy!
O frabjous day! Callooh! Callay!"
   He chortled in his joy.

'Twas brillig, and the slithy toves
    Did gyre and gimble in the wabe;
All mimsy were the borogoves,
    And the mome raths outgrabe.

Study Questions

1. What is the rhyme scheme?
2. Find an example of onomatopoeia, alliteration, and assonance.
3. What is the most memorable thing about this poem? Is it effective? Try diagramming or parsing the first verse.

Their Neighbors' Fault
by John Godfrey Saxe

Why human kind should ever be
So keen their neighbors' faults to see,
While (wonderful to tell!) their own
Are to themselves almost unknown,
This ancient fable clearly shows:
Once on a time—the story goes—
Great Jove, the wise Olympian King,
Proclaimed to each created thing,
That he would hold a special court
Where all might come and make report
Of aught that each might deem it wise
To change in feature, form, or size.
He promised quickly to redress
All imperfections, large or less;
Whatever error or defect
Each in his person might detect.
First came the *Monkey*. Naught had he
Of special fault—that *he* could see!

A paragon of wit and grace,
Who had—almost—a human face!
One seeks a finer form in vain,
Pray, why should *he* complain?
"But look at Bruin!" cried the ape:
"Was ever such a clumsy shape?
And then for life, condemned to wear
That ugly suit of shaggy hair!"
"Nay," said the bear, "I find my form
As I could wish. My fur is warm,
And looks, I think, extremely fine,
Good Master Ape, compared with thine!
But see the *Elephant!* His size
Is much too huge!—and I advise
(So ludicrous the beast appears)
To stretch his tail and crop his ears!"
"Nay," quoth the Elephant, who deems
His figure clear of all extremes,
"I can't complain—I'm quite content!"
But then he marveled what it meant
The *Whale* should be so huge and fat!
The *Ant* was sorry for the *Gnat!*
The *Gnat* reproached the tiny *Flea!*
How could one live so small as she?
Thus all the animals, in turn,
The faults of others could discern;
But not a creature, large or small,
His own defects could see at all!

Study Question

1. What is the point of this poem?

How to Tell the Wild Animals

by Carolyn Wells

If ever you should go by chance
    To jungles in the East,
And if there should to you advance
    A large and tawny beast,
If he roars at you as you're dyin'
You'll know it is the Asian Lion.

Or if some time when roaming round,
    A noble wild beast greets you,
With black stripes on a yellow ground,
    Just notice if he eats you.
This simple rule may help you learn
The Bengal Tiger to discern.

If strolling forth, a beast you view,
    Whose hide with spots is peppered,
As soon as he has lept on you,
    You'll know it is the Leopard.
'Twill do no good to roar with pain,
He'll only lep and lep again.

Though to distinguish beasts of prey
    A novice might nonplus,
The Crocodiles you always may
    Tell from Hyenas thus:
Hyenas come with merry smiles;
But if they weep, they're Crocodiles.

Study Questions

1. What is the rhyme scheme?
2. What is funny about this poem?

I Never Saw a Moor

by Emily Dickinson

I never saw a moor,
I never saw the sea;
Yet know I how the heather looks,
And what a wave must be.

I never spoke with God,
Nor visited in heaven;
Yet certain am I of the spot
As if a chart were given.

Study Questions

1. Restate the theme of this poem.
2. What is the rhyme scheme?
3. "Moor" can mean either a Muslim person from northwest Africa, or it can mean an open, grassy area. Which is it here, and how do you know?

Hymn to the Night

by Henry Wadsworth Longfellow

I heard the trailing garments of the Night
    Sweep through her marble halls!
I saw her sable skirts all fringed with light
    From the celestial walls!

I felt her presence, by its spell of might,
    Stoop o'er me from above;
The calm, majestic presence of the Night,
    As of the one I love.

The Rhetorical Stage: Poetry Selections: Section I

I heard the sounds of sorrow and delight,
    The manifold, soft chimes,
That fill the haunted chambers of the Night,
    Like some old poet's rhymes.

From the cool cisterns of the midnight air
    My spirit drank repose;
The fountain of perpetual peace flows there,—
    From those deep cisterns flows.

O holy Night! from thee I learn to bear
    What man has borne before!
Thou layest thy finger on the lips of Care,
    And they complain no more.

Peace! Peace! Orestes-like I breathe this prayer!
    Descend with broad-winged flight,
The welcome, the thrice-prayed for, the most fair,
    The best-beloved Night!

Study Questions

1. The line "trailing garments of the Night" gives one a feeling of quietness and repose. The whole sense or feeling of the poem is restful. To which senses does the poet appeal to achieve this impression?
2. Is night more restful than day, usually? How does Night "layest (her) finger on the lips of Care"?
3. In line nine, were the sounds he heard real or imaginary?
4. Where is personification used in this poem?
5. Where is there a simile in the poem?
6. Which line tells you that the poet bears a great sorrow?

Barter

by Sara Teasdale

Life has loveliness to sell,
    All beautiful and splendid things,
Blue waves whitened on a cliff,
    Soaring fire that sways and sings,
And children's faces looking up
Holding wonder like a cup.

Life has loveliness to sell,
    Music like a curve of gold,
Scent of pine trees in the rain,
    Eyes that love you, arms that hold,
And for your spirit's still delight,
Holy thoughts that star the night.

Spend all you have for loveliness,
    Buy it and never count the cost;
For one white singing hour of peace
    Count many a year of strife well lost,
And for a breath of ecstasy
Give all you have been or could be.

Study Questions

1. What does it mean to barter?
2. What are some of the things Life has to sell? What does the poet think we should be willing to offer in exchange?
3. Quote a line with a complete picture. Could you draw it?
4. Find a simile in the poem.

Fame

by Father John Banister Tabb

Their noonday never knows
What names immortal are:
'Tis night alone that shows
How star surpasseth star.

Study Questions

1. Few artists enjoy fame in their own day. It is only after many
   years have passed that a judgment is made about the merit of
   their work. Keeping this in mind, what is meant by "noonday"
   in this poem?
2. What is the comparison in the poem?

Father Damien

by Father John Banister Tabb

O God, the cleanest offering
Of tainted earth below,
Unblushing to Thy feet we bring—
"A leper white as snow!"

Study Questions

1. Father Damien was a Belgian priest who went to the leper
   colony of Molokai to serve as a chaplain. After twelve years of
   selfless service he contracted the disease and died three years
   later. What is the earth's "cleanest offering"? And with what is
   earth tainted?
2. The last line is a scriptural quote, from the fifth chapter of 2
   Kings. It is found in the story of Naaman, the Syrian general

who was cured of his leprosy. The meaning of the phrase as used in this poem is different from its meaning in Scripture. What is the difference?

Prayer of a Soldier in France
by Joyce Kilmer

My shoulders ache beneath my pack
(Lie easier, Cross, upon His back).

I march with feet that burn and smart
(Tread, Holy Feet, upon my heart).

Men shout at me who may not speak
(They scourged Thy back and smote Thy cheek).

I may not lift a hand to clear
My eyes of salty drops that sear.

(Then shall my fickle soul forget
Thy Agony of Bloody Sweat?)

My rifle hand is stiff and numb
(From Thy pierced palm red rivers come).

Lord, Thou didst suffer more for me
Than all the hosts of land and sea.

So let me render back again
This millionth of Thy gift. Amen.

Study Questions

1. What form of rhyme is this?
2. Look up Colossians 1:24. How does it fit with this poem?
3. Which lines are the heart of this prayer?

High Flight

by John Gillespie Magee, Jr.

Oh, I have slipped the surly bonds of earth,
And danced the skies on laughter-silvered wings;
Sunward I've climbed and joined the tumbling mirth
Of sun-split clouds—and done a hundred things
You have not dreamed of—wheeled and soared and swung
High in the sunlit silence. Hov'ring there,
I've chased the shouting wind along and flung
My eager craft through footless halls of air.
Up, up the long delirious burning blue
I've topped the wind-swept heights with easy grace,
Where never lark, or even eagle, flew;
And, while with silent, lifting mind I've trod
The high untrespassed sanctity of space,
Put out my hand, and touched the face of God.

Study Questions

1. The unexpected combinations of words in this poem make it a delight to read. What are some of those combinations?
2. The first two lines contain alliteration; what sound is used? Where is there an instance of personification?
3. This poem was written by a nineteen-year-old pilot with the Royal Canadian Air Force who died in action in the Second World War. Which lines show the boyish joy of the author? Which his reverent spirit?

Guilielmus Rex

by Thomas Bailey Aldrich

The folk who lived in Shakespeare's day
And saw that gentle figure pass
By London Bridge, his frequent way—
They little knew what man he was.

The pointed beard, the courteous mien,
The equal port to high and low,
All this they saw or might have seen—
But not the light behind the brow!

The doublet's modest gray or brown,
The slender sword-hilt's plain device,
What sign had these for prince or clown?
Few turned, or none, to scan him twice.

Yet t'was the king of England's kings!
The rest with all their pomps and trains
Are moulded, half-remembered things—
'Tis he alone that lives and reigns!

Study Questions

1. The folks who lived in Shakespeare's time noticed some things about the playwright, according to the poet. What did they notice? And what did they fail to see?
2. The title of this poem, in English, is "King William", and the poet says in the last stanza that Shakespeare alone of England's kings still lives and reigns. How is Shakespeare a king of England? And how does he still reign?
3. Compare this poem to "Fame" by Father Tabb. How are they alike?

4. Shakespeare was in fact a successful playwright in his own time. Why would the author, knowing this, still insist that the general public of Shakespeare's time did not recognize his gifts?

O Captain! My Captain!
by Walt Whitman

O Captain! my Captain! our fearful trip is done;
The ship has weather'd every rack, the prize we sought is won;
The port is near, the bells I hear, the people all exulting,
While follow eyes the steady keel, the vessel grim and daring:

But O heart! heart! heart!
O the bleeding drops of red,
Where on the deck my Captain lies,
Fallen cold and dead.

O Captain! my Captain! rise up and hear the bells;
Rise up—for you the flag is flung—for you the bugle trills;
For you bouquets and ribbon'd wreaths—for you the shores a-
crowding;
For you they call, the swaying mass, their eager faces turning:

Here Captain! dear father!
This arm beneath your head;
It is some dream that on the deck
You've fallen cold and dead.

My Captain does not answer, his lips are pale and still;
My father does not feel my arm, he has no pulse or will;
The ship is anchor'd safe and sound, its voyage closed and
done;
From the fearful trip the victor ship comes in with object won:

Exult, O shores, and ring, O bells!
   But I, with mournful tread.
     Walk the deck my Captain lies,
      Fallen cold and dead.

Study Questions

1. Which figure of speech is sustained throughout this poem about Abraham Lincoln? Explain the various parts of this figure.
2. Why, in the last stanza, does the poet say, "Exult, O shores, and ring, O bells!"
3. What is the rhyme scheme?

Preparedness
by Edwin Markham

For all your days prepare,
   And meet them all alike:
When you are the anvil, bear—
   When you are the hammer, strike.

Study Question

1. Express the central thought of this poem in your own words.

Daffodils

by William Wordsworth

I wander'd lonely as a cloud
    That floats on high o'er vales and hills,
When all at once I saw a crowd,
    A host of golden daffodils;
Beside the lake, beneath the trees,
Fluttering and dancing in the breeze.

Continuous as the stars that shine
    And twinkle on the Milky Way,
They stretch'd in never-ending line
    Along the margin of a bay:
Ten thousand saw I, at a glance,
Tossing their heads in sprightly dance.

The waves beside them danced, but they
    Out-did the sparkling waves in glee:
A poet could not but be gay,
    In such a jocund company:
I gazed—and gazed—but little thought
What wealth the show to me had brought:

For oft, when on my couch I lie,
    In vacant or in pensive mood,
They flash upon the inward eye
    Which is the bliss of solitude;
And then my heart with pleasure fills,
And dances with the daffodils.

Study Questions

1. What kind of poetry is this, lyric or narrative?
2. What is the rhyme scheme?
3. What figure of speech do you find in the first stanza?
4. In addition to the picture of the daffodils, what other thought
   does the poet express, at least implicitly?

The Fool's Prayer

by Edward Rowland Sill

The royal feast was done; the King
   Sought some new sport to banish care,
And to his jester cried: "Sir Fool,
   Kneel now, and make for us a prayer!"

The jester doffed his cap and bells,
   And stood the mocking court before;
They could not see the bitter smile
   Behind the painted grin he wore.

He bowed his head, and bent his knee
   Upon the monarch's silken stool;
His pleading voice arose: "O Lord,
   Be merciful to me, a fool!

"No pity, Lord, could change the heart
   From red with wrong to white as wool;
The rod must heal the sin: but, Lord,
   Be merciful to me, a fool!

" 'T is not by guilt the onward sweep
   Of truth and right, O Lord, we stay;
'T is by our follies that so long
   We hold the earth from heaven away.

"These clumsy feet, still in the mire,
   Go crushing blossoms without end;
These hard, well-meaning hands we thrust
   Among the heart-strings of a friend.

"The ill-timed truth we might have kept—
    Who knows how sharp it pierced and stung!
The word we had not sense to say—
    Who knows how grandly it had rung!

"Our faults no tenderness should ask,
    The chastening stripes must cleanse them all;
But for our blunders—oh, in shame
    Before the eyes of heaven we fall.

"Earth bears no balsam for mistakes;
    Men crown the knave, and scourge the tool
That did his will; but Thou, O Lord,
    Be merciful to me, a fool!"

The room was hushed; in silence rose
    The King, and sought his gardens cool,
And walked apart, and murmured low,
    "Be merciful to me, a fool!"

Study Questions

1. What is the message of the fool to the court in general and the king in particular?
2. Is there an equivocation on the word "fool", that is, is the same word used in two senses in this poem?
3. How did the king respond to the rebuke given him?
4. What is the rhyme scheme?
5. In the first stanza can you find an instance of alliteration?

When I Was One and Twenty

by A. E. Houseman

When I was one-and-twenty
   I heard a wise man say,
"Give crowns and pounds and guineas
   But not your heart away;
Give pearls away and rubies
   But keep your fancy free."
But I was one-and-twenty
   No use to talk to me.

When I was one-and-twenty
   I heard him say again,
"The heart out of the bosom
   Was never given in vain;
'Tis paid with sighs a-plenty
   And sold for endless rue."
And I am two-and-twenty
   And oh, 'tis true, 'tis true.

Study Questions

1. What was the advice of the wise man in the first stanza?
2. What did he say would happen, and was it true?
3. Why didn't the young man take the advice? Is he sorry?

Opportunity

by Edward Rowland Sill

This I beheld, or dreamed it in a dream:—
There spread a cloud of dust along a plain;
And underneath the cloud, or in it, raged
A furious battle, and men yelled, and swords
Shocked upon swords and shields. A prince's banner
Wavered, then staggered backward, hemmed by foes.

A craven hung along the battle's edge,
And thought, "Had I a sword of keener steel—
That blue blade that the king's son bears—but this
Blunt thing!—" he snapped and flung it from his hand.
And lowering crept away and left the field.

Then came the king's son, wounded, sore bestead,
And weaponless, and saw the broken sword,
Hilt-buried in the dry and trodden sand,
And ran and snatched it, and with battle-shout
Lifted afresh he hewed his enemy down,
And saved a great cause that heroic day.

Study Questions

1. Contrast the two characters in the poem. How do they differ?
2. What is the central thought of the poem?

Answers to the Study Questions

"In Coventry"   *p. 223*

1. The poem treats the coming of autumn as though the change of season was a change taking place in his summer friends. They are behaving differently toward him, treating him coolly and distantly. He feels they are deserting him, leaving him out, excluding him.
2. The leaves are spoken of as friends who used to chatter. The birds are also friends who are withdrawing. The sun is acting coolly: he seems distant; he smiles less brightly.

"The Vulture"   *p. 224*

1. "Don't eat between meals" is the central idea, but it is much more amusingly (and thus more memorably) put here than when simply stated.

"The Height of the Ridiculous"   *p. 225*

1. This seems to be primarily an exercise in fun. Part of the humor is achieved by having the rather smug writer of the poem suffer from his own competence. If he hadn't been as good at his craft as he was, and as he proclaimed himself to be, he wouldn't have had to suffer through ten days of care for his servant.
2. The speaker seems to be a self-satisfied person, perhaps looking for an excuse for a certain lack of humor in his verse. One wonders about his veracity.
3. The rhyme scheme is *abcb*.

"How Cyrus Laid the Cable"   *p. 226*

1. There is a point, whether it is the first intention of the author or not. Those who succeed are those who do not give up. Compare this poem to "Opportunity", by Edward Rowland Sill (p. 116).

2. The rhyme scheme is *abcb*.

3. This is narrative poetry.

4. "Bold **C**yrus Field he **s**aid, **s**ays he" contains alliteration.

"Why Tigers Can't Climb" *p. 228*

1. A tiger, who was slow-witted, asked his aunt, the clever cat, to teach him how to hunt. She showed him how to stalk and pounce upon his prey. The nephew decided to try out his new-found knowledge on his sleek and plump aunt. He jumped at her, and she, quicker than he, ran up a cedar tree. Then she said that she was glad she had not taught him to climb. And that is why tigers cannot climb; this lesson in the fundamentals of crime was cut short.

2. The rhyme scheme is *aabbcc*, that is, the first two lines rhyme, the second two lines rhyme, and the third two lines rhyme. This is an example of couplets.

3. Personification is the figure of speech used.

"My Familiar" *p. 230*

1. This is narrative poetry, because it tells a story.

2. The rhyme scheme is *abcbdefe*.

3. At least one of the reasons it is funny is the unexpected turn at the end of each section. And yes, we should take care not to assume liberties that might in fact be annoying to our hosts.

"When I Was in Love" *p. 232*

1. The great wonder was the good behavior of the young man, which suggests that he had been something of a problem until then.

2. The tone of this poem, though it seems cocky and amused, is rather sad. The young man is aware of his reputation and acknowledges the truth of it by saying that when he was in love he was different; he was clean and brave. Now he's not.

"Portrait by a Neighbor" *p. 233*

1. The rhyme scheme is *abcb*.
2. There are similes employed in "She walks . . . *Like* a woman in a dream", and "lawn *like* a meadow".
3. This is a person who is somewhat eccentric, living in her own world by her own time-frame. One has a suspicion that the author is describing herself.

"The Ticket Agent" *p. 234*

1. The ticket agent looks upon his job as work, as though he were just like any other merchant, clerk, or salesman. The author, on the other hand, thinks this is a job of great romance, one which "deals in dreams".
2. The theme of the poem is first revealed in the fourth line, "Small pass-keys to the world's Romance". Not everyone will agree about the most memorable line, but I like "He deals in dreams, and calls it—work!"

"The Feast of Padre Chala" *p. 235*

1. A number of priests from different religious orders have come to Tocaima to celebrate the feast day of Saint Thomas of Tocaima. They have a wonderful meal prepared for them. While they are eating, the parrot of the pastor calls out, "Pray for us! Pray for us, O great Saint Thomas!" The priests begin to speculate about which Saint Thomas the parrot is speaking of. Four different candidates are urged: Saint Thomas the Apostle, Saint Thomas Aquinas, Saint Thomas of Canterbury, and Saint Thomas of Villanova. While they argue, a falcon comes and carries off the parrot. Suddenly, the parrot begins to screech, "Pray for us, O great Saint Thomas!" The falcon, startled, lets the parrot go, and it returns to its perch. The pastor, Padre Chala, drops to his knees and says that this miraculous

happening has settled the previous question, "Praise Saint Thomas of Tocaima—none can question now or doubt him!"

2. The ending is surprising because Padre Chala seems to see, or at least say, that this drama with the parrot has settled the previous question—but it is hard for us to see how!

3. The rhyming words in this poem are in the middle of each line, rather than at the end.

4. Bells tinkling is an example of onomatopoeia.

5. The religious orders mentioned in the story are the Recoletos, the Jesuits, the Dominicans, the Carmelites, the Augustinians, the Escolapians, and the Marists. Our Lady de la Pena is probably the name of a parish.

6. See the answer to question number one.

"Robinson Crusoe's Story"   *p. 239*

1. Robinson Crusoe's ship, the *Piccadilly Daisy*, was lost with all her crew except Robinson Crusoe. He found himself alone on an island and proceeded to make himself a tavern, where he sat to watch for people. He found one other human being on the island, a man whom he named Friday. Friday helped Robinson Crusoe keep his tavern tidy.

   Robinson Crusoe keeps a garden, and he lives on toasted lizards, prickly pears, parrot gizzards, and beetle-pie. He had furry clothes, which he scraped and sanded, boiled and tanned. On sunny days he takes scientific excursions with his parrot, goat, dog, and cat. They collect various specimens. On rainy days they all stay home and study. They live a regular life, retiring at eleven and rising at seven.

2. The rhyme scheme is *aabccb*.

3. I would say that the purpose of this poem is fun, pure and simple.

1. The rhyme scheme of the main portion of the poem is *abab*. The first and last stanzas are *abcbdefe*, but the rest of the stanzas are *aabb*, with internal rhyme that carries the rhythm of the poem.

2. There are many examples of personification in this poem; some of them are "the stars o'erhead were dancing heel and toe" (fourth stanza) and "the heavens scowled" (twelfth stanza).

3. Examples of alliteration abound: **bl**ooms and **bl**ows (second stanza), **c**ursed **c**old (fifth stanza), **h**urried, **h**orror-driven (seventh stanza), **br**awn and **br**ains (seventh stanza), **l**ong, **l**ong night, by the **l**one fire**l**ight (eighth stanza), **r**ound in a **r**ing (eighth stanza), **h**eaped the fuel **h**igher (eleventh stanza), **c**old and **c**alm (fourteenth stanza), and so on.

4. "Stabbed like a driven nail", in the third stanza, is an example of a simile. "Greasy smoke in an inky cloak", in the twelfth stanza, is a metaphor.

5. Sam McGee is a man from Tennessee who is looking for gold up near the Pole. He is always cold, and he finally dies from the cold. Before his death Sam asks his friend to cremate his body, rather than bury him in the ground. Sam says he just can't face the icy cold of the grave. Cap, Sam's friend, agrees to do so. This is not easy or pleasant, but a promise to a dying friend is a debt that must be paid, so Cap looks for a way to fulfill his friend's request. Eventually Cap comes upon a ship bound in the ice, and he uses the boiler of that ship as a crematorium. He stokes the boiler and puts the corpse of Sam McGee in it. Then he waits for a while, until he thinks the cremation must be done. When Cap opens the boiler, he finds Sam McGee, alive and well, and warm for the first time since he left Tennessee.

"Matilda" *p. 246*

1. "The Boy Who Cried Wolf".
2. The rhyme scheme is couplets.
3. Perhaps he chose to capitalize these words for emphasis.

"Strictly Germ-Proof" *p. 248*

1. An example of assonance is in the tenth line, "They trimmed its frisky whiskers with a pair of hard-boiled shears".
2. There is a simile in the seventh line, "cold *as* Banished Hope".
3. Three examples of alliteration are line seven, "**fr**oze it in a **fr**eezer", the last line, "The **B**unny and the **B**aby", and the first and last lines, "**P**rophylactic **P**up".
4. The definitions of these words are as follows: **antiseptic**: opposing sepsis, putrefaction, or decay; **prophylactic**: preventing or guarding from disease; **permanganate**: a salt of permanganic acid, an aqueous solution that is strongly oxidizing; **carbolated**: full of carbonic acid; **sulphurated**: combined or treated with sulphur; **fumigated**: to apply smoke, vapor, or gas as a means of disinfecting; **micrococcus**: any of a genus of spherical bacteria occurring in plates or irregular groups and living on dead matter or as parasites; **iodoform**: a clear compound used as a healing and antiseptic dressing for wounds and sores; **hygenic**: of or pertaining to health or hygiene, sanitary.
5. This is an example of ironic humor involving hyperbole. The author doesn't approve of excessive concern with germs, and he conveys this by giving an exaggerated account of the reaction to an unsanitary playmate.

"The Sycophantic Fox and the Gullible Raven" *p. 249*

1. "The Fox and the Raven" is the fable from which this is taken.
2. *Ababcc* is the rhyme scheme.
3. "**S**ubtle **s**peech", "**sh**ameless **s**inner" are examples of alliteration.

4. The two meanings of "after dinner" add to the humor.

"The Purple Cow" and "Cinq Ans Après" p. 251

1. Many people must have commented upon the first poem and asked Mr. Burgess about it. It seems he found it to be an albatross around his neck.
2. *Abab*; in each case the rhyme of the second and fourth line is accomplished by using the same word.
3. It is likely that the words Mr. Burgess wished to emphasize are those he capitalized.

"The Embarrassing Episode of Little Miss Muffet" p. 252

1. The rhyme scheme is complex and very clever. Every other line has an internal rhyme, and the alternate lines end with identical words. Thus, in the first line "muffet" and "tuffet" rhyme, while the second and fourth lines both end in "us". However, the third to last syllable of each of the lines ending identically rhymes. So the second line says "rest of us", and the fourth line says "best of us". (This is an example of triple rhyme, which is found almost exclusively in humorous poetry.)
2. The word "whey" is used in two senses. It means "whey" as in "curds and whey", and "way" as in "get in the way".
3. This is narrative poetry, but it is also nonsense.

"Jabberwocky" p. 254

1. It varies. The first, second, fourth, and last stanzas have *abab* as the rhyme scheme. The others are *abcb*. Line three in the third and sixth stanzas has internal rhyme, and in the fifth stanza, both lines one and three have internal rhyme.
2. "Burbled" is a good example of onomatopoeia. "**G**yre and **g**imble" and "**C**allooh! **C**allay!" are examples of alliteration; "v**or**pal sw**or**d" is an example of assonance.

3. The most memorable thing about this poem is the amazing invented language. It is extremely effective, as you can see by the following analysis.

" 'Twas" is a contraction of "it was'; "it' is the subject of the first of two independent clauses in a compound sentence and "was" is the verb. "Brillig" is a predicate noun or possibly an adjective. "And" is a conjunction, "the" an article modifying "toves", and "slithy" an adjective also modifying "toves". "Toves" is a noun and the subject of the second independent clause. "Did gyre and gimble" is a compound verb joined by the conjunction "and". "In" is a preposition, "the" an article modifying "wabe", and "wabe" a noun used as the prepositional object. "In the wabe" is an adverbial prepositional phrase.

"All" is an adverb modifying "mimsy", which is a predicate adjective said of "borogoves". "Were" is the verb, and "the" an article modifying "borogoves", the subject of the clause. "And" is a conjunction, "the" an article, and "mome" an adjective, both modifying "raths", which is a noun and the subject of the verb "outgrabe".

"Their Neighbors' Fault" p. 255

1. The point of the poem is twofold: that it is much easier to see others' faults than it is to see our own, and that we are often mistaken in what we view as another's fault. In each case the animal in the poem saw himself as perfect, but thought that one or more of the other animals had some serious flaw. And the very feature that each saw as a flaw was one the owner thought of as a gift.

"How to Tell the Wild Animals" p. 257

1. The rhyme scheme is *ababcc*.
2. In each stanza there is some unexpected and absurd twist. In the first and fourth stanzas it is in the last two lines; in the second

stanza it is in the fourth line; and in the third stanza it is in the third and fourth lines.

"I Never Saw a Moor" *p. 258*

1. This poem points out that we are all willing to accept the existence of natural objects that we have not seen, and the description of their appearance, so to believe in heaven is certainly just as reasonable. There is an implicit notion, namely, that we believe in the existence of natural things we haven't seen on the authority of those who tell us of them. The certitude of such knowledge is only as good as the honesty and understanding of the person who has given us the information. In the case of supernatural objects, our belief in their existence is similarly dependent for certitude on the authority of the one telling us about them. In this case, however, our source is God, who can neither deceive nor be deceived. We are actually more certain of the existence of heaven than we are of natural objects we have not seen.
2. The rhyme scheme is *abcb*.
3. It is the open, grassy area, and you can tell from the structure of the poem that line 3 of the first stanza refers to line 1.

"Hymn to the Night" *p. 258*

1. The senses of hearing, touch, and sight might all be cited. The first stanza has "I *heard* the trailing garments of the Night" and "I *saw* her sable skirts all fringed with light". The second stanza mentions *feeling* her presence, and the fourth stanza says, "*cool* cisterns of the midnight air". In the third stanza the sense of hearing is again invoked: "I *heard* the sounds".
2. Night *is* usually more restful than day, simply because the world is quiet and one is expected to rest. Most of the daytime is full of activities, busy with daily duty and recreation. The night allows both the cessation of activity and sleep, which silences the concerns of the day.

3. The sounds were imaginary, as the poet manifests by saying "fill the haunted chambers of the Night".
4. Personification is used in a number of verses. Night is personified in her trailing garments, marble halls, sable skirts, and her finger, which she lays on the lips of Care (another personification).
5. "Chimes . . . like some old poet's rhymes" is a simile.
6. The first verse of the last stanza indicates that the poet has a great sorrow. He is praying for peace, as did Orestes, the Greek youth who killed his mother and was punished by the Furies.

"Barter" *p. 260*

1. "Barter" means to exchange goods without using money.
2. "Blue waves whitened on a cliff", "soaring fire that sways and sings", "children's faces looking up/ Holding wonder like a cup", "music like a curve of gold", "scent of pine trees in the rain", "eyes that love you", "arms that hold", and "holy thoughts that star the night" are all instances of the loveliness that Life has to sell. They bring with them a "white singing hour of peace", for which we should be willing to offer "many a year of strife", or they may bring "a breath of ecstasy", for which you should give all you have been or could be (giving your all or working up to your full capacity might be another way of putting it). It is worth noting that the list of lovely things includes four of the five objects of the outer senses, as well as objects of intelligence.
3. "Blue waves whitened on a cliff", "soaring fire that sways and sings", and "children's faces looking up/ Holding wonder like a cup" are all complete pictures that could be sketched.
4. Line eight, "music like a curve of gold", is a simile.

"Fame" *p. 261*

1. "Noonday" is the time of life in which an artist is working, the middle of his active life.

2. The stars are in the sky at noon and shine just as brightly as at night, but their light is dimmed by the more brilliant light of the sun. At night, however, one sees the stars and their comparative radiance clearly. So it is with many artists; during their lifetime their work is not seen clearly, but after their death (or cessation of the most productive time of life), looking back with the judgment of time, an informed estimatation of their work can be made.

"Father Damien" p. 261

1. Earth's "cleanest offering" is a man who has sacrificed himself for love of God and his neighbor. The man spoken of here overcame the "taint" of original sin and lived his life for others, even to his own death. It is sin with which earth is tainted.
2. In both cases the men in question were white from the disease of leprosy, but Father Damian contracted the sickness by his close association with the lepers whom he was serving. The avaricious servant, Giezi, who was the subject of the phrase's original use, contracted the disease as a punishment for his behavior.

"Prayer of a Soldier in France" p. 262

1. This poem is written in couplets.
2. The poet sees his sufferings as an opportunity to "fill up those things that are wanting of the sufferings of Christ."
3. The last four lines of the poem are the heart of the prayer.

"High Flight" p. 263

1. Some of the unexpected and pleasant combinations of words are "slipped the surly bonds of earth", "danced the skies", "laughter-silvered wings", "tumbling mirth/Of sun-split clouds", "footless halls of air", "long, delirious, burning blue", "touched the face of God". There are other wonderfully vivid

descriptions: "high in the sunlit silence", "chased the shouting wind", "flung/ My eager craft", "topped the wind-swept heights", "silent, lifting mind", and "high untrespassed sanctity of space".

2. The "s" sound is used. The clouds are personified in "tumbling mirth".

3. The first eight lines are joyful and the last six are reverent.

"Guilielmus Rex" *p. 264*

1. They would have noticed Shakespeare's regular route by London Bridge, his pointed beard, and courteous bearing. They would have noticed his equal treatment of all, high-born or low. They would have seen his modest clothing and sword hilt. None of these, however, would have displayed his genius—the "light" behind his brow.

2. There is a way in which a king occupies the highest position in his realm. Shakespeare has that status with respect to English poets. He was the most gifted of all, and his works have been and are still read and loved by millions of people, for whom he is the king of verse.

3. This poem agrees with "Fame", because both say that in the noonday of an artist's life he is not valued as he will be later. "Fame" speaks generally of artists; this poem considers a particular case wherein the general point is seen.

4. The author of this poem thinks that the general public did not realize the incredible depth of Shakespeare's sight and his gift of conveying what he saw. It is possible to enjoy Shakespeare's stories without realizing the true mastery he displays. The author implies that if the public had realized what they had in their midst, Shakespeare would have been more than simply a successful writer of plays. This is not an unreasonable position because it is often in comparison that one sees the objects compared most clearly. When Shakespeare is compared to other

poets his excellence becomes more apparent, and since his time there have been more poets with whom to compare him.

"O Captain! My Captain!" p. 265

1. This poem contains a sustained metaphor; the captain is Abraham Lincoln, the ship is the United States, and the fearful trip is the Civil War.
2. The poet is talking about the victory in the Civil War; while he's glad about the victory, his joy is overshadowed by the sadness of Lincoln's death.
3. The rhyme scheme is *aabbcded*.

"Preparedness" p. 266

1. Do your daily duty according to your state in life.

"Daffodils" p. 267

1. This is an instance of lyric poetry. It is marked by imagination, melody, emotion, and the creation of a single, unified impression on the reader. While it has something of a plot, this is less important than the ideas and feelings expressd in the poem; in a narrative poem the plot is essential.
2. The rhyme scheme is *ababcc*.
3. The first stanza has two instances of personification: the notion of the cloud being lonely and the daffodils dancing.
4. The poet expresses his pleasure in the memory of the picture he sees. When he initially saw the lovely scene of the daffodils dancing he didn't realize the twofold pleasure he had received, the pleasure of the initial sight and the memory of the sight, which would cheer him in his pensive mood.

"The Fool's Prayer" p. 269

1. The fool says that it is not by reason of serious sin that most of

us impede truth and right, but by reason of our follies. One example of such folly is the king's sin in asking the fool to pray "for sport". These follies include, as well, not noticing what we should, so that we make well-intentioned remarks that cause sorrow to our friends, and, on the other hand, noticing and speaking about what we should not, true though the remarks might be. There are also the things we notice and should speak of, but do not. It is for these sorts of mistakes, these follies, that we must ask God for mercy. The serious sins we must be punished for, but for the blunders we make we need to feel shame and ask pardon.

2. The word "fool" is used in two senses: fool as in a jester of the court (line 3), and fool as in one who is foolish, who commits follies (lines 12 onward).

3. The king accepted the rebuke in good part, was ashamed of his ineptitude, and asked God for mercy.

4. The rhyme scheme is *abcb*.

5. The second line contains an alliteration, "**S**ought **s**ome new **s**port to bani**sh** care".

"When I Was One and Twenty"   *p. 271*

1. The wise man told the young man not to give his heart away, that is, not to fall in love.

2. The warning of the wise man was that if one falls in love there will be sighs and endless rue, in other words, there will be regrets and unhappiness.

3. He didn't take the advice because he was one-and-twenty, that is, immature. There is certainly a note of regret in the poem.

"Opportunity"   *p. 272*

1. The craven does not fight for his cause, giving as a reason that he thinks himself ill-equipped. He breaks the blade, which he thinks inadequate to his needs, and throws it away. The prince,

wounded and weaponless, comes upon the broken blade, the blade the craven thought was worthless when it was whole, and using it, saves the cause for which he fights. The prince is brave and wins because he is willing to use what comes to hand. The craven is a coward and uses whatever excuse comes to hand to enable him to abandon his duty.

2. The central thought is that one should not waste time wishing for assets someone else has, nor should we use our lack as an excuse for failure. Most success comes from within a person, not from having the right equipment or resources.

POETRY SELECTIONS

with Study Questions and Answers

SECTION II

Terms to Know for the Study of Poetry

These terms are useful for the analysis of the poetry that follows. Read the definitions and talk about them before beginning to study the poems in this section. Then go through the poems, using the study questions. When that is completed, come back to these terms, find an example of each and discuss them again in the light of the poems in which they are used. Some of the terms that the study questions use were listed in the previous section, and it would be valuable to look back at those definitions.

Rhythm: Rhythm can be defined simply as the regular repetition of stressed and unstressed syllables. In "No **rov** ing **foot** shall **crush** thee **here** / No **bu** sy **hand** pro **voke** a **tear**" (from "To a Wild Honeysuckle", by Philip Freneau), the first syllable is not stressed, the second syllable is stressed, and the following words repeat that pattern.

Foot: A foot in this context is the division of a line of poetry into groups of two or three syllables, each group having a stressed syllable. There are different kinds of patterns created using the accented and unaccented syllables within one foot. Often these patterns are mixed; that is, there are certain regular variations in rhythm that are likely to be found in verse, such as iambic and anapestic feet within the same line. The following are the basic patterns that should be known:

Iambic: a "marching" or duple rhythm involving one stressed and one unstressed syllable. It is a rising pattern, that is, beginning with an unstressed syllable and ending with a stressed syllable. This is the most common rhythm in English poetry.

> I **heard**/ the **trail**/ ing **gar**/ ments **of**/ the **Night**
> **Sweep** through/ her **mar**/ ble **halls**!
> *"Hymn to the Night", by Henry Wadsworth Longfellow*

Trochaic: another "marching" rhythm, with one stressed and one unstressed syllable, but it is a falling pattern, that is, beginning with a stressed syllable and ending with an unstressed syllable.

> **Serve** the/ **Lord** with/ **glad** ness!
> *Psalm 100*

Anapestic: a "dancing" or triple rhythm involving two unstressed syllables followed by a stressed syllable. It is a rising pattern, as is the iambic.

> The As **sy**/ rian came **down**/ like a **wolf**/ on the **fold**.
> And his **co**/ horts were **gleam**/ ing in **pur**/ ple and **gold**;
> *"The Destruction of Sennacherib", by George Gordon Lord Byron*

Dactylic: another "dancing" rhythm, which is also falling. The first syllable is stressed, followed by two unstressed syllables. In the following example every foot is a dactyl except for the last.

This is the/ **for** est pri/ **me** val, the/ **mur** mur ing/
pines and the/ **hem** locks.

Evangeline, by Henry Wadsworth Longfellow

These various rhythms may be found within a single poem, though often a poem is written in a single rhythm.

Meter: The meter of a poem is determined by the number of feet in a line. If there is one foot the meter is monometer. If there are two feet, the meter is dimeter; if three, the meter is trimeter; if four, the meter is tetrameter; if five, the meter is pentameter; if six, the meter is hexameter; if seven, the meter is heptameter. Therefore, feet are often identified by type and number, such as the following:

Iambic Trimeter: This is the iambic pattern with three feet in a line.

I **nev**/ er **saw**/ a **moor**,
I **nev**/ er **saw**/ the **sea**;

"I Never Saw a Moor", by Emily Dickinson

Iambic Tetrameter: This is the iambic pattern with four feet in a line.

And **child**/ren's **fa**/ ces **look**/ ing **up**

"Barter", by Sara Teasdale

Iambic Pentameter: This is the iambic pattern with five feet.

An **nounced**/ by **all**/ the **trum**/ pets **of**/ the **sky**,
Ar **rives**/ the **snow**,/ and, **driv**/ ing **o'er**/ the **fields**,

"The Snow Storm", by Ralph Waldo Emerson

Similarly, the other types of rhythm come in various numbers of feet, such as the following:

trochaic trimeter, the trochaic pattern with three feet
trochaic tetrameter, the trochaic pattern with four feet
anapestic tetrameter, the anapestic pattern with four feet
dactylic dimeter, the dactylic pattern with two feet
dactylic hexameter, the dactylic pattern with six feet

An example of the last is:

> **This** is the/ **for** est pri/ **me** val,
> the/ **mur** mur ing/ **pines** and the/ **hem** locks.
>
> *Evangeline, by Henry Wadsworth Longfellow*

Scan: To scan a verse means to divide it into feet and indicate which syllable is accented.

Blank verse: This is the term given to unrhymed lines of iambic pentameter.

Couplet: two successive verses rhyming with each other.

> My shoulders ache beneath my *pack*
> (Lie easier, Cross, upon His *back*).
>
> *"Prayer of a Soldier in France", by Joyce Kilmer*

Tercet: a group of three successive verses rhyming with each other.

Quatrain: The quatrain consists of four lines, usually with one of two rhyme schemes. Either the first and third, and second and fourth lines may rhyme, or the first and fourth and second and third may rhyme.

> He who, from zone to zone,   a
> Guides through the boundless sky thy certain flight,   b
> In the long way that I must tread alone,   a
> Will lead my steps aright.   b
>
> *"To a Waterfowl", by William Cullen Bryant*

Who knows what days I answer for today? a
 Giving this bud I give the flower. I bow b
 This yet unfaded and a faded brow; b
Bending these knees and feeble knees, I pray. a

"The Young Neophyte", by Alice Meynell

Sestet: The sestet consists of six lines and several possible rhyme schemes, such as *ababcc*, *abbacc*, or *abcabc*.

Octave: The octave is made up of eight lines and various rhyme schemes. The most frequently used is *ababcdcd*.

The Head and the Heart

by John Godfrey Saxe

The head is stately, calm, and wise,
  And bears a princely part;
And down below in secret lies
  The warm, impulsive heart.

The lordly head that sits above,
  The heart that beats below,
Their several office plainly prove,
  Their true relation show.

The head, erect, serene, and cool,
  Endowed with Reason's art,
Was set aloft to guide and rule
  The throbbing, wayward heart.

And from the head, as from the higher,
  Comes every glorious thought;
And in the heart's transforming fire
  All noble deeds are wrought.

Yet each is best when both unite
  To make the man complete;
What were the heat without the light?
  The light, without the heat?

Study Questions

  1. What is the central theme of the poem?
  2. What figure of speech does the poet employ?
  3. What is the rhyme scheme?

Travel

by Edna St. Vincent Millay

The railroad track is miles away,
   And the day is loud with voices speaking,
Yet there isn't a train goes by all day
   But I hear its whistle shrieking.

All night there isn't a train goes by,
   Though the night is still for sleep and dreaming
But I see its cinders red on the sky,
   And hear its engine steaming.

My heart is warm with the friends I make,
   And better friends I'll not be knowing,
Yet there isn't a train I wouldn't take,
   No matter where it's going.

Study Questions

1. What do you think about the desire expressed in the poem to be off, no matter where?
2. The first two stanzas illustrate vividly one capacity of the human soul. What is it?
3. What is the rhyme scheme?

An Old Woman of the Roads

by Padraic Colum

O to have a little house!
To own the hearth and stool and all!
The heaped up sods upon the fire,
The pile of turf against the wall!

To have a clock with weights and chains
And pendulum swinging up and down!
A dresser filled with shining delph,
Speckled with white and blue and brown!

I could be busy all the day
Cleaning and sweeping hearth and floor,
And fixing on their shelf again
My white and blue and speckled store!

I could be quiet there at night
Beside the fire and by myself,
Sure of a bed, and loth to leave
The ticking clock and the shining delph!

Och! but I'm weary of mist and dark,
And roads where there's never a house or bush,
And tired I am of bog and road
And the crying wind and the lonesome hush!

And I am praying to God on high,
And I am praying Him night and day,
For a little house—a house of my own—
Out of the wind's and the rain's way.

Study Questions

1. Name the attributes of the little house for which the old woman is longing. What is the contrasting picture drawn in the poem?
2. Which lines contain the most vivid images?
3. How does the poem affect the reader? What emotion does it tend to evoke?

A Parting Guest

by James Whitcomb Riley

What delightful hosts are they—
    Life and Love!
Lingeringly I turn away,
    This late hour, yet glad enough
They have not withheld from me
    Their high hospitality.
So, with face lit with delight
    And all gratitude, I stay
Yet to press their hands and say,
    "Thanks.—So fine a time! Good night."

Study Questions

1. Which line shows who the hosts are?
2. Which line shows the poet is getting into old age? Which that he has enjoyed his span of life?
3. What is the theme of this work?
4. What is the rhyme scheme?

The Wild Honeysuckle

by Philip Freneau

Fair flower, that dost so comely grow,
    Hid in this silent, dull retreat,
Untouched thy honied blossoms blow,
    Unseen thy little branches greet:
      No roving foot shall crush thee here,
      No busy hand provoke a tear.

By nature's self in white arrayed,
  She bade thee shun the vulgar eye,
And planted here the guardian shade,
  And sent soft waters murmuring by,
    Thus quietly thy summer goes,
    Thy days declining to repose.

Smit with those charms, that must decay,
  I grieve to see your future doom;
They died —nor were those flowers more gay,
  Then flowers that did in Eden bloom;
    Unpitying frosts and Autumn's power,
    Shall leave no vestige of this flower.

From morning suns and evening dews
  At first thy little being came;
If nothing once, you nothing lose,
  For when you die you are the same;
    The space between is but an hour,
    The frail duration of a flower.

Study Questions

1. What is the comparison that is being made in this poem?
2. Which line in the poem expresses the idea of "from beginning to end"?
3. How does the poet describe the honeysuckle? Compare this description to that in "The Violet".
4. Who is the "She" referred to in line 8?
5. Is the poet talking about the natural or the supernatural level?
6. What is the rhyme scheme?
7. Scan this poem. What kind of meter is used?

The Chambered Nautilus

by Oliver Wendell Holmes

This is the ship of pearl, which, poets feign,
   Sails the unshadowed main,—
   The venturous bark that flings
On the sweet summer wind its purpled wings
In gulfs enchanted, where the Siren sings,
   And coral reefs lie bare,
Where the cold sea-maids rise to sun their streaming hair.

Its webs of living gauze no more unfurl;
   Wrecked is the ship of pearl!
   And every chambered cell,
Where its dim dreaming life was wont to dwell,
As the frail tenant shaped his growing shell,
   Before thee lies revealed,—
Its irised ceiling rent, its sunless crypt unsealed!

Year after year beheld the silent toil
   That spread his lustrous coil;
   Still, as the spiral grew,
He left the past year's dwelling for the new,
Stole with soft step its shining archway through,
   Built up its idle door,
Stretched in his last-found home, and knew the old no more.

Thanks for the heavenly message brought by thee,
   Child of the wandering sea,
   Cast from her lap, forlorn!
From thy dead lips a clearer note is born
Then ever Triton blew from wreathèd horn!
   While on mine ear it rings,
Through the deep caves of thought I hear a voice that sings:—

Build thee more stately mansions, O my soul,
  As the swift seasons roll!
  Leave thy low-vaulted past!
Let each new temple, nobler than the last,
Shut thee from heaven with a dome more vast,
  Till thou at length art free,
Leaving thine outgrown shell by life's unresting sea!

Study Questions

1. What is the rhyme scheme in this poem?
2. Where does the poem refer to the ability the nautilus has of using his shell like a boat, while extending himself out of the shell like a sail?
3. In the first stanza the animal is referred to as alive. Does this change in the subsequent stanzas?
4. What is the color of the shell? How is the shell formed?
5. What does the last stanza mean?

The Snow-Storm

by Ralph Waldo Emerson

Announced by all the trumpets of the sky,
  Arrives the snow; and, driving o'er the fields,
  Seems nowhere to alight; the whited air
  Hides hills and woods, the river, and the heaven,
  And veils the farm-house at the garden's end.
  The sled and traveller stopped, the courier's feet
  Delayed, all friends shut out, the housemates sit
  Around the radiant fireplace, enclosed
  In a tumultuous privacy of storm.
    Come see the north wind's masonry.
  Out of an unseen quarry, evermore

Furnished with tile, the fierce artificer
Curves his white bastions with projected roof
Round every windward stake or tree or door;
Speeding, the myriad-handed, his wild work
So fanciful, so savage; nought cares he
For number or proportion. Mockingly
On coop or kennel he hangs Parian wreaths;
A swan-like form invests the hidden thorn;
Fills up the farmer's lane from wall to wall,
Maugre the farmer's sighs; and at the gate
A tapering turret overtops the work.
And when his hours are numbered, and the world
Is all his own, retiring as he were not,
Leaves, when the sun appears, astonished Art
To mimic in slow structures, stone by stone,
Built in an age, the mad wind's night-work,
The frolic architecture of the snow.

Study Questions

1. Emerson intended in this poem to draw a sketch of a winter day. Did he succeed?
2. Which lines invoke the most vivid picture of the storm?
3. What is the theme of the poem? Its central thought?
4. Is there a rhyme scheme in this poem?

The Falconer of God

by William Rose Benét

I flung my soul to the air like a falcon flying.
I said, "Wait on, wait on, while I ride below!
   I shall start a heron soon
   In the marsh beneath the moon—
A strange white heron rising with silver on its wings,
     Rising and crying
   Wordless, wondrous things;
The secret of the stars, of the world's heart-strings
   The answer to their woe.
Then stoop thou upon him, and grip him and hold him so!

   My wild soul waited on as falcons hover.
   I beat the reedy fens as I trampled past.
   I heard the mournful loon
   In the marsh beneath the moon.
And then with feathery thunder—the bird of my desire
     Broke from the cover
   Flashing silver fire.
High up among the stars I saw his pinions spire.
   The pale clouds gazed aghast
As my falcon stooped upon him, and gripped and held him
   fast.

My soul dropped through the air—with heavenly plunder?—
Gripping the dazzling bird my dreaming knew?
   Nay! But a piteous freight,
   A dark and heavy weight
Despoiled of silver plumage, its voice forever stilled,—
     All of the wonder
   Gone that ever filled
Its guise with glory. Oh, bird that I have killed,

How brilliantly you flew
Across my rapturous vision when first I dreamed of you!

Yet I fling my soul on high with new endeavor,
And I ride the world below with a joyful mind.
I shall start a heron soon
In the marsh beneath the moon—
A wondrous silver heron its inner darkness fledges!
I beat forever
The fens and the sedges.
The pledge is still the same—for all disastrous pledges,
All hopes resigned!
My soul still flies above me for the quarry it shall find.

Study Questions

1. If the heron symbolizes earthly beauty and the falcon the soul of man, or the human spirit, and the solitary hunter the human person in pursuit of ideal beauty, what is the central thought of this poem?
2. Which lines suggest the wonderful brilliance of Beauty? Which describe the disillusionment of the falconer?
3. Why is the poem titled "The Falconer of God"?
4. What is the rhyme scheme?
5. Find an example of alliteration in the poem.

The Rhetorical Stage: Poetry Selections: Section II

The Housewife's Prayer

by Blanche Mary Kelly

Lady, who with tender word
Didst keep the house of Christ the Lord,
Who didst set forth the bread and wine
Before the Living Wheat and Vine,
Reverently didst make the bed
Whereon was laid the Holy Head
That such a cruel pillow prest
For our behoof, on Calvary's crest;
Be beside me while I go
About my labors to and fro.
Speed the wheel and speed the loom,
Guide the needle and the broom,
Make my bread rise sweet and light,
Make my cheese come foamy white,
Yellow may my butter be
As cowslips blowing on the lea.
Homely though my tasks and small,
Be beside me at them all.
Then when I shall stand to face
Jesu in the judgment place,
To me thy gracious help afford,
Who are the Handmaid of the Lord.

Study Questions

1. How is the first section (lines 1–8) related to the rest of the poem?
2. To whom do the words "Living Wheat and Vine" refer?
3. Which figure of speech do you find in line four? Lines 15 and 16?
4. In lines 11 and 12 there is an instance of vowel assonance. What is it?

Rouge Bouquet

by Joyce Kilmer

In a wood they call the Rouge Bouquet
There is a new-made grave today,
Built by never a spade nor pick
Yet covered with earth ten meters thick.
There lie many fighting men,
   Dead in their youthful prime,
Never to laugh nor love again
   Nor taste the Summertime
For Death came flying through the air
And stopped his flight at the dugout stair,
Touched his prey and left them there,
   Clay to clay.
He hid their bodies stealthily
In the soil of the land they fought to free
   And fled away.
Now over the grave abrupt and clear
   Three volleys ring;
And perhaps their brave young spirits hear
   The bugle sing:
"Go to sleep!
Go to sleep!
Slumber well where the shell screamed and fell.
Let your rifles rest on the muddy floor,
You will not need them any more.
Danger's past;
Now at last,
Go to sleep!"

There is on earth no worthier grave
To hold the bodies of the brave
Than this place of pain and pride

Where they nobly fought and nobly died.
Never fear but in the skies
   Saints and angels stand
Smiling with their holy eyes
   On this new-come band.
St. Michael's sword darts through the air
And touches the aureole on his hair
As he sees them stand saluting there,
   His stalwart sons:
And Patrick, Brigid, Columkill
Rejoice that in veins of warriors still
   The Gael's blood runs.
And up to Heaven's doorway floats,
   From the wood called Rouge Bouquet,
A delicate cloud of bugle notes
   That softly say:
"Farewell! Farewell.
Comrades true, born anew, peace to you!
Your souls shall be where the heroes are
And your memory shine like the morning-star.
Brave and dear,
Shield us here.
Farewell!"

Study Questions

1. This poem is a tribute by Joyce Kilmer to his comrades, men who fought and died in World War I. If you were to put this poem in prose, what would it say?
2. How do you interpret "clay to clay"?
3. Which figures of speech are in the following lines: line 8, lines 9 and 10, line 22, line 30, line 48, line 50?

The Lake Isle of Innisfree
by William Butler Yeats

I will arise and go now, and go to Innisfree,
And a small cabin build there, of clay and wattles made:
Nine bean-rows will I have there, a hive for the honey-bee,
And live alone in the bee-loud glade.

And I shall have some peace there, for peace comes dropping
    slow,
Dropping from the veils of the morning to where the cricket
    sings;
There midnight's all a glimmer, and noon a purple glow,
And evening full of the linnet's wings.

I will arise and go now, for always night and day
I hear lake water lapping with low sounds by the shore;
While I stand on the roadway, or on the pavements gray,
I hear it in the deep heart's core.

Study Questions

1   What sounds are brought to mind by this poem? What appeal
    is made to the sense of sight?
2. How does the sound of the phrase "dropping slow" contribute
    to the effect of the poem?

3. What is the single most important item the poet wants to find in Innisfree?
4. Find an example of alliteration in the third stanza. What about the following line?

The Kings

by Louise Imogen Guiney

A man said unto his Angel:
"My spirits are fallen low,
And I cannot carry this battle:
O brother! Where might I go?

"The terrible Kings are on me
With spears that are deadly bright;
Against me so from the cradle
Do fate and my fathers fight."

Then said to the man his Angel:
"Thou wavering witless soul,
Back to the ranks! What matter
To win or to lose the whole,

"As judged by the little judges
Who hearken not well, not see?
Not thus, by the outer issue,
The Wise shall interpret thee.

"Thy will is the sovereign measure
And only event of things:
The puniest heart defying,
Were stronger than all these Kings.

"Though out of the past they gather,
Mind's Doubt, and Bodily Pain,
And pallid Thirst of the Spirit
That is kin to the other twain,

"And Grief, in a cloud of banners,
And ringletted Vain Desires,
And Vice, with spoils upon him
Of thee and thy beaten sires,—

"While Kings of Eternal evil
Yet darken the hills about,
Thy part is with broken saber
To rise on the last redoubt;

"To fear not sensible failure,
Nor covet the game at all,
But fighting, fighting, fighting,
Die, driven against the wall."

Study Questions

1. In the first two stanzas the man makes a complaint to his angel.
   What is it, and what does he wish to do?
2. What does the angel say in response? Who are the "little
   judges"? What is the outer issue?
3. Why is the will the sovereign measure? And why is the "puniest
   heart defying" stronger than all the kings?
4. What do the kings gather against men? And what is the right
   response to this?
5. Find an example of alliteration in the second stanza of the
   poem.
6. What is the rhyme scheme?

Loss of Faith

by Alfred J. Barrett

The life of grace and glory is the same.
The life of grace is, by another name,
Heaven on earth, and death is but a change
In range—
And nothing strange!

There lies between our dreaming and our seeing
One pulsing continuity of being.
Ah, when the life of glory we achieve
Why grieve?
We only lose our having to believe.

Study Questions

1. What is the meaning of "glory" in the first line?
2. What does the poet say the life of grace is? Why?
3. When the poet uses the words "dreaming" and "seeing" in line 6, what does he mean?
4. What does the poet mean by his last line?
5. What is the rhyme scheme?

Prospice (Look Ahead!)

by Robert Browning

Fear death?—to feel the fog in my throat,
   The mist in my face,
When the snows begin, and the blasts denote
   I am nearing the place,
The power of the night, the press of the storm,
   The post of the foe;

Where he stands, the Arch Fear in a visible form,
    Yet the strong man must go:
For the journey is done and the summit attained,
    And the barriers fall,
Though a battle's to fight ere the guerdon be gained,
    The reward of it all.
I was ever a fighter, so—one fight more,
    The best and the last!
I would hate that death bandaged my eyes, and forbore,
    And bade me creep past.
No! Let me taste the whole of it, fare like my peers
    The heroes of old,
Bear the brunt, in a minute pay glad life's arrears
    Of pain, darkness and cold.
For sudden, the worst turns the best to the brave,
    The black minute's at end,
And the elements' rage, the fiend-voices that rave,
    Shall dwindle, shall blend,
Shall change, shall become first a peace out of pain,
    Then a light, then thy breast,
O thou soul of my soul! I shall clasp thee again,
    And with God be the rest!

Study Questions

1. This poem was written shortly after the death of Robert Browning's wife, Elizabeth Barrett Browning. The title means "look forward". To what is the author looking forward?
2. To what does the poem compare death?
3. How does the poet wish to meet his end?
4. Where does the mood of the poem change? What accounts for this change?
5. Give the central thought of the poem.
6. What is the rhyme scheme?

How the Great Guest Came

by *Edwin Markham*

Before the Cathedral in grandeur rose,
At Ingelburg where the Danube goes;
Before its forest of silver spires
Went airily up to the clouds and fires:
Before the oak had ready a beam,
While yet the arch was stone and dream—
There where the altar was later laid,
Conrad, the cobbler, plied his trade.
Doubled all day on his busy bench,
Hard at his cobbling for master and hench,
He pounded away at a brisk rat-tat,
Shearing and shaping with pull and pat,
Hide well-hammered and pegs sent home,
Till the shoe was fit for the Prince of Rome.
And he sang as the threads went to and fro:
"Whether 'tis hidden or whether it show,
Let the work be sound, for the Lord will know."

Tall was the cobbler, and gray and thin,
And a full moon shone where the hair had been.
His eyes peered out, intent and afar,
As looking beyond the things that are;
He walked as one who is done with fear,
Knowing at last that God is near.
Only the half of him cobbled the shoes:
The rest was away for the heavenly news.
Indeed, so thin was the mystic screen
That parted the Unseen from the Seen,
You could not tell from the cobbler's theme,
If his dream were truth or his truth were dream.

It happened one day at the year's white end,
Two neighbors called on their old-time friend;
And they found the shop, so meager and mean,
Made gay with a hundred boughs of green.
Conrad was stitching with face ashine,
But suddenly stopped as he twitched a twine:
"Old friends, good news! At dawn today,
As the cocks were scaring the night away,
The Lord appeared in a dream to me,
And said, 'I am coming your guest to be!'
So I've been busy with branches of fir.
The wall is washed and the shelf is shined,
And over the rafter the holly twined.
He comes today, and the table is spread
With milk and honey and wheaten bread."

His friends went home; and his face grew still
As he watched for the shadow across the sill.
He lived all the moments o'er and o'er,
When the Lord should enter the lowly door—
The knock, the call, the latch pulled up,
The lighted face, the offered cup.
He would wash the feet where the spikes had been;
He would kiss the hands where the nails went in;
And then at last he would sit with Him,
And break the bread as the day grew dim.

While the cobbler mused there passed his pane
A beggar drenched by the driving rain.
He called him in from the stony street
And gave him shoes for his bruised feet.
The beggar went and there came a crone,
Her face with wrinkles of sorrow sown.
A bundle of faggots bowed her back,

And she was spent with the wrench and rack.
He gave her his loaf and steadied her load
As she took her way on the weary road.
Then came to his door a little child,
Lost and afraid in the world so wild,
In the big, dark world. Catching it up,
He gave it the milk in the waiting cup,
And led it home to its mother's arms,
Out of the reach of the world's alarms.

The day went down in the crimson west
And with it the hope of the blessed Guest,
And Conrad sighed as the world turned gray:
"Why is it, Lord, that your feet delay?
Did You forget that this was the day?"
Then soft in the silence a Voice he heard:
"Lift up your heart, for I kept my word,
Three times I came to your friendly door;
Three times my shadow was on your floor,
I was the beggar with bruised feet;
I was the woman you gave to eat;
I was the child on the homeless street!"

Study Questions

1. There are two broad categories of poetry, lyric and narrative. Lyric poetry is marked by imagination, melody, emotion, and the creation of a single, unified impression on the reader. Narrative poetry tells a story. Which sort of poetry is this poem an instance of?
2. Look up Matthew 25:34–40. "How the Great Guest Came" is an illustration of what Our Lord explains in Saint Matthew's Gospel. Did you see the ending of this poem coming?

Little Boy Blue

by Eugene Field

The little toy dog is covered with dust,
  But sturdy and staunch he stands;
The little toy soldier is red with rust,
  And his musket moulds in his hands.
Time was when the little toy dog was new,
  And the soldier was passing fair;
And that was the time when our Little Boy Blue
  Kissed them and put them there.

"Now don't you go till I come," he said,
  "And don't you make any noise!"
So toddling off to his trundle-bed,
  He dreamt of the pretty toys.
And as he was dreaming, an angel song
  Awakened our Little Boy Blue,—
Oh! the years are many, the years are long,
  But the little toy friends are true!

Ay, faithful to Little Boy Blue they stand,
  Each in the same old place,
Awaiting the touch of a little hand,
  The smile of a little face;
And they wonder, as waiting the long years through,
  In the dust of that little chair,
What has become of our Little Boy Blue
  Since he kissed them and put them there.

Study Questions

1. How, in the last stanza, does the poet convey to us his sense of sadness?

The Rhetorical Stage: Poetry Selections: Section II

2. The first part of the poem is narrative in character; the reader is waiting to see what the explanation for the disuse of the toys is. Where does this explanation occur, and where does the tone change?
3. What is the rhyme scheme?
4. What figure of speech is used in the poem?

Christmas

by Sir John Betjeman

The bells of waiting Advent ring,
    The Tortoise stove is lit again
And lamp-oil light across the night
    Has caught the streaks of winter rain
In many a stained-glass window sheen
    From Crimson Lake to Hooker's Green.

The holly in the windy hedge
    And round the Manor House the yew
Will soon be stripped to deck the ledge,
    The altar, font and arch and pew,
So that the villagers can say
    "The church looks nice" on Christmas Day.

Provincial public houses blaze
    And Corporation tramcars clang,
On lighted tenements I gaze
    Where paper decorations hang,
And bunting in the red Town Hall
    Says "Merry Christmas to you all."

And London shops on Christmas Eve
  Are strung with silver bells and flowers
As hurrying clerks the City leave
  To pigeon-haunted classic towers,
And marbled clouds go scudding by
  The many-steepled London sky.

And girls in slacks remember Dad,
  And oafish louts remember Mum,
And sleepless children's hearts are glad,
  And Christmas-morning bells say "Come!"
Even to shining ones who dwell
  Safe in the Dorchester Hotel.

And is it true? And is it true,
  This most tremendous tale of all,
Seen in a stained-glass window's hue,
  A Baby in an ox's stall?
The Maker of the stars and sea
  Become a Child on earth for me?

And is it true? For if it is,
  No loving fingers tying strings
Around those tissued fripperies,
  The sweet and silly Christmas things,
Bath salts and inexpensive scent
  And hideous tie so kindly meant,

No love that in a family dwells,
  No caroling in frosty air,
Nor all the steeple-shaking bells
  Can with this single Truth compare—
That God was Man in Palestine
  And lives to-day in Bread and Wine.

The Rhetorical Stage: Poetry Selections: Section II

1. The first five stanzas can be divided against the last three. What would be the basis for the division?
2. What is the "punch line" of the poem?
3. In the first line there is a personification; what is it?
4. What is the rhyme scheme?

The Day Is Done

by Henry Wadsworth Longfellow

The day is done, and the darkness
    Falls from the wings of Night,
As a feather is wafted downward
    From an eagle in his flight.

I see the lights of the village
    Gleam through the rain and the mist,
And a feeling of sadness comes o'er me,
    That my soul cannot resist:

A feeling of sadness and longing,
    That is not akin to pain,
And resembles sorrow only
    As the mist resembles rain.

Come, read to me some poem,
    Some simple and heartfelt lay,
That shall soothe this restless feeling,
    And banish the thoughts of day.

Not from the grand old masters,
    Not from the bards sublime,
Whose distant footsteps echo
    Through the corridors of Time.

For, like strains of martial music,
    Their mighty thoughts suggest
Life's endless toil and endeavor;
    And tonight I long for rest.

Read from some humbler poet,
    Whose songs gushed from his heart,
As showers from the clouds of summer,
    Or tears from the eyelids start;

Who, through long days of labor,
    And nights devoid of ease,
Still heard in his soul the music
    Of wonderful melodies.

Such songs have power to quiet
    The restless pulse of care,
And come like the benediction
    That follows after prayer.

Then read from the treasured volume
    The poem of thy choice,
And lend to the rhyme of the poet
    The beauty of thy voice.

And the night shall be filled with music
    And the cares, that infest the day,
Shall fold their tents, like the Arabs,
    And as silently steal away.

1. What is the ending mood of the poem?
2. The poet says that his restless feeling will not be soothed by the "grand old masters" or the "bards sublime". Why? And would there be a time when Longfellow would want to turn to them?
3. What is the rhyme scheme of the poem?

The Tables Turned

by William Wordsworth

Up! up! my Friend, and quit your books;
Or surely you'll grow double:
Up! up! my Friend, and clear your looks;
Why all this toil and trouble?

The sun, above the mountain's head,
The freshening lustre mellow
Through all the long green fields has spread,
His first sweet evening yellow.

Books! 'tis a dull and endless strife:
Come, hear the woodland linnet,
How sweet his music! on my life,
There's more of wisdom in it.

And hark! how blithe the throstle sings!
He, too, is no mean preacher:
Come forth into the light of things,
Let Nature be your Teacher.

She has a world of ready wealth,
Our minds and hearts to bless—

Spontaneous wisdom breathed by health,
Truth breathed by cheerfulness.

One impulse from a vernal wood
May teach you more of man,
Of moral evil and of good,
Than all the sages can.

Sweet is the lore which Nature brings;
Our meddling intellect
Mis-shapes the beauteous forms of things:—
We murder to dissect.

Enough of Science and of Art;
Close up those barren leaves;
Come forth, and bring with you a heart
That watches and receives.

Study Questions

1. What does the title of the poem suggest to you? It might help to
   know that this poem was Wordsworth's answer to a critic who
   accused him of being preoccupied with nature to the neglect of
   formal study.
2. Summarize the two positions, that of Wordsworth and that of
   the critic, as presented in this poem.
3. Which manifestations of nature does Wordsworth select to
   contrast the life of formal study and the study of nature?

The Virgin

by William Wordsworth

Mother! Whose virgin bosom was uncrost
With the least shade of thought to sin allied;
Woman! above all women glorified,
Our tainted nature's solitary boast;
Purer than foam on central ocean tost;
Brighter than eastern skies at daybreak strewn
With fancied roses, than the unblemished moon
Before her wane begins on heaven's blue coast:

Thy image falls to earth. Yet some, I ween,
Not unforgiven, the suppliant knee might bend
As to a visible power, in which did blend
All that was mixed and reconciled in thee
Of a mother's love with maiden purity,
Of high with low, celestial with terrene.

Study Questions

1. Which two dogmas of the Catholic Faith are indicated in this poem? Select the lines that refer to both and explain their meaning.
2. What three images does Wordsworth use to express Mary's purity? How does his choice fit with the thoughts he expresses in "The Tables Turned"?

The Destruction of Sennacherib

by George Gordon Byron

The Assyrian came down like the wolf on the fold,
And his cohorts were gleaming in purple and gold;
And the sheen of their spears was like stars on the sea,
When the blue wave rolls nightly on deep Galilee.

Like the leaves of the forest when Summer is green,
That host with their banners at sunset were seen;
Like the leaves of the forest when Autumn hath blown,
That host on the morrow lay withered and strown.

For the Angel of Death spread his wings on the blast,
And breathed in the face of the foe as he passed;
And the eyes of the sleepers waxed deadly and chill,
And their hearts but once heaved, and forever grew still!

And there lay the steed with his nostril all wide,
But through it there rolled not the breath of his pride;
And the foam of his gasping lay white on the turf,
And cold as the spray of the rock-beating surf.

And there lay the rider distorted and pale,
With the dew on his brow and the rust on his mail;
And the tents were all silent, the banners alone,
The lances unlifted, the trumpet unblown.

And the widows of Ashur are loud in their wail,
And the idols are broke in the temple of Baal;
And the might of the Gentile, unsmote by the sword,
Hath melted like snow in the glance of the Lord!

1. Look up 2 Kings 19. What scene is being described in this poem?
2. Was Sennacherib's army large? Were they well equipped? How do you know?
3. Compare the poem to the account in Scripture. How do they differ and how are they the same? On which particular verse is this poem based?
4. Give the similes used in the poem.
5. What is the rhyme scheme? What is the meter?

Lepanto

by G. K. Chesterton

SECTION I

White founts falling in the Courts of the Sun,
And the Soldan of Byzantium is smiling as they run;
There is laughter like the fountains in that face of all men
    feared,
It stirs the forest darkness, the darkness of his beard;
It curls the blood-red crescent, the crescent of his lips;
For the inmost sea of all the earth is shaken with his ships.
They have dared the white republics on the capes of Italy,
They have dashed the Adriatic round the Lion of the Sea,
And the Pope has cast his arms abroad for agony and loss,
And called the kings of Christendom for swords about the
    Cross.
The cold queen of England is looking in the glass;
The shadow of Valois is yawning at the Mass;
From evening isles fantastical rings faint the Spanish gun,
And the Lord upon the Golden Horn is laughing in the sun.

Dim drums throbbing, in the hills half heard,
Where only on a nameless throne a crownless prince has
      stirred,
Where, risen from a doubtful seat and half-attained stall,
The last knight of Europe takes weapons from the wall,
The last and lingering troubadour to whom the bird has sung,
That once went singing southward when all the world was
      young.
In that enormous silence, tiny and unafraid,
Comes up along a winding road the noise of the Crusade.
Strong gongs groaning as the guns boom far,
Don John of Austria is going to the war,
Stiff rags straining in the night blasts cold
In the gloom black-purple, in the glint old-gold,
Torchlight crimson on the copper kettledrums,
Then the tuckets, then the trumpets, then the cannon, and he
      comes.
Don John laughing in the brave beard curled,
Spurning of his stirrups like the thrones of all the world,
Holding his head up for a flag of all the free.
Love light of Spain—hurrah!
Death light of Africa!
Don John of Austria
Is riding to the sea.

SECTION III

Mahound is in his paradise above the evening star;
(Don John of Austria is going to the war.)
He moves a mighty turban on the timeless houri's knees.
His turban that is woven of the sunsets and the seas.
He shakes the peacock gardens as he rises from his ease,
And he strides among the treetops and is taller than the trees;
And his voice through all the garden is a thunder sent to bring

Black Azrael and Ariel and Ammon on the wing.
Giants and the Genii,
Multiplex of wing and eye,
Whose strong obedience broke the sky
When Solomon was king.

They rush in red and purple from the red clouds of the morn,
From the temples where the yellow gods shut up their eyes in
    scorn;
They rise in green robes roaring from the green hells of the
    sea
Where fallen skies and evil hues and eyeless creatures be,
On them the sea valves clusters and the gray sea forests curl,
Splashed with a splendid sickness, the sickness of the pearl;
They swell in sapphire smoke out of the blue cracks of the
    ground—
They gather and they wonder and give worship to Mahound.
And he saith, "Break up the mountains where the hermit-folk
    can hide,
And sift the red and silver sands lest bone of saint abide,
And chase the Giaours flying night and day, not giving rest,
For that which was our trouble comes again out of the west,
We have set the seal of Solomon on all things under sun,
Of knowledge and of sorrow and endurance of things done.
But a noise is in the mountains, in the mountains, and I know
The voice that shook our palaces—four hundred years ago:
It is he that saith not 'Kismet'; it is he that knows not Fate;
It is Richard, it is Raymond, it is Godfrey at the gate!
It is he whose loss is laughter when he counts the wager
    worth,
Put down your feet upon him, that our peace be on the
    earth."
For he heard drums groaning and he heard guns jar,
(Don John of Austria is going to the war.)

Sudden and still—hurrah!
Bolt from Iberia!
Don John of Austria
Is gone by Alcalar.

St. Michael's on his Mountain in the sea roads of the north
(Don John of Austria is girt and going forth.)
Where the gray seas glitter and the sharp tides shift
And the seafolk labor and red sails lift.
He shakes his lance of iron and he claps his wings of stone;
The noise is gone through Normandy; the noise is gone
    alone;
The North is full of tangled things and texts and aching eyes,
And dead is all the innocence of anger and surprise,
And Christian killeth Christian in a narrow dusty room,
And Christian dreadeth Christ that hath a newer face of
    doom.
And Christian hateth Mary that God kissed in Galilee—
But Don John of Austria is riding to the sea.
Don John calling through the blast and the eclipse
Crying with the trumpet, with the trumpet of his lips.
Trumpet that sayeth *ha!*
Domino gloria!
Don John of Austria
Is shouting to the ships.

King Philip's in his closet with the Fleece about his neck
(Don John of Austria is armed upon the deck.)
The walls are hung with velvet that is black and soft as sin,
And little dwarfs creep out of it and little dwarfs creep in.
He holds a crystal phial that has colors like the moon,
He touches, and it tingles, and he trembles very soon,
And his face is as a fungus of a leprous white and gray

Like plants in the high houses that are shuttered from the day,
And death is in the phial, and the end of noble work,
Don John of Austria has fired upon the Turk.
Don John's hunting, and his hounds have bayed—
Booms away past Italy the rumor of his raid
Gun upon gun, ha! ha!
Gun upon gun, hurrah!
Don John of Austria
Has loosed the cannonade.

SECTION V

The Pope was in his chapel before day or battle broke,
(Don John of Austria is hidden in the smoke.)
The hidden room in man's house where God sits all the year,
The secret window whence the world looks small and very
    dear.
He sees as in a mirror on the monstrous twilight sea
The crescent of his cruel ships whose name is mystery;
They fling great shadows foe-wards, making Cross and Castle
    dark,
They veil the plumed lions on the galleys of St. Mark;
And above the ships are palaces of brown, black-bearded
    chiefs,

And below the ships are prisons, where with multitudinous
    griefs,
Christian captives sick and sunless, all a laboring race repines
Like a race in sunken cities, like a nation in the mines.
They are lost like slaves that swat, and in the skies of morning
    hung
The stairways of the tallest gods when tyranny was young.
They are countless, voiceless, hopeless as those fallen or
    fleeing on
Before the high kings' horses in the granite of Babylon.
And many a one grows witless in his quiet room in hell
Where a yellow face looks inward through the lattice of his
    cell,
And he finds his God forgotten, and he seeks no more a
    sign—
(But Don John of Austria has burst the battle line!)
Don John pounding from the slaughter-painted poop.
Purpling all the ocean like a bloody pirate's sloop,
Scarlet running over on the silvers and the golds,
Breaking of the hatches up and bursting of the holds,
Thronging of the thousands up that labor under sea
White for bliss and blind for sun and stunned for liberty.
Vivat Hispania!
Domino gloria!
Don John of Austria
Has set his people free!
Cervantes on his galley sets the sword back in the sheath
(Don John of Austria rides homeward with a wreath.)
And he sees across a weary land a straggling road in Spain,
Up which a lean and foolish knight forever rides in vain,
And he smiles, but not as Sultans smile, and settles back the
    blade.
(But Don John of Austria rides home from the Crusade.)

Study Questions

Section I

    This battle took place in 1571; the pope referred to is Pope Saint Pius V. There are many historical details given in the poem. For instance, who is the cold queen of England? And why is she looking in the mirror? What is the situation portrayed in this section? Who has the upper hand? What is the reaction of the Christian leaders to the Pope's call? See how many of the people referred to in this poem you can name.

Section II

    How is Don John of Austria characterized? What colors are used in the section? Are there examples of alliteration? What is the rhyme scheme?

Section III

    What attributes are given to Mahound by the poet? How does he react to this new crusade? Whom does he command? And to whom is Don John compared? Can you find an instance of imagery? Of metaphor?

Section IV

    Which lines indicate that Saint Michael has issued a call to arms? What causes Christian to "killeth Christian"? And why does "Christian dreadeth Christ"? What is Chesterton's opinion of King Philip II? How has Don John of Austria responded to the call?

Section V

    Where was the Pope? This section of the poem recounts the vision that Pope Pius V saw. What was the position of the Christian captives? What other specific features of the battle did the Pope see? Why is Cervantes alluded to at the end of the poem?

The Passionate Shepherd to His Love

by Christopher Marlowe

Come live with me and be my Love,
And we will all the pleasures prove
That hills and valleys, dales and fields,
Or woods, or steepy mountain yields.

And we will sit upon the rocks,
And see the shepherds feed their flocks
By shallow rivers, to whose falls
Melodious birds sing madrigals.

And I will make thee beds of roses
And a thousand fragrant posies;
A cap of flowers, and a kirtle
Embroider'd all with leaves of myrtle;

A gown made of the finest wool
Which from our pretty lambs we pull;
Fair linèd slippers for the cold,
With buckles of the purest gold;

A belt of straw and ivy buds,
With coral clasps and amber studs:
And if these pleasures may thee move,
Come live with me, and be my Love.

Thy silver dishes for thy meat
As precious as the gods do eat,
Shall on an ivory table be
Prepared each day for thee and me.

The shepherd swains shall dance and sing
For thy delight each May morning:
If these delights thy mind may move,
Then live with me and be my Love.

Study Questions

1. What does the shepherd promise his love, if she will come and live with him?
2. Given that these are the things he promises, what are the kinds of joys he seems to think essential to happiness? Do you think he is right? Has he omitted anything important?
3. Scan one stanza.

The Nymph's Reply to the Shepherd

by Sir Walter Raleigh

If all the world and love were young,
And truth in every shepherd's tongue,
These pretty pleasures might me move
To live with thee and be thy Love.

But Time drives flocks from field to fold;
When rivers rage and rocks grow cold;
And Philomel becometh dumb;
The rest complains of cares to come.

The flowers do fade, and wanton fields
To wayward Winter reckoning yields:
A honey tongue, a heart of gall,
Is fancy's spring, but sorrow's fall.

The gowns, thy shoes, thy beds of roses,
Thy cap, thy kirtle, and thy posies
Soon break, soon wither—soon forgotten,
In folly ripe, in reason rotten.

Thy belt of straw and ivy-buds,
Thy coral clasps and amber studs,—
All these in me no means can move
To come to thee and be thy Love.

But could youth last and love still breed,
Had joys no date nor age no need,
Then these delights my mind might move
To live with thee and be thy Love.

Study Questions

1. How is this poem a reply to Marlowe's? Be specific.
2. Is the form of this poem the same as the previous one?
3. Which of the two poems seems to be better poetry? Consider
   the use of imagery, cadence, figurative language, and meter in
   each of them.
4. Does either poem give the complete picture of courtship and
   married love?

A Song

by Thomas Carew

Ask me no more where Jove bestows,
When June is past, the fading rose;
For in your beauty's orient deep
These flowers, as in their causes, sleep.

Ask me no more whither do stray
The golden atoms of the day;
For, in pure love, heaven did prepare
Those powders to enrich your hair.

Ask me no more whither doth haste
The nightingale, when May is past;
For in your sweet dividing throat
She winters, and keeps warm her note.

Ask me no more where those stars' light
That downwards fall in dead of night;
For in your eyes they sit, and there
Fixèd become, as in their sphere.

Ask me no more if east or west
The Phoenix builds her spicy nest;
For unto you at last she flies,
And in your fragrant bosom dies.

Study Questions

1. Notice the couplet form. Why did the poet divide the poem into five stanzas, even though it is written in couplets?
2. What are the five questions the poet asks? What are the answers?
3. What, then, is the theme of the poem?
4. "Dividing throat" refers to the ability to sing in harmony or in parts. How is that term used in stanza three?
5. The phoenix is a mythological bird that destroys itself and then rises from its own ashes. How is this image used in the last stanza?
6. Why is the title appropriate?

To Celia

by Ben Jonson

Drink to me only with thine eyes,
 And I will pledge with mine;
Or leave a kiss but in the cup
 And I'll not look for wine.
The thirst that from the soul doth rise,
 Doth ask a drink divine;
But might I of Jove's nectar sup,
 I would not change for thine.

I sent thee late a rosy wreath,
 Not so much honouring thee,
As giving it a hope that there
 It could not wither'd be.
But thou thereon didst only breathe,
 And sent'st it back to me;
Since when it grows and smells, I swear
 Not of itself, but thee!

Study Questions

1. Under what circumstances does the poet say he will not look
   for wine? Why not?
2. What does the last verse of the first stanza say? What is Jonson
   saying he wouldn't change for Jove's nectar?
3. What property does Celia's breath seem to have?
4. What is the rhyme scheme?

To the Virgins, to Make Much of Time

by Robert Herrick

Gather ye rosebuds while ye may,
   Old Time is still a-flying;
And this same flower that smiles to-day
   To-morrow will be dying.

The glorious lamp of heaven, the sun,
   The higher he's a-getting,
The sooner will his race be run,
   And nearer he's to setting.

That age is best which is the first,
   When youth and blood are warmer;
But being spent, the worse, and worst
   Times still succeed the former.

Then be not coy, but use your time,
   And while ye may, go marry;
For, having lost but once your prime,
   You may for ever tarry.

Study Questions

1. What images does the poet use to contrast youth and old age?
2. Robert Browning's poem "Rabbi Ben Ezra" has these lines:
   Grow old along with me!
   The best is yet to be,
   The last of life, for which the first was made;
   Our times are in His hand
   Who saith, "A whole I planned;
   Youth shows but half; trust God, see all, nor be afraid!"

How does this compare to the sentiment in "To the Virgins"?

A General Communion

by Alice Meynell

I saw the throng, so deeply separate,
  Fed at only one board—
The devout people, moved, intent, elate,
  And the devoted Lord.

O struck apart! not side from human side,
  But soul from human soul,
As each asunder absorbed the multiplied,
  The ever unparted, whole.

I saw this people as a field of flowers,
  Each grown at such a price
The sum of unimaginable powers
  Did no more than suffice.

A thousand single central daisies they,
  A thousand of the one;
For each the entire monopoly of day;
  For each the whole of the devoted sun.

Study Questions

1. Can you find an example of hyperbole?
2. The central idea of this poem is the Mystical Body of Christ. Mrs. Meynell brings to mind both the individuality of each human being, as well as their union in Christ as their Head. Find the lines where this theme is developed.
3. What do you think "the entire monopoly of day" means?

Love (III)

by George Herbert

Love bade me welcome: yet my soul drew back,
    Guilty of dust and sin.
But quick-eyed Love, observing me grow slack
    From my first entrance in,
Drew nearer to me, sweetly questioning
    If I lacked anything.

"A guest," I answered, "worthy to be here":
    Love said, "You shall be he."
"I, the unkind, ungrateful? Ah, my dear,
    I cannot look on thee."
Love took my hand, and smiling did reply,
    "Who made the eyes but I?"

"Truth, Lord; but I have marred them; let my shame
    Go where it doth deserve."
"And know you not," says Love, "who bore the blame?"
    "My dear, then I will serve."
"You must sit down," says Love, "and taste my meat."
    So I did sit and eat.

Study Questions

1. This poem is an allegory. What is it an allegory of?
2. What is the rhyme scheme?
3. The soul is unwilling to enter into the banquet because of dust
   and sin. What does Love say to that excuse?

The Pulley

by George Herbert

When God at first made Man,
Having a glass of blessings standing by,
"Let us" (said He) "pour on him all we can;
Let the world's riches, which dispersèd lie,
    Contract into a span."

So strength first made a way;
Then beauty flowed, then wisdom, honour, pleasure.
When almost all was out, God made a stay,
Perceiving that, alone of all his treasure,
    Rest in the bottom lay.

"For if I should" (said He)
"Bestow this jewel also on My creature,
He would adore My gifts instead of Me,
And rest in Nature, not the God of Nature;
    So both should losers be.

"Yet let him keep the rest,
But keep them with repining restlessness;
Let him be rich and weary, that at least,
If goodness lead him not, yet weariness
    May toss him to My breast."

Study Questions

1. What are the treasures God gives to man?
2. Sometimes one word has more than one meaning. Can you find an example of this in the poem?
3. Why does God refrain from adding rest to these treasures?
4. Count the number of accents in each line. What is the pattern?

5. Can you find an example of vowel assonance in the first stanza?
6. What is the rhyme scheme?
7. There are a number of contrary images in the poem. How many can you find?
8. Give the central thought of this poem in your own words.

Requiem

by Robert Louis Stevenson

Under the wide and starry sky
Dig the grave and let me lie.
Glad did I live and gladly die,
    And I laid me down with a will.

This be the verse you grave for me:
Here he lies where he longed to be;
Home is the sailor, home from the sea,
    And the hunter home from the hill.

Study Questions

1. Where did Stevenson wish to be buried?
2. How did he live and die?
3. What is the mood created by the poem?

The Bells

by Edgar Allan Poe

Hear the sledges with the bells—
   Silver bells!
What a world of merriment their melody foretells!
   How they tinkle, tinkle, tinkle,
      In the icy air of night!
   While the stars that oversprinkle
   All the heavens, seem to twinkle
      With a crystalline delight;
   Keeping time, time, time,
   In a sort of Runic rhyme,
To the tintinnabulation that so musically wells
   From the bells, bells, bells, bells,
      Bells, bells, bells,—
From the jingling and the tinkling of the bells.

   Hear the mellow wedding bells,
      Golden bells!
What a world of happiness their harmony foretells!
   Through the balmy air of night
   How they ring out their delight!
      From the molten-golden notes,
         And all in tune,
      What a liquid ditty floats
To the turtle dove that listens, while she gloats
         On the moon!
   Oh, from out the sounding cells,
What a gush of euphony voluminously wells!
         How it swells!
         How it dwells
      On the Future! how it tells
      Of the rapture that impels

To the swinging and the ringing
    Of the bells, bells, bells,
    Of the bells, bells, bells, bells,
        Bells, bells, bells,—
To the rhyming and the chiming of the bells!

    Hear the loud alarum bells—
        Brazen bells!
What a tale of terror now their turbulency tells!
    In the startled ear of night
    How they scream out their affright!
    Too much horrified to speak
    They can only shriek, shriek,
        Out of tune,
In a clamorous appealing to the mercy of the fire,
In a mad expostulation with the deaf and frantic fire,
    Leaping higher, higher, higher,
    With a desperate desire,
        And a resolute endeavor,
        Now—now to sit or never,
    By the side of the pale-faced moon.
    Oh, the bells, bells, bells!
    What a tale their terror tells
        Of despair!
    How they clang, and clash, and roar!
    What a horror they outpour
On the bosom of the palpitating air!
    Yet the ear it fully knows,
        By the twanging,
        And the clanging,
    How the danger ebbs and flows;
    Yet the ear distinctly tells,
        In the jangling,
        And the wrangling,

How the danger sinks and swells,
By the sinking or the swelling in the anger of the bells—
        Of the bells—
    Of the bells, bells, bells, bells,
        Bells, bells, bells,—
In the clamor and the clangor of the bells!

        Hear the tolling of the bells—
            Iron bells!
What a world of solemn thought their monody compels!
        In the silence of the night,
        How we shiver with affright
    At the melancholy menace of their tone!
        For every sound that floats
        From the rust within their throats
            Is a groan.
        And the people—ah, the people—
        They that dwell up in the steeple,
            All alone,
    And who tolling, tolling, tolling,
        In that muffled monotone,
    Feel a glory in so rolling
        On the human heart a stone—
    They are neither man nor woman—
    They are neither brute nor human—
        They are Ghouls:
    And their king it is who tolls;
    And he rolls, rolls, rolls,
            Rolls
        A paean from the bells!
    And his merry bosom swells
        With the paean of the bells!
    And he dances, and he yells;
    Keeping time, time, time,

In a sort of Runic rhyme,
   To the paean of the bells—
     Of the bells:
  Keeping time, time, time,
  In a sort of Runic rhyme,
   To the throbbing of the bells—
     Of the bells, bells, bells,—
   To the sobbing of the bells;
  Keeping time, time, time,
     As he knells, knells, knells,
  In a happy Runic rhyme,
    To the rolling of the bells—
  Of the bells, bells, bells—
    To the tolling of the bells,
  Of the bells, bells, bells, bells—
    Bells, bells, bells—
To the moaning and the groaning of the bells!

Study Questions

1. A different mood is expressed in each of the four stanzas. What
   are they? What might be the reason for the order of the stanzas?
   Or for the various lengths of the stanzas?
2. Which sound produces the impression of sleigh bells? What
   figure of speech is this?
3. Which sounds give the wedding bells smooth, mellow tones?
4. In the third stanza there are some unpleasant sounds: the short *a*
   followed by *r* or *ng*, also the harsh gutturals of *k* and hard *c*, and
   the sibilants *s*, *z*, and *sh*. Why are they used here?

Answers to Study Questions

Please note that these answers are not the only possible answers to many of the questions asked. Encourage your student to reflect upon the poems and the questions that are asked about them. If he does that and arrives at an answer that differs from those given here, his answer may well be better. Don't direct the student's attention to the "right answer" instead of an honest attempt to figure out the meaning of the poem on his own.

"The Head and the Heart"   *p. 293*

1. The central theme is that man needs to have both his intellect and will in line to do great things.
2. The poet employs personification in the poem. Both the head and the heart are spoken of as though they were separately existing entities, endowed with human qualities.
3. The rhyme scheme is *abab*.

"Travel"   *p. 294*

1. People will have different responses to this question, but it does seem that there is something disordered in such a desire. We should always make an attempt to do our daily duty, where we are. This doesn't mean that one should never desire to change jobs or situations, but that the desire for change for its own sake is not a good thing.
2. There is an amazing capacity in the human soul to have a "single-track mind", to shut out, for the moment, all but a desired experience. If this capacity is rightly ordered, that is, ordered to carrying out God's will, it is a great gift.
3. The rhyme scheme is *abab*.

"An Old Woman of the Roads"   p. 294

1. The little house that the old woman longs for has a hearth with a sod fire, a pile of turf for fuel, and a stool to sit on before the fire. It has a clock and a dresser with blue and white, shining dishes. It has a bed and is warm and snug, out of the wind and the rain's way. The contrasting picture is drawn in the fifth stanza, where the old woman says she's so tired of the mist and dark, the lonely roads, the bog, the crying wind, and loneliness.
2. There are many vivid images; the second stanza gives just the right details for us to picture a cozy little house, satisfying, without gaudiness. The fifth stanza is also vivid, with the contrasting picture, the lonely, cold, and weary road.
3. The poem evokes pity and longing for the old woman to have her desire.

"A Parting Guest"   p. 296

1. The second line shows who the hosts are.
2. The third and fourth lines show that the poet is growing old. The poet expresses his enjoyment of life by saying "yet glad enough/ They have not withheld from me/ Their high hospitality" and "face lit with delight/ And all gratitude."
3. The theme of this work is that life itself, and the love that fills it, is very pleasant. The author faces separation from this world with reluctance, but with gratitude for all he has been given.
4. The rhyme scheme is complex, *abacddeaae*.

"The Wild Honeysuckle"   p. 296

1. The comparison is the life of a flower to the life of man. The last verse is a reflection on the brevity of human life, which thought was occasioned by observing the shortness of a honeysuckle's life.
2. "The space between", in line 23, is another way of saying "from beginning to end".

3. The poet describes a honeysuckle as "fair", "comely", "honied", "little", "white arrayed", and says that it is hidden, untouched, and unseen. Both "The Wild Honeysuckle" and "The Violet" help us picture a small, unpretentious flower, but in the case of "The Violet" we are bidden to try to be like the flower, while in the "The Wild Honeysuckle" we are reminded of the mortality we have in common with the flower.

4. "She" is nature.

5. The poet is clearly talking about the natural level, since it is on this level we die as do the flowers. On the supernatural level we will live forever, either with God or without Him.

6. The rhyme scheme is *ababcc*.

7. The meter used is iambic tetrameter.

"The Chambered Nautilus" p. 298

1. The rhyme scheme is *aabbbcc*.

2. "This is the ship of pearl . . . / The venturous bark that flings/ On the sweet summer wind its purpled wings" and "Its webs of living gauze" refer to this ability.

3. The second and subsequent stanzas are about the nautilus once it is destroyed, revealing its internal structure.

4. The nautilus is referred to as a ship of pearl, with irised ceiling. It is probably iridescent. The shell is formed by the nautilus; as each chamber becomes too small for his increased growth, he abandons it, patiently building himself a new one by adding another chamber. Then he moves into the new chamber, builds a wall across the old, and lives in the new until he outgrows it.

5. In the last stanza the poet appeals to his soul to take a lesson from the chambered nautilus, imitating its constant growth and willingness to move to a more suitable home. He entreats his soul to let each new home be nobler than the last, till at length it is free to leave the outgrown shell entirely.

1. I think so. Reading this poem calls to mind the isolation and peace that occur in the wake of a snowstorm and paints a picture of the consequences of the storm in the exterior world.

2. Different lines might well be chosen as the most vivid; I like "the fierce artificer/ Curves his white bastions with projected roof/ Round every windward stake or tree or door." It reminds me of my backyard in Minnesota after the snow. But there are other candidates, for example, "Mockingly/ On coop or kennel he hangs Parian wreaths;/ A swan-like form invests the hidden thorn".

3. The theme of the poem seems to be a snowstorm and its effects, both interior and exterior. The central thought might be stated as, "The architecture of nature, manifested in a snowstorm, is wrought quickly and imitated with difficulty."

4. There is no rhyme scheme. Though most of the poetry we study has a rhyme scheme, rhyme is not necessary for poetry. Most of Shakespeare is without rhyme, though it is the greatest poetry in the English language. There are numerous characteristics that belong to poetry and make it what it is. Meter, imagery, and the various figures of speech are all important. This poem employs meter (primarily iambic pentameter), alliteration ("Announced by all the trumpe**t**s of the **s**ky,/ Arrive**s** the **s**now; and, driving o'er the field**s**,/ **S**eems nowhere to alight"), and a number of figures of speech (e.g., personification—"the north wind's masonry", "the fierce artificer/ curves his white bastions", "nought cares he for number or proportion", "he hangs Parian wreaths"; metaphor—"trumpets of the sky"; imagery—"veils the farm-house", "radiant fireplace").

"The Falconer of God" *p. 301*

1. At least one interpretation of the poem is that the soul of man is ever seeking true beauty, and that, in the pursuit of this beauty, he is often fooled by earthly loveliness. He thinks that such lovely things will tell him the "secret of the stars, of the world's heart-strings/ The answer to their woe." But soon the soul, gripping and holding fast to the beloved object, hoping for the heavenly plunder of his dreams, finds that what he has instead is "a piteous freight,/ A dark and heavy weight". Yet the soul continues on, confident that it will find its object ("My soul still flies above me for the quarry it shall find"), but we know it will not be in earthly things, for all such are "silver herons" with "inner darkness", "all disastrous pledges".

2. These lines suggest the brilliance of Beauty: "A strange white heron rising with silver on its wings,/ Rising and crying/ Wordless, wondrous things;/ The secret of the stars, of the world's heart-strings/ The answer to their woe." Also the descriptive phrase when the falconer first thinks he has captured Beauty, "—the bird of my desire/ Broke from the cover/ Flashing silver fire", gives a sense of how Beauty appears. The falconer's disappointment and disillusionment are shown in the third stanza, "Nay! But a piteous freight,/ A dark and heavy weight/ Despoiled of silver plumage, its voice forever stilled,—/ All of the wonder/ Gone that ever filled/ Its guise with glory."

3. The title signifies what the falconer is really looking for, and who the Beauty is that will satisfy the soul.

4. The rhyme scheme is amazingly complex: *abccdaddbb.*

5. An example of alliteration is the *f* sound in the first line, or the *s* sound in the third and fifth lines, but there are others as well.

"The Housewife's Prayer" *p. 303*

1. The Blessed Mother did these same housewifely tasks that every mother does. She did them for Our Lord (as do we), and

she knows how important and how difficult they are. The poet asks the Blessed Mother to help her in her tasks, knowing that Mary will understand the need, the importance, and the difficulty of her daily duty.

2. These words refer to Our Lord as He will be in the Blessed Eucharist.

3. In line four there is a metaphor, "Living Wheat and Vine", and in lines 15 and 16 there is a simile, butter yellow *as* cowslips.

4. "Speed the wheel and speed the loom,/ guide the needle and the broom" is an instance of vowel assonance.

"Rouge Bouquet" *p. 304*

1. In a wood called the Rouge Bouquet, an enemy shell killed many fighting men. They were in their "youthful prime", and now they are lying ten meters under the earth, in the land they were fighting to free. There was a firing of rifles, and the bugle played, in honor of the dead. The bugle seemed to be saying, "Go to sleep, your work is done, and the danger is past." The cadence of the words fits the rhythm of "Taps".

   This is a worthy place for the dead to lie, because this is the place where they so nobly fought and died. In heaven the saints and angels welcome the newcomers, and Saint Michael salutes them, happy to see his stalwart Irish sons. And from the Rouge Bouquet the sound of the bugle notes carries up to heaven saying, "Good-bye, true comrades, your souls shall be in heaven, and your memory will remain clearly before us who are left. Shield us, please."

2. It reminds one of the words of the priest on Ash Wednesday, "Remember, man, that you are dust and to dust you will return."

3. Line 8—imagery, lines 9 and 10—personification, line 22—metaphor (death is portrayed as sleep) and internal rhyme, line 30—alliteration, line 48—internal rhyme, line 50—simile.

"The Lake Isle of Innisfree"   *p. 306*

1. Sounds that are brought to mind in this poem are the humming
   of the bees, the cricket song, the sound of the linnet's wings,
   and lake water lapping. The visual images in the poem are a
   small clay and twig cabin with a bean garden and bee-hives.
   There is a glimmer in the nighttime and a purple glow at noon.
2. The sound of the vowels in this phrase slows down the rythmn
   of the words, so that the sound fits with the meaning of the
   words.
3. Peace is the main attraction of living in Innisfree.
4. "Lake water lapping with low sounds" is an example of allitera-
   tion. In the following line there is an example of assonance, "on
   the roadway, or on the pavements gray".

"The Kings"   *p. 307*

1. The complaint the man makes is that he is too downhearted to
   continue the battle of life. He says that from his cradle both his
   environment and his heredity have been against him. He wishes
   to leave this battle and asks where he might go.
2. The angel tells him to get back to the ranks of those who fight.
   He says that it doesn't matter whether the man wins or loses ac-
   cording to the standards of the world. The "little judges" are
   those who judge by the "outer issue" of worldly gain and loss.
3. The will is the sovereign measure because charity resides in the
   will. It is by our love of God and love of neighbor for God's sake
   that we will be judged (1 Cor 13). If one's heart is right, filled
   with the love of God, then one's actions will reflect that orien-
   tation. Such a person will do good and turn away from evil, and
   in the end, it is this that will determine who wins the victor's
   crown.
4. The kings gather doubt, pain, thirst of the spirit, grief, vain de-
   sires, and vice. The right response is to keep fighting against

such weapons, fearing not worldly failure, but steadfastly resist-
ing evil right to the death.

5. "Do fate and my fathers fight" is an example of alliteration.
6. The rhyme scheme is *abcb*.

"Loss of Faith" *p. 309*

1. "Glory" here means the life of the glorified in heaven, those
   who seeing do not have to believe. The poet is showing us why
   death is nothing strange; the life of grace is heaven on earth, and
   heaven is the life of glory, so in a certain way we already share in
   this life. The only difference is the difference between believing
   as we do now, and seeing as we will in heaven.
2. The life of grace is heaven on earth; it is a sharing in the life of
   God.
3. By "dreaming" he indicates the same thing as Saint Paul when he
   speaks of "seeing through a veil darkly"; we live by faith here on
   earth. But in heaven we will see directly what we now believe.
4. We lose our having to believe because now we see.
5. The rhyme scheme is *aabbb*.

"Prospice (Look Ahead!)" *p. 309*

1. The author is looking forward to being reunited to his wife.
2. He compares death to an enemy who must be overcome by
   battle.
3. The poet wishes to meet his end like the heroes of old, aware
   and fighting to the end. He is willing to pay for his happy life,
   for his being involved with life to the very end, by a death of
   pain and darkness and cold. He knows that will last only for a
   minute.
4. The transistion in mood occurs with the transistion in thought,
   from the fight to the peace and reunion of the last lines. The
   change starts with, "Shall dwindle, shall blend" and continues
   to the end.

5. The central idea of the poem is that the poet does not fear death, for he knows both that it is inevitable and the way to the life beyond, where he will be reunited with his love, and under the authority of God.
6. The the rhyme scheme is *ababcdcd*, etc.

"How the Great Guest Came"   *p. 313*

1. This is an instance of narrative poetry.

"Little Boy Blue"   *p. 314*

1. The poet's use of the toy figures waiting and waiting without any possibility of achieving the result awaited conveys his sadness.
2. The explanation occurs in lines 13 and 14, and the tone of the poem becomes explicitly sad at the same point.
3. The rhyme scheme is *ababcdcd*.
4. The poem uses personification.

"Christmas"   *p. 315*

1. The first five stanzas are all prosaic and secular, about Christmas in its simply natural manifestations, while the last three are about the supernatural truth of God made Man, and the pre-eminence of that truth.
2. The last two lines are the "punchline" of the poem.
3. To say Advent waits is to endow Advent with human characteristics.
4. The rhyme scheme is *ababcc*, and all the stanzas are regular except the first. In the first stanza the first and third lines do not rhyme, but the third line has an internal rhyme.

"The Day is Done"   *p. 317*

1. The ending mood of the poem is calm and peaceful, following the opening mood of sadness.

2. He says the "grand old masters" and "bards sublime" are like the "strains of martial music", their thoughts suggest the "endless toil and endeavor" of life. Such sentiments will not soothe. One might turn to this kind of poetry when it is time to get to work, but not at nightfall when rest is desired. Similarly, when one is tired, at the end of a long day, sweet and quiet music is preferred to lively and stirring music.

3. The rhyme scheme is *abcb*.

"The Tables Turned" p. 319

1. The title tells the reader the author's intention to answer, he thinks cogently, the criticisms leveled at his poetry.

2. Wordsworth thinks that one should turn to nature to pursue wisdom. He says wisdom will come spontaneously in the natural environment, which encourages health and cheerfulness. It teaches lessons by encouraging a right ordering in men. That's why impulses inspired by contact with nature will teach morals; the man thus nurtured will be in conformity with nature and will then respond rightly to his circumstances. The author says that in formal study we don't see things as they are; rather, we destroy them to study them—but then we are studying the destroyed thing, rather than the living. Come, he says, to nature, and bring a receptive heart. Then you will learn the living and life-giving truth.

   The position of Wordsworth's critic has to be surmised from what is said here, so it is hard to be sure, but evidently the critic thought that simply trusting to nature would not produce learned men. He probably suggested that illiteracy would result from a lack of formal study, and that most men need human teachers to understand the world around them. Given the content of the fifth and sixth stanzas, the critic might also have suggested that people need to learn how to be good, that they are not so by nature, and that study of great thinkers can help them learn to become good.

3. The songs of the linnet and the throstle, and the vernal wood, are used to contrast nature's lessons to the teaching of "barren" books. Also, the beauty of nature is called to mind in the second stanza where the colors in nature are placed before the reader.

"The Virgin" *p. 321*

1. The Immaculate Conception and the Virginity of the Mother of God are both indicated. Mary was conceived without original sin, the only creature of whom this is true. Wordsworth says in the second line that Mary was without the least stain of sin, and in the fourth line that she is the only creature of whom this is true. (Jesus was also, of course, without sin, but he is not a creature.)

2. He likens the purity of Mary to the foam of the ocean, the brightness of the eastern skies at daybreak, and the unblemished full moon. These images are all visual images taken from nature, so he has turned to nature for help in expressing his thoughts, which fits with his ideas in the previous poem. However, nature would not give him these ideas in the first place. One needs more than unaided nature to learn the truth, especially the truths of the faith. It is true, nevertheless, that all study must be in conformity with nature, and measured against reality, or it is false.

"The Destruction of Sennacherib" *p. 322*

1. This is a poem recounting the intervention of the Lord to save Isreal, under the reign of King Hezekiah, from the Assyrian army under the leadership of Sennacherib.

2. In Scripture the Assyrians are boasting about how they have defeated all the opposing nations. This leads to the surmise that the army was both large and well equipped. Further, it says that the angel of the Lord slew 185,000 in the Assyrian camp. That's a large number. In the poem, Lord Byron translates this large

number into visual images, "And the sheen of their spears was like stars on the sea," and, "Like the leaves of the forest when Summer is green,/ That host with their banners at sunset were seen". Byron mentions spears, banners, horses, mail, tents, lances, and trumpets, all accoutrements of a well-equipped army.

3. The poem is based on verse 35 in 2 Kings, chap. 19. There isn't any mention of the horses and riders in the account in Scripture, and the poem doesn't discuss the demise of Sennecharib by the hands of his own sons. The poem is more descriptive, making a picture for the reader of the events recounted in the Bible. Both Scripture and the poem tell the basic facts. The Isrealites were being threatened by the Assyrian army, and God saved his people by sending His angel to kill the Assyrian foe in their sleep.

4. "The Assyrian . . . like a wolf on the fold," "the sheen of their spears was like stars on the sea," "Like the leaves of the forest . . . That host with their banners," "the foam . . . cold as the spray of the rock-beating surf", and "the might of the Gentile . . . hath melted like snow".

5. The rhyme scheme is *aabb*, couplets. The meter is anapestic—a "dancing" or triple rhythm involving one stressed and two unstressed syllables. It is a rising rhythm, as is the iambic pattern.

    The As **syr**/ ian came **down**/ like a **wolf**/ on the **fold**,
    And his **co**/ horts were **gleam**/ ing in **pur**/ ple and **gold**

"Lepanto"   *p. 323*

Section I

The Sultan of Constantinople (Soldan of Byzantium) has taken control of the Mediterranean, and the Pope has called upon the kings of Christendom to come to the aid of their Christian brothers. The Queen of England, Elizabeth, is not interested in helping, nor is the King of France (here referred to as the "shadow" of the Valois because he had only nominal control of the government).

The Spanish guns are ringing faint. The Soldan of Byzantium is the Sultan of Constantinople; the cold queen is Elizabeth, who was reputedly very vain; the shadow of the Valois is Charles IX of France, a very weak king; the crownless prince is Don John of Austria, who was illegitimate; Mahound is the name for one of the gods that Christians thought Muslims worshiped; Azreal is the angel of death; Ariel is a spirit of the air; Ammon is a god of the Egyptians; Richard, Raymond, and Godfrey were Christian Crusaders who defeated the Turks at different times; Cervantes is the author of *Don Quixote*, a story about a brave and idealistic (though somewhat simple) knight.

Section II

Don John of Austria sits on a nameless throne, without a crown. He has a doubtful seat, and a half-attained seat. But he is the last knight of Europe, the last troubadour, and he alone, laughing in his brave beard, heeds the call of the Holy Father. "Dark purple", "old-gold", "crimson", and "copper" are colors mentioned in the stanza. Some examples of alliteration are: "**d**im **d**rums", "**h**ills **h**alf **h**eard", "**w**eapons from the **w**all", "**l**ast and **l**ingering", "**s**inging **s**outhward", "**g**ongs **g**roaning as the **g**uns", "**st**iff rags **st**raining", "In the **g**loom black-purple, in the **g**lint old-**g**old", "torchlight **c**rimson on the **c**opper **k**ettle-drums", "the **t**uckets, then the **t**rumpets", "the **c**annon, and he **c**omes", "**b**rave **b**eard curled", "**h**olding his **h**ead", "**f**lag of all the **f**ree", and "**l**ove **l**ight". The rhyme scheme is couplets.

Section III

Mahound, otherwise known as Mohammed, is characterized as physically powerful, very tall, with a voice like thunder. He is also very powerful in terms of wielding power. His subjects rush to obey him, even "Black Azreal and Ariel and Ammon on the wing". Mohammed is very concerned about this new Crusade. He says that he recognizes Don John, that he is King Richard, and Raymond, and Sir Godfrey back again. They did not give up, they did not say that fate was against them, and they laughed at their losses if the losses were in a good cause; and Mohammed sees that Don John is made of the same metal. The "turban woven of sunsets and seas" is an instance of imagery; the "voice is thunder" is a metaphor.

Section IV

"He shakes his lance of iron and he claps his wings of stone;/ The noise is gone through Normandy" is an issue of the call to arms. Christian is killing Christian for the same reason that "Christian dreadeth Christ", who has a new face of doom, and "Christian hateth Mary". The Protestant revolution has occurred. Chesterton did not think well of King Philip II; he suggested that Philip was a luxurious coward. Don John has responded vigorously.

Section V

The Pope was in his chapel when he saw his vision. The Christian captives were galley slaves, kept in darkness. They are sick and numerous, with no recourse and no hope. The Pope saw Don John fighting valiantly and effectively. Specifically he sees "on the monstrous twilight sea" the crescent of the ships of Mohammed and the great shadows they cast, "making Cross and Castle dark". Above the ships he sees the palaces of the Mohammedans and below the ships the prisons where the Christian captives are kept. The Pope sees Don John burst the battle line, pounding forward in his ship, "purpling all the ocean like a bloody pirate's sloop,/ Scarlet running over on the silvers and the golds," rescuing the Christians working as galley slaves in the holds of the enemy's ships. The prisoners come forth, white in their happiness, blind from the bright sun, which they have not seen for a long time, and stunned to think that they are free. Don John, like Don Quixote (the knight created by Cervantes), is a knight of the impossible, fighting the fight that no one else is willing to undertake.

1. The shepherd promises many material and natural pleasures that are yielded by the countryside. They'll *watch* the shepherds and their flocks as they sit by the river and *listen* to the birds. He will make her a bed of roses and *fragrant* posies, along with floral ornaments. (There is an appeal to the various senses throughout the poem.) She'll have a *fine (soft)* wool gown and *lined (soft)* slippers with *beautiful* golden buckles, a belt make of straw and ivy buds, "with *coral* clasps and *amber* studs". Further, they will use *silver* dishes for their wonderful *meat*, which will be prepared on an *ivory* table. The shepherds will *dance* and *sing* for her entertainment. All the senses are invoked in the recounting of promised enjoyments. There will be pleasurable things to see, to hear, to smell, to taste, and to feel.

2. The shepherd concentrates exclusively on natural, material pleasures. There is no sense that there is any other kind of joy, such as comes from having children, or growing old together, or growing toward virtue together. His thoughts are concerned only with the pleasures of sense in the here and now. Therefore he has omitted the more important and lasting joys of marriage and so seems not to be aware of the fleeting character of the picture he has drawn.

3.   Come **live**/ with **me**/ and **be**/ my **Love**,
                And **we**/ will **all**/ the **plea**/ sures **prove**
                That **hills**/ and **val**/ leys, **dales**/ and **fields**,
                Or **woods**/ or **steep**/ y **moun**/ tain **yields**.

This poem in written in iambic tetrameter, with an *aabb* rhyme scheme. The last line of the stanza is, as it were, missing the unstressed syllable of the first foot. This does not mean that the line is not iambic tetrameter, but is rather an additional way for the poet to create his effect. Since one is expecting the regular unstressed, stressed beat, the lack of it in a particular foot will call attention to the meter and in a certain way intensifies the effect of the cadence.

"The Nymph's Reply to the Shepherd" *p. 331*

1. In general this poem calls attention to the obvious omissions of "The Passionate Shepherd to His Love". The first stanza of this poem answers the first stanza of the previous poem. Sir Walter Raleigh points out that youth is not a permanent condition of the world, and not every shepherd who might be making these promises is trustworthy.

   The second stanza goes on to answer the second stanza of the first poem. It points out that time must be taken into account, and the natural changes in the material world.

   The third stanza speaks to the third stanza of "The Passionate Shepherd". Again, Raleigh calls to mind the changes time brings, and the winter of life, which follows the carefree summer. He points out that as the sorrows of fall follow the fancies of spring so to, it is implied, the sorrows of age and change follow the delights of youth. This is like the heart of gall underneath the honey tongue.

   The fourth stanzas are also to be read together. Raleigh says that it's all very well to talk about the lovely clothes that will be worn, but the clothes too are subject to change and decay. They break, wither, and are forgotten. To act on the basis of such promises is ripe, or complete, folly, and not a reasonable course of action.

   Having determined this, in the fifth stanza Raleigh says clearly that the pleasures promised in the fourth and fifth stanzas of Marlowe's poem are not adequate to move the shepherd's love, or, it is implied, any reasonable person, to accept the proffered proposal.

   The last stanza restates the general objection that youth will not last, that joys date, and age makes changes and demands of its own. If this were not the true state of things, Raleigh says, the passionate shepherd's proposal might move her, but as it is, no!

2. The form of both poems is similar. In both the rhyme scheme is *aabb*, and both are written in iambic tetrameter. Further, as described above, they follow a similar sequence of ideas.

3. In spite of the similarities, however, the first poem is better simply as poetry. One sees a picture emerge through the poem, and the appeal to the various senses is made effectively. The cadence is smoother than the second poem, rather soft and mellow. Notice in the last stanza the proliferation of *m*'s. This gives a certain calm and peaceful feel to the poem.

   The purpose of the second poem is not to paint a picture or appeal to the senses but to make an appeal to reason. It does not have the same smooth and peaceful effect; it seems rather harsh, and as if it is intended to draw one up short. Are you familiar with the scene in C. S. Lewis' *The Silver Chair*, where Puddleglum counteracts the spell of the wicked serpent by stamping on the fire and introducing the unpleasant smell of burnt Marshwiggle into the air? "The Nymph's Reply to the Shepherd" is like that. It is not as superficially pleasant, but its truth is bracing.

4. Neither of these poems gives the full picture of courtship and married love. Time, and the changes it brings, must be taken into account, but there are joys that are appropriate to each stage of life. True love, that is, love that is founded on God and intends the good of the other person, has a permanent quality that will not alter with time's alterations. Look at Sonnet CXVI by Shakespeare for another consideration of this subject.

"A Song" *p. 332*

1. He divided it into the stanzas to distinguish the five separate questions he wished to discuss.

2. The five questions and answers are (1) Where does Jove bestow the fading rose? These flowers sleep in the beauty of his beloved. (2) Where do the golden atoms of the day go? They go to her hair. (3) Where does the nightingale go when May is past? It is found in her throat. (4) Where do the shooting stars go? They sit in her eyes. (5) Does the Phoenix build its nest in the east or in the west? She builds it in his beloved's bosom.

3. The theme of the poem is the wonderfulness of the beloved. Nature, science, and mythology are all appealed to in an effort to find adequate expressions of the poet's admiration.

4. It is used to indicate that the beloved has a lovely, perhaps trained, voice.

5. It is used as an image of immortality. The beloved contains such life, such interest, that she will be a constant source of renewal.

6. There is a sense in which every poem is a song, taken in its most general sense. However, we tend to name something a song when it expresses the poet's personal hopes, fears, ideals, sorrows, joys, or loves. This poem is an expression of personal love. Singing is what one is often moved to by joy, and here the poet so enjoys his beloved that he is inspired to sing about her. It has also been suggested that the five stanzas might be taken to be like the five fingers used to play an instrument, each with a specific task.

"To Celia" p. 334

1. The poet says he will not look for wine in his cup if Celia will leave a kiss in it. He thinks that her kiss is more satisfying than any wine could be.

2. The last verse of the stanza says that if the poet had the cup with her kiss in it, he would not change it even for one with the nectar of the gods. He has said that the thirst of the soul needs to be satisfied with a divine drink, and since he wouldn't change her cup for Jove's, he implies that the cup of her kiss is more divine.

3. Celia's breath causes the wreath sent to her to grow and smell like her; it gives a share in her life to the wreath. This fits with the suggestion of divinity made in the first stanza. (Note that the divinity mentioned here never goes beyond Jove. Jonson is not intending a comparison with God.)

4. The rhyme scheme is *abcbabcb*.

"To the Virgins, to Make Much of Time" p. 335

1. In the first stanza the poet uses the images of rosebuds and dying roses to contrast youth and age. In the second stanza the images of the sun rising and setting highlight the difference in the times of life. He also says that one's blood is warmer in youth, sugesting that in old age the blood is cooler.

2. These two poems present very different points of view. "To the Virgins" takes a physical view of life, where the powers are in fact at their height during the earlier years of life. "Rabbi Ben Ezra" takes a fuller view, seeing that it would be a pretty strange plan that had the best first and all the rest of life a dull appendage. The experience gained in earlier years is meant to give a certain breadth of understanding to man, which makes life more intelligible and therefore more interesting as time goes on.

"A General Communion" p. 336

1. "A thousand single central daisies they" is an example of hyperbole, since it is most unlikely that there were a thousand people at Mass, but the overstatement of the number does draw the reader's attention to fact that any number may be fed in this way and will each receive the whole.

2. These three quotes develop this theme, "the throng, so deeply separate,/ Fed at only one board—", "each asunder absorbed the multiplied,/ The ever unparted, whole", "A thousand single central daisies they,/ A thousand of the one". In each both the

individuality and the oneness of the churchgoers is brought to mind.

3. The sun shines as brightly for each daisy as if it were the only one. The fact that it is shining on a thousand other daisies in no way dimishes its power.

"Love (III)" p. 337

1. This poem is an allegory of the relationship between God and sinful man. Here the soul and Love stand for all men and God.
2. The rhyme scheme is *ababcc*.
3. Love tells the soul that He has borne the blame for the soul's sin, so it is no longer to be adverted to; the debt has been paid.

"The Pulley" p. 338

1. God gave strength, beauty, wisdom, honor, and pleasure.
2. "Rest" has more than one meaning. It primarily means the rest that is opposed to restlessness, rest meaning peace, contentment, satisfaction. In the first line of the fourth stanza it is used to mean "the remaining", and this shift in meaning calls the reader's attention to the word and emphasizes its centrality in the poem.
3. God doesn't add rest because then man would be satisfied with his lot in life. He would be content with things as they are and would adore the gifts instead of the giver.
4. The pattern is 3,5,5,5,3, that is, three accented syllables in the first line (iambic trimeter), five accented syllables in each of the next three lines (generally, iambic pentameter), and three accented syllables in the last line (iambic trimeter).
5. "When God **at** first made **Man**,/ **Ha**ving a **glass** of **bles**sings **stan**ding by" is an example of vowel assonance.
6. The rhyme scheme is *ababa*.
7. There is the contrariety of "rest" and "restless", "dispersed" and "contract", "weariness" and "toss", "pulley" and "rest".

8. The title is significant in understanding the thrust of the poem. Saint Augustine says, "Our hearts are restless until they rest in Thee." This poem uses that idea and proposes that God allows us to be restless so that we *will* turn to Him, that the lack of satisfaction men find in natural goods will lead them to seek further and look to the supernatural.

"Requiem" p. 339

1. He wished to be buried under the "wide and starry sky".
2. He both lived and died gladly.
3. The mood created is one of peace and rest. There is neither despair about life nor sadness in death, just a sense of coming home.

"The Bells" p. 340

1. The first stanza is joyful. The second is happy and full of pleasant anticipation. The third has a sense of distress and despair, even horror. The fourth is menacing and malevolent. The reason for the order of the stanzas might be a (wrong) view of the course of life. In childhood life starts pleasantly, even joyfully. The next stage is young adulthood, with its anticipation of a full and productive life. In the following phase one finds those promises unfulfilled, and the person despairs. This brings one to the last stage, which brings death, and happiness only to the ghouls. The length of the stanzas might be related either to the poet's view of the relative truth of these views, or to the chronological relation of these stages of life.
2. The *t* sound brings to mind the sleigh bells. This is onomatopoeia.
3. The *m* sound contributes to smooth, mellow tones of the wedding bells.
4. The harsh, guttural sounds are used to create the mood of despair and unhappiness found in this stanza.

POETRY SELECTIONS

with Study Questions and Answers

SECTION III

Terms to Know for the Study of Poetry

Ballad: A ballad is a short narrative poem, which was originally composed to be sung. The supernatural is likely to play an important part in the events of the poem; physical courage and love are frequent themes. The action usually involves the common people rather than the nobility, and domestic episodes are common. Often the first two stanzas identify the hero, the next two stanzas tell the story, and the remaining stanzas give the action in a series of little scenes, utilizing dialogue to do so. Motives tend to be suggested and implied rather than directly expressed. As in most poetry, the concrete expression is preferred to the abstract, and not much attention is paid to characterization or description. There is usually a single episode of a extremely dramatic nature presented.

The ballad is composed in stanzas of couplets of iambic pentameter (see previous section, page 290) or, in the **ballad stanza**, a quatrain rhyming (again, see the previous section, page 291) *abcb*, with alternating iambic tetrameter and iambic trimeter lines (once again, see page 290). Often there is a refrain with what is known as "incremental repetition", a stanza that repeats the preceding stanza with the variations necessary to continue the story. (See "Edward,

Edward" and "Get Up and Bar the Door" for examples of the ballad.)

There are two other kinds of narrative poems, epic and metrical romance, which we will discuss here, but which will not be represented in this study of English poetry because of their length.

Cavalier lyric: This kind of poetry was developed by the followers of King Charles. It is often keen, clever, sometimes flippant, sometimes sensual. However, there are two frequently occurring components of this type of poetry that are worth noting:

—in it one is exhorted to make the most of today because tomorrow inevitably encompasses the passage of the material world, e.g., "Flowers fade and women grow old"; and

—as a further consequence of the death of material loveliness, one should seek the beauty of mind and spirit.

Cavalier poetry is intended to engage the mind, in contrast to Elizabethan lyrics, which are first intended to stir the heart. "To Lucasta, on Going to the Wars", by Richard Lovelace, is representative of Cavalier verse.

Conceit: The conceit is a type of poetic metaphor. It designates a fanciful or ingenious idea expressed through an analogy, pointing to a striking parallel between two seemingly unlike things. It may be brief, or it may be the framework of an entire poem. There are two types of conceits, the Petrarchan and the metaphysical. The first is used in love poems and sonnets, often comparing the loved one to some object, such as a rose, a ship, or a summer's day. The second is used in metaphysical poetry, wherein complex and startling intellectual analogies are made. "Batter My Heart", by John Donne, uses the conceit in this sense.

Elegy: The elegy has death or mourning as its theme. It is quiet in mood and tends to be contemplative in nature. Gray's "Elegy in a Country Churchyard" is one example.

Epic: An epic is an extended narrative poem, in which stories are told in verse form and organized as a series of related episodes. Each episode is complete in itself, but the poem is unified by a central heroic figure and by the fact that the whole of the poem is important to the history of a nation or a race. The style is formal or dignified. The *Iliad* and the *Odyssey* are examples of this type of poetry.

Lyric poetry: Lyric poetry differs from narrative poetry by its subjectivity. Narrative poems are objective, that is, they tell a story for its own sake, not as a chronicle of the author's personal feelings, emotions, or views of life. The lyric poem expresses some personal feeling, emotion, or point of view. Lyric poetry may tell a story, but not for its own sake. Such a poem is a vehicle for the expression of the author's attitude or philosophy of life.

Lyric poetry has a definite unity; it is about one single thought, feeling, or situation. It is a relatively brief, intense, emotional expression. Since it is short, the emotion is compressed and intensified. Songs, odes, sonnets, and elegies are all types of lyric poetry.

Metaphysical poetry: Metaphysical poetry is a type of poetry that treats of the great concerns of man: God, love, sin, suffering, and death. It satirizes the prevailing ideals and practices of the time in which it was written and usually contains serious philosophic truths. Metaphysical poetry is considered to be a kind of lyric poetry, though there are those who see it as contrasted with most lyric poetry in its emphasis on thought rather than feeling. One commentator calls it "the emotional apprehension of thought" or felt thought. Look for the following elements in metaphysical poetry:

—dramatic speech;

—use of words and expressions from everyday speech;

—an argumentative approach to the theme;

—a strict logical structure to the poem;

—the use of religious imagery for sensual love and sensual imagery for religious experience;

—imagery from science, attempting to find points of similarity between widely differing things. (Such a technique tends to reveal the "sacramentality" of creation. Use of objects in the natural order as symbols of theological and philosophical truths brings to light the fact that the order of grace builds upon and is in harmony with the natural order.)

"The Pulley", by George Herbert, is an example of metaphysical poetry.

Metrical romance: The metrical romance is a narrative poem that has a romantic theme. It usually deals with love, chivalry, and religion. The *Idylls of the King*, by Alfred Lord Tennyson, is a good example of the metrical romance.

Ode: An ode addresses some object or person in an exalted manner. It is usually intended to be accompanied by music. Keats' "Ode on a Grecian Urn" is an illustration of this form of lyric poetry.

Song: A song expresses the poet's personal hopes, fears, ideals, sorrows, joys, or loves. It may have a religious, national, or personal significance. "To Celia", by Ben Johnson, is an instance of a song that has lasted through the years.

Sonnet: Sonnets are poetry in a certain definite verse form. They were originally intended to be sung and were accompanied by music. There are two types of sonnets in English poetry: the Italian and the English or Shakespearean. The Italian sonnet has a fixed rhyming scheme in its fourteen lines. The first eight lines are called an octave, for which the rhyme scheme is *abbaabba*, while the last six lines, or sestet, have a rhyme scheme of *cdecde* or *cdcdcd*. The octave presents the subject matter of the poem, and the sestet contains the poet's reflection on the subject matter. "The World Is Too

Much with Us", by William Wordsworth, and "How Do I Love Thee", by Elizabeth Barrett Browning, are examples of this form.

The English sonnet has three quatrains and a couplet. The rhyme scheme is *abab, cdcd, efef, gg*. Like the Italian sonnet it has two distinct parts; the first twelve lines express a problem, and the couplet contains either the poet's reflections on the problem or a solution. "Sonnet XXX: When to the Sessions of Sweet Silent Thought", by William Shakespeare, is an example of a sonnet in the English form.

Edward, Edward

Author Unknown

"Why dois your brand sae drap wi bluid,
    Edward, Edward,
Why dois your brand° sae drap wi bluid,   *sword*
    And why sae sad gang° yee O?"   *go*
"O I hae killed my hauke sae guid,
    Mither, mither,
O I hae killed my hauke sae guid,
    And I had nae mair bot hee O."

"Your haukis bluid was nevir sae reid,
    Edward, Edward,
Your haukis bluid was nevir sae reid,
    My deir son I tell thee O."
"O I hae killed my reid-roan steid,
    Mither, Mither,
O I hae killed my reid-roan steid,
    That erst was sae fair and frie O."   *That once was fair and spirited, O.*

"Your steid was auld, and ye hae gat mair,
    Edward, Edward,
Your steid was auld, and ye hae gat mair,
    Sum other dule ye drie O."   *Some other grief you suffer, O.*
"O I hae killed my fadir deir,
    Mither, mither,
O I hae killed my fadir deir,
    Alas, and wae is mee O!"

"And whatten penance wul ye drie for that,
    Edward, Edward?
And whatten penance will ye drie for that?
    My deir son, now tell me O."

"Ile set my feit in yonder boat,
    Mither, mither,
Ile set my feit in yonder boat,
    And Ile fare ovir the sea O."

"And what wul ye doe wi your towirs and your ha,
    Edward, Edward?
And what wul you doe wi your towirs and your ha,
    That were sae fair to see O?"
"Ile let thame stand tul they doun fa,
    Mither, mither,
Ile let thame stand tul they doun fa,
    For here nevir mair I bee O."

"And what wul ye leive to your bairns and your wife,
    Edward, Edward?
And what wul ye leive to your bairns and your wife
    When ye gang ovir the sea O?"
"The warld is room, late them beg thrae life,
    Mither, mither,
The warld is room, late them beg thrae life,
    For thame nevir mair wul I see O."

"And what wul ye leive to your ain mither deir,
    Edward, Edward?
And what wul ye leive to your ain mither deir?
    My deir son, now tell me O."
"The curse of hell frae me sall ye beir,
    Mither, mither,
The curse of hell frae me sall ye beir,
    Sic counseils ye gave to me O."

1. What form of poetry is this? What characteristics of the form does it have?
2. What has Edward done? Who incited him to do this deed? Why didn't he immediately tell what he had done?
3. What kind of a person is the mother? What would you guess the relationship of the mother and son has been?
4. What is the climax of the story?

Get Up and Bar the Door

Author Unknown

It fell about the Martinmas° time,   *Feast of Saint Martin, November 11*
   And a gay time it was then,
When our goodwife got puddings to make,
   And she's boild them in the pan.

The wind sae cauld blew south and north,
   And blew into the floor;
Quoth our goodman to our goodwife,
   "Gae out and bar the door."

"My hand is in my hussykap°,   *household duties*
   Goodman, as ye may see;
An it should nae be barrd this hundred year,
   It's no be barrd for me°."   *"for me": as far as I am concerned*

They made a paction tween them twa,
   They made it firm and sure,
That the first word whaeer should speak,
   Shoud rise and bar the door.

Then there came two gentlemen,
    At twelve o clock at night,
And they could see neither house nor hall,
    Nor coal nor candle-light.

"Now whether is this a rich man's house,
    Or whether is it a poor?"
But neer a word wad ane o them speak,
    For barring of the door.

And first they ate the white puddings
    And then they ate the black;
Tho muckle° thought the goodwife to hersel,   *much*
    Yet neer a word she spake.

Then said the one unto the other,
    "Here, man, tak ye my knife;
Do ye tak off the auld man's beard,
    And I'll kiss the goodwife."

"But there's nae water in the house,
    And what shall we do than?"
"What ails ye at the pudding-broo,   *What is the matter with the pudding broth?*
    That boils into the pan?"

O up then started our goodman,
    An angry man was he:
"Will ye kiss my wife before my een,
    And scad me wi' pudding-bree?"

Then up and started our goodwife,
    Gied three skips on the floor:
"Goodman, you've spoken the foremost word,
    Get up and bar the door."

1. In your own words tell what happened in this story. Is the action explicitly stated, or is it implied?
2. Is this poem written in the traditional ballad stanza and meter?

The Burning Babe

by Robert Southwell, S.J.

As I in hoary winter's night
   Stood shivering in the snow,
Surprised I was with sudden heat
   Which made my heart to glow;

And lifting up a fearful eye
   To view what fire was near,
A pretty Babe, all burning bright,
   Did in the air appear;

Who, scorchèd with excessive heat,
   Such floods of tears did shed,
As though His floods should quench His flames,
   Which with His tears were bred.

"Alas!" quoth He, "but newly born,
   In fiery heats I fry,
Yet none approach to warm their hearts
   Or feel my fire, but I;

"My faultless breast the furnace is;
   The fuel, wounding thorns;
Love is the fire, and sighs the smoke;
   The ashes, shames and scorns.

"The fuel Justice layeth on,
   And Mercy blows the coals,
The metal in this furnace wrought
   Are men's defilèd souls.

"For which, as now on fire I am,
   To work them to their good,
So will I melt into a bath,
   To wash them in My blood."

With this He vanish'd out of sight
   And swiftly shrunk away,
And straight I callèd unto my mind
   That it was Christmas Day.

Study Questions

1. This is a Christmas poem, but it differs from the usual Christmas theme. Describe the difference.
2. List the metaphors in the poem. Is there a "conceit"? What about personification?
3. Can you find an instance of alliteration in the poem?
4. What is the rhyme scheme? The meter?

To the Memory of My Beloved Master, William Shakespeare

by Ben Jonson

To draw no envy, Shakespeare, on thy name,
Am I thus ample° to thy book and fame,   *abundant in praise*
While I confess thy writings to be such
As neither man nor Muse can praise too much.
'Tis true, and all men's suffrage.° But these ways   *opinion, decision*

Were not the paths I meant unto thy praise:
For silliest ignorance on these may light,
Which, when it sounds at best, but echoes right;
Or blind affection, which doth ne'er advance
The truth, but gropes, and urgeth all by chance;
Or crafty malice might pretend this praise,
And think to ruin where it seemed to raise. . . .
But thou art proof against them, and, indeed,
Above th' ill fortune of them, or the need.
I therefore will begin. Soul of the age!
The applause! delight! the wonder of our stage!
My Shakespeare, rise; I will not lodge thee by
Chaucer* or Spenser, or bid Beaumont lie   *(English poets; playwright)*
A little further to make thee a room:
Thou art a monument without a tomb,
And art alive still while thy book doth live,
And we have wits to read and praise to give.
That I not mix thee so, my brain excuses,
I mean with great, but disproportioned Muses;
For, if I thought my judgment were of years,°   *mature*
I should commit° thee surely with thy peers,   *compare*
And tell how far thou didst our Lyly outshine,
Or sporting Kyd, or Marlowe's mighty line. *(Contemporary playwrights)*
And though thou hadst small Latin and less Greek,
From thence to honor thee I would not seek
For names, but call forth thund'ring Aeschylus,
Euripides, and Sophocles to us,   *(Ancient Greek dramatists)*
Pacuvius, Accius, him of Cordova dead,   *(Ancient Roman dramatists)*
To life again, to hear thy buskin° tread   *a high boot worn by actors of tragedy*
And shake a stage; or when thy socks° were on,   *thin slippers worn by*
Leave thee alone for the comparison   *comic actors*
Of all that insolent Greece or haughty Rome

* *All well-known poets. Chaucer is considered the father of English literature.*

Sent forth, or since did from their ashes come.
Triumph, my Britain; thou hast one to show
To whom all scenes of Europe homage owe.
He was not of an age, but for all time!
And all the Muses still were in their prime
When like Apollo he came forth to warm
Our ears, or like a Mercury to charm.
Nature herself was proud of his designs,
And joyed to wear the dressing of his lines,
Which were so richly spun, and woven so fit,
As, since, she will vouchsafe no other wit:
The merry Greek, tart Aristophanes,   *(Greek author of comedies)*
Neat Terence, witty Plautus now not please, *(Roman authors of comedies)*
But antiquated and deserted lie,
As they were not of Nature's family.
Yet must I not give Nature all; thy Art,
My gentle Shakespeare, must enjoy a part.
For though the poet's matter Nature be,
His Art doth give the fashion; and that he
Who casts to write a living line must sweat
(Such as thine are) and strike the second heat
Upon the muses' anvil; turn the same,
And himself with it, that he thinks to frame,
Or for the laurel° he may gain a scorn;   *a symbolic crown of achievement*
For a good poet's made as well as born.
And such wert thou! Look how the father's face
Lives in his issue, even so the race
Of Shakespeare's mind and manners brightly shines
In his well-turnèd and true-filèd lines,
In each of which he seems to shake a lance,
As brandished at the eyes of ignorance.
Sweet swan of Avon, what a sight it were
To see thee in our waters yet appear,
And make those flights upon the banks of Thames

That so did take Eliza and our James!   *(Queen Elizabeth and King James I)*
But stay; I see thee in the hemisphere
Advanced and made a constellation there!
Shine forth, thou star of poets, and with rage
Or influence chide or cheer the drooping stage,
Which, since thy flight from hence, hath mourned like night,
And despairs day, but for thy volume's light.

Study Questions

1. This poem can be broken down into at least five sections (possibly one or two more, depending on how you view the central thought of each section). Break it down into its sections.
2. What is the theme or central thought of this poem?
3. Explain the following: "But these ways were not the paths I meant unto thy praise", "Thou art a monument without a tomb", and "Yet I must not give Nature all; thy Art, My gentle Shakespeare, must enjoy a part".
4. What are the meter and stanza form of this poem?

The Rhetorical Stage: Poetry Selections: Section III

Sonnet LXI
From the *Amoretti*
by Edmund Spenser

The glorious image of the Maker's beauty,
My sovereign saint, the idol of my thought,
Dare not henceforth, above the bounds of duty,
T' accuse of pride, or rashly blame for ought.
For being, as she is, divinely wrought,
And of the brood of angels heavenly born,
And with the crew of blessed saints upbrought,
Each of which did her with their gifts adorn—
The bud of joy, the blossom of the morn,
The beam of light, whom mortal eyes admire;
What reason is it then but she should scorn
Base things that to her love too bold aspire!
Such heavenly form ought rather worshipt be
Than dare be loved by men of mean degree.

Study Questions

1. What scriptural reference does the first line call to mind? Does it refer to material or spiritual beauty?
2. What is the form of this sonnet?
3. What is the central idea of this poem? Which particular details develop this theme?

Sonnets

by William Shakespeare

XVIII

Shall I compare thee to a summer's day?
Thou art more lovely and more temperate:
Rough winds do shake the darling buds of May,
And summer's lease hath all too short a date:
Sometime too hot the eye of heaven shines,
And often is his gold complexion dimm'd;
And every fair from fair sometime declines,
By chance or nature's changing course untrimm'd;
But thy eternal summer shall not fade,
Nor lose possession of that fair thou owest;
Nor shall Death brag thou wander'st in his shade,
When in eternal lines to time thou grow'st:
 So long as men can breathe, or eyes can see,
 So long lives this, and this gives life to thee.

Study Questions

1. Shakespeare asks a question in the first line. How does he answer it?
2. Shakespeare asserts that "thy eternal summer shall not fade". What does he mean?
3. What is the basic thought in this sonnet? How does the couplet add to it?

XIX

Devouring Time, blunt thou the lion's paws,
And make the earth devour her own sweet brood;
Pluck the keen teeth from the fierce tiger's jaws,
And burn the long-lived phoenix in her blood;
Make glad and sorry seasons as thou fleets,
And do whate'er thou wilt, swift-footed Time,
To the wide world and all her fading sweets;
But I forbid thee one most heinous crime:
O, carve not with thy hours my love's fair brow,
Nor draw no lines there with thine antique pen;
Him in thy course untainted do allow
For beauty's pattern to succeeding men.
   Yet do thy worst, old Time: despite thy wrong,
   My love shall in my verse ever live young.

Study Questions

1. How is Time personified? What images illustrate the effects of Time?
2. What does the poet say is the "heinous crime" that Time is forbidden?
3. Should Time commit this "crime", how will the poet defeat him?

XXXVI

Let me confess that we two must be twain,
Although our undivided loves are one:
So shall those blots that do with me remain,
Without thy help, by me be borne alone.
In our two loves there is but one respect,
Though in our lives a separable spite,
Which though it alter not love's sole effect,
Yet doth it steal sweet hours from love's delight.
I may not evermore acknowledge thee,
Lest my bewailed guilt should do thee shame,
Nor thou with public kindness honor me,
Unless thou take that honor from thy name:
    But do not so; I love thee in such sort,
    As thou being mine, mine is thy good report.

Study Questions

1. What is the situation that this sonnet addresses?
2. The first wave of thought considers the effects of the situation. What thought does the couplet add to the sonnet?
3. What is the rhyme scheme? What is the meter?

CXXXVIII

When my love swears that she is made of truth,
I do believe her, though I know she lies,
That she might think me some untutor'd youth,
Unlearned in the world's false subtleties.
Thus vainly thinking that she thinks me young,
Although she knows my days are past the best,
Simply I credit her false-speaking tongue:
On both sides thus is simple truth suppress'd.
But wherefore says she not she is unjust?
And wherefore say not I that I am old?
O, love's best habit is in seeming trust,
And age in love loves not to have years told:
    Therefore I lie with her and she with me,
    And in our faults by lies we flatter'd be.

Study Questions

1. Why doesn't the speaker tell her that what she says is untrue?
2. Does he really believe her?
3. What does the speaker say is love's best habit? Is he right?
4. Compare this sonnet to CXVI. Which seems to be a better representation of reality?

CXVI

Let me not to the marriage of true minds
Admit impediments. Love is not love
Which alters when it alteration finds,
Or bends with the remover to remove:
O, no! it is an ever-fixed mark,
That looks on tempests and is never shaken;
It is the star to every wandering bark,
Whose worth's unknown, although his height be taken.
Love's not Time's fool, though rosy lips and cheeks
Within his bending sickle's compass come;
Love alters not with his brief hours and weeks,
But bears it out even to the edge of doom.
  If this be error and upon me proved,
  I never writ, nor no man ever loved.

Study Questions

1. What are "true minds"?
2. Why does the poet say, "Love's not Time's fool"? And why does Time have a "bending sickle"?
3. The first sentence is the statement of the theme of the sonnet. The following sentences elaborate that theme. State the theme in your own words and give the points that Shakespeare uses in support of it.
4. What figures of speech are used in the sonnet?

XXX

When to the sessions of sweet silent thought
I summon up remembrance of things past,
I sigh the lack of many a thing I sought,
And with old woes new wail my dear time's waste:
Then can I drown an eye, unused to flow,
For precious friends hid in death's dateless night,
And weep afresh love's long since cancell'd woe,
And moan the expense of many a vanish'd sight:
Then can I grieve at grievances foregone,
And heavily from woe to woe tell o'er
The sad account of fore-bemoaned moan,
Which I new pay as if not paid before.
    But if the while I think on thee, dear friend,
    All losses are restored and sorrows end.

Study Questions

1. In the first line Shakespeare compares what he is doing to being involved in a court session. What is summoned?
2. What is the form used in this sonnet? What are the two basic thoughts expressed in the sonnet? Each quatrain expresses a variation on the main thought of the first part. What are those variations?
3. Find some examples of alliteration.
4. Shakespeare uses a number of conceits. Can you find one?

XXIX

When, in disgrace with fortune and men's eyes,
I all alone beweep my outcast state,
And trouble deaf heaven with my bootless cries,
And look upon myself, and curse my fate,
Wishing me like to one more rich in hope,
Featured like him, like him with friends possess'd,
Desiring this man's art, and that man's scope,
With what I most enjoy contented least;
Yet in these thoughts myself almost despising,
Haply I think on thee,—and then my state,
Like to the lark at break of day arising
From sullen earth, sings hymns at heaven's gate;
    For thy sweet love remembered, such wealth brings
    That then I scorn to change my state with kings.

Study Questions

1. Describe the mood of the first eight lines.
2. What breaks and changes this mood?
3. Find the lines in the earlier part of the sonnet that are the exact opposite of the last three lines.
4. Is this an Italian or English sonnet?
5. What image in the poem is used to describe the change of feeling in the author?

LV

Not marble, nor the gilded monuments
Of princes, shall outlive this powerful rhyme;
But you shall shine more bright in these contents
Than unswept stone, besmeared with sluttish time.
When wasteful war shall statues overturn,
And broils root out the work of masonry,
Nor Mars his sword nor war's quick fire shall burn
The living record of your memory.
'Gainst death and all-oblivious enmity
Shall you pace forth; your praise shall still find room
Even in the eyes of all posterity
That wear this world out to the ending doom.
    So, till the judgment that yourself arise,
    You live in this, and dwell in lovers' eyes.

Study Questions

1. Who is the "you" of the third line? (Look at the last line—what dwells in lovers' eyes?)
2. What are "these contents" of the third line?
3. What is the thought of the first quatrain? the second? the third? the couplet?
4. Why is great literature said to be eternal?

LXXIII

That time of year thou mayst in me behold
When yellow leaves, or none, or few, do hang
Upon those boughs which shake against the cold,
Bare ruined choirs, where late the sweet birds sang.
In me thou see'st the twilight of such day
As after sunset fadeth in the west;
Which by and by black night doth take away,
Death's second self, that seals up all in rest.
In me thou see'st the glowing of such fire,
That on the ashes of his youth doth lie,
As the death-bed whereon it must expire,
Consumed with that which it was nourished by.
    This thou perceivest, which makes thy love more strong,
    To love that well which thou must leave ere long.

Study Questions

1. What is "death's second self"?
2. Can you find a conceit in the last quatrain? What is it?
3. Shakespeare uses three figures of speech, images, which tell us about the time of life he is discussing. What are they?
4. What is the second wave of thought in this sonnet?

Sonnet 41

by Philip Sidney

Having this day my horse, my hand, my lance
Guided so well that I obtained the prize,
Both by the judgment of the English eyes
And of some sent from that sweet enemy France,
Horsemen my skill in horsemanship advance,
Town folks my strength; a daintier judge applies
His praise to sleight which from good use doth rise;
Some lucky wits impute it but chance;
Others, because of both sides I do take
My blood from them who did excel in this,
Think Nature me a man-at-arms did make.
How far they shot awry! The true cause is,
Stella looked on, and from her heavenly face
Sent forth the beams which made so fair my race.

Study Questions

1. What is the form of the sonnet? Is it Italian or English? Where does the first wave of thought end?
2. What are the two thoughts in the poem?
3. What is the rhyme scheme?
4. Explain the meaning of lines 9–11.

Two Sonnets from *Divina Commedia*
by Henry Wadsworth Longfellow

Sonnet I

Oft have I seen at some cathedral door
A laborer, pausing in the dust and heat,
Lay down his burden, and with reverent feet
Enter and cross himself, and on the floor
Kneel to repeat his paternoster o'er;
Far off the noises of the world retreat;
The loud vociferations of the street
Become an undistinguishable roar.
So, as I enter here from day to day
And leave my burden at this minster gate,
Kneeling in prayer and not ashamed to pray,
The tumult of the time disconsolate
To inarticulate murmurs dies away,
While the eternal ages watch and wait.

Sonnet IV

I lift mine eyes, and all the windows blaze
With forms of Saints and holy men who died,
Here martyred and hereafter glorified;
And the great Rose upon its leaves displays
Christ's Triumph, and the angelic roundelays,
With splendor upon splendor multiplied;
And Beatrice again at Dante's side
No more rebukes, but smiles her words of praise.
And then the organ sounds, and unseen choirs
Sing the old Latin hymns of peace and love
And benedictions of the Holy Ghost;
And the melodious bells among the spires
O'er all the house-tops and through heaven above
Proclaim the elevation of the Host!

1. The group of sonnets from which these are taken are commentary on Dante's great work, *The Divine Comedy*. With this in mind see if you can find a double comparison in the first sonnet. What is it?
2. Judging by Sonnet IV, what is the subject of the *Paradiso* section of Dante's work?
3. Compare the emotion in these sonnets. How do they differ?
4. In "The Day is Done", Longfellow speaks of which poems he turns to when he feels in a certain mood. Would this poem fit that need?
5. What is the rhyme scheme of these sonnets?

The Owl Critic

by James Thomas Fields

"Who stuffed that white owl?" No one spoke in the shop;
The barber was busy, and he couldn't stop;
The customers, waiting their turns, were all reading
The *Daily*, the *Herald*, the *Post*, little heeding
The young man who blurted out such a blunt question;
Not one raised a head, or even made a suggestion;
   And the barber kept on shaving.

"Don't you see, Mister Brown,"
Cried the youth with a frown,
"How wrong the whole thing is,
How preposterous each wing is,
How flattened the head, how jammed down the neck is—
In short, the whole owl, what an ignorant wreck 'tis!

"I make no apology;
I've learned owleology,

I've passed days and nights in a hundred collections,
And cannot be blinded to any deflections
Arising from unskilful fingers that fail
To stuff a bird right, from his beak to his tail.
Mister Brown! Mister Brown!
Do take that bird down,
Or you'll soon be the laughing stock all over town!"
    And the barber kept on shaving.

"I've studied owls,
And other night fowls,
And I tell you
What I know to be true!
An owl cannot roost
With his limbs so unloosed;
No owl in this world
Ever had his claws curled,
Ever had his legs slanted,
Ever had his bill canted,
Ever had his neck screwed
Into that attitude.
He can't do it, because
'Tis against all bird laws.
Anatomy teaches,
Orinthology preaches,
An owl has a toe
That can't turn out so!
I've made the white owl my study for years,
And to see such a job almost moves me to tears!

"Mister Brown, I'm amazed
You should be so crazed
As to put up a bird
In that posture absurd!

To look at that owl really brings on a dizziness;
The man who stuffed him don't half know his business!"
   And the barber went on shaving.

"Examine those eyes,
I'm filled with surprise
Taxidermists should pass
Off on you such poor glass;
So unnatural they seem
They'd make Audubon scream,
And John Burroughs laugh
To encounter such chaff.
Do take that bird down;
Have him stuffed again, Brown!"
   And the barber went on shaving.

"With some sawdust and bark
I could stuff in the dark
An owl better than that.
I could make an old hat
Look more like an owl
Than that horrid fowl,
Stuck up there so stiff like a side of coarse leather;
In fact, about him there's not one natural feather."

Just then with a wink and a sly normal lurch,
The owl, very gravely, got down from his perch,
Walked round, and regarded his fault-finding critic,
(Who thought he was stuffed) with a glance analytic,
And then fairly hooted, as if he would say:
"Your learning's at fault, this time, anyway;
Don't waste it again on a live bird, I pray.
I'm an owl; you're another. Sir Critic, good-day!"
   And the barber kept on shaving.

Study Questions

1. Which kind of poetry is this, lyric or narrative?
2. What is the rhyme scheme?
3. What is the point of the story?

To Lucasta, Going to the Wars

by Richard Lovelace

Tell me not, Sweet, I am unkind
    That from the nunnery
Of thy chaste breast and quiet mind,
    To war and arms I fly.

True, a new mistress now I chase,
    The first foe in the field;
And with a stronger faith embrace
    A sword, a horse, a shield.

Yet this inconstancy is such
    As thou too shalt adore;
I could not love thee, Dear, so much,
    Loved I not Honour more.

Study Questions

1. Does this poem appeal to the emotion or to the intellect?
2. Put into prose the content of this poem.
3. In each of the three stanzas there is a clash of images, a surprising juxtaposition, that makes the hearer stop and think. What are these images?
4. Do you agree with the last, very famous, two lines?

At the Aquarium

by Max Eastman

Serene the silver fishes glide,
Stern-lipped, and pale, and wonder-eyed.
As, through the aged deeps of ocean,
They glide with wan and wavy motion.
They have no pathway where they go,
They flow like water to and fro,
They watch, with never-winking eyes,
They watch, with staring, cold surprise,
The level people in the air,
The people peering, peering there:
Who wander also to and fro,
And know not why or where they go,
Yet have a wonder in their eyes,
Sometimes a pale and cold surprise.

Study Questions

1. Compare the people to the fish. How does the author see their likeness to one another?
2. Where does the element of surprise first appear in the poem?
3. What is the central thought behind this description?
4. What is the rhyme scheme?

To a Waterfowl

by William Cullen Bryant

Whither, midst falling dew,
While glow the heavens with the last steps of day,
Far, through their rosy depths, dost thou pursue
    Thy solitary way?

Vainly the fowler's eye
Might mark thy distant flight to do thee wrong,
As, darkly painted on the crimson sky,
    Thy figure floats along.

Seek'st thou the plashy brink
Of weedy lake, or marge of river wide,
Or where the rocking billows rise and sink
    On the chafed ocean side?

There is a Power whose care
Teaches thy way along that pathless coast,—
The desert and illimitable air,—
    Lone wandering, but not lost.

All day thy wings have fanned,
At that far height, the cold, thin atmosphere,
Yet stoop not, weary, to the welcome land,
    Though the dark night is near.

And soon that toil shall end;
Soon shalt thou find a summer home, and rest,
And scream among thy fellows; reeds shall bend,
    Soon, o'er thy sheltered nest.

Thou'rt gone, the abyss of heaven
Hath swallowed up thy form; yet, on my heart
Deeply hath sunk the lesson thou hast given,
    And shall not soon depart:

He who, from zone to zone,
Guides through the boundless sky thy certain flight,
In the long way that I must tread alone,
    Will lead my steps aright.

Study Questions

1. What effect did the sight of the lone waterfowl, wending its sure way, have on the poet? Put this poem into prose. What is the theme of the poem?
2. Find an instance of alliteration and of assonance in the poem.
3. What color occurs in the poet's description?
4. If you were counting the number of accent words in each line, what would the pattern be?

To Althea, from Prison

by Richard Lovelace

When Love with unconfinèd wings
Hovers within my gates,
And my divine Althea brings
To whisper at the grates;
When I lie tangled in her hair
And fetter'd to her eye,
The birds that wanton in the air
Know no such liberty.

When flowing cups run swiftly round
With no allaying Thames,
Our careless heads with roses bound,
Our hearts with loyal flames;
When thirsty grief in wine we steep,
When healths and draughts go free,
Fishes, that tipple in the deep,
Know no such liberty.

When, like committed linnets, I
With shriller throat shall sing
The sweetness, mercy, majesty,
And glories of my King;
When I shall voice aloud how good
He is, how great should be,
Enlargèd winds, that curl the flood,
Know no such liberty.

Stone walls do not a prison make,
Nor iron bars a cage;
Minds innocent and quiet take
That for an hermitage;

If I have freedom in my love
And in my soul am free,
Angels alone, that soar above,
Enjoy such liberty.

Study Questions

1. What is the meter of the poem? What is the rhyme scheme?
2. Each of the first three stanzas make a statement about true free-
   dom. Also, each stanza makes a comparison between the poet
   and other creatures. Express the central thought of each of the
   stanzas, and show how the fourth stanza is a logical conclusion
   of the first three.

Repentance
by John Donne

At the round earth's imagined corners, blow
Your trumpets, angels, and arise, arise
From death, you numberless infinities
Of souls, and to your scattered bodies go,
All whom the flood did, and fire shall o'erthrow,
All whom war, death, age, agues, tyrannies,
Despair, law, chance, hath slain, and you whose eyes
Shall behold God and never taste death's woe.

But let them sleep, Lord, and me mourn a space,
For if above all these my sins abound,
'Tis late to ask abundance of Thy grace
When we are there; here on this lowly ground
Teach me how to repent; for that's as good
As if Thou hadst seal'd my pardon with Thy blood.

1. What is the rhyme scheme of this sonnet?
2. The first wave of thought describes what event? How does Donne describe the two types of people?
3. What does the first line mean?
4. What is the second wave of thought?

Batter My Heart

by John Donne

Batter my heart, three-personed God; for You
As yet but knock, breathe, shine, and seek to mend;
That I may rise and stand, o'erthrow me, and bend
Your force to break, blow, burn, and make me new.
I, like a usurped town, to another due,
Labor to admit You, but, O, to no end;
Reason, Your viceroy in me, me should defend,
But is captived, and proves weak or untrue.

Yet dearly I love You, and would be lovèd fain,
But am betrothed unto Your enemy;
Divorce me, untie or break that knot again;
Take me to You, imprison me, for I,
Except You enthrall me, never shall be free,
Nor ever chaste, except You ravish me.

Study Questions

1. What effect does the alliteration in line four have?
2. There are two metaphors used in this poem. What are they? And how are they used?
3. Can you find an example of a conceit?
4. What elements of metaphysical poetry can you find in the poem?

Why So Pale and Wan?

by Sir John Suckling

Why so pale and wan, fond lover?
    Prithee, why so pale?
Will, when looking well can't move her,
    Looking ill prevail?
    Prithee, why so pale?

Why so dull and mute, young sinner?
    Prithee, why so mute?
Will, when speaking well can't win her,
    Saying nothing do 't?
    Prithee, why so mute?

Quit, quit for shame! This will not move;
    This cannot take her.
If of herself she will not love,
    Nothing can make her:
    The devil take her!

Study Questions

1. What aspect of Cavalier poetry does this poem exhibit?
2. What is the rhyme scheme of the poem? What is the meter? Does the meter change during the poem? Where and why?
3. What is Sir John Suckling's advice?

Elegy Written in a Country Churchyard
by Thomas Gray

The Curfew tolls the knell of parting day,
    The lowing herd wind slowly o'er the lea,
The plowman homeward plods his weary way,
    And leaves the world to darkness and to me.

Now fades the glimmering landscape on the sight,
    And all the air a solemn stillness holds,
Save where the beetle wheels his droning flight,
    And drowsy tinklings lull the distant folds;

Save that, from yonder ivy-mantled tow'r
    The moping owl does to the moon complain
Of such, as wandering near her secret bow'r,
    Molest her ancient solitary reign.

Beneath those rugged elms, that yew-tree's shade,
    Where heaves the turf in many a mold'ring heap,
Each in his narrow cell for ever laid,
    The rude Forefathers of the hamlet sleep.

The breezy call of incense-breathing Morn,
    The swallow twitt'ring from the straw-built shed,
The cock's shrill clarion, or the echoing horn,
    No more shall rouse them from their lowly bed.

For them no more the blazing hearth shall burn,
    Or busy housewife ply her evening care;
No children run to lisp their sire's return,
    Or climb his knees the envied kiss to share.

Oft did the harvest to their sickle yield,
    Their furrow oft the stubborn glebe has broke;
How jocund did they drive their team afield!
    How bow'd the woods beneath their sturdy stroke!

Let not Ambition mock their useful toil,
    Their homely joys, and destiny obscure;
Nor Grandeur hear with a disdainful smile
    The short and simple annals of the poor.

The boast of heraldry, the pomp of pow'r,
    And all that beauty, all that wealth e'er gave,
Awaits alike th' inevitable hour:
    The paths of glory lead but to the grave.

Nor you, ye Proud, impute to These the fault,
    If Memory o'er their tomb no Trophies raise,
Where through the long-drawn aisle and fretted vault,
    The pealing anthem swells the note of praise.

Can storied urn or animated bust
    Back to its mansion call the fleeting breath?
Can Honour's voice provoke the silent dust,
    Or Flatt'ry soothe the dull cold ear of Death?

Perhaps in this neglected spot is laid
    Some heart once pregnant with celestial fire;
Hands that the rod of empire might have sway'd,
    Or waked to ecstasy the living lyre.

But Knowledge to their eyes her ample page
    Rich with the spoils of time did ne'er unroll;
Chill Penury repress'd their noble rage,
    And froze the genial current of the soul.

Full many a gem of purest ray serene,
　　The dark unfathomed caves of ocean bear:
Full many a flower is born to blush unseen,
　　And waste its sweetness on the desert air.

Some village Hampden that with dauntless breast
　　The little tyrant of his fields withstood;
Some mute inglorious Milton here may rest,
　　Some Cromwell guiltless of his country's blood.

Th' applause of list'ning senates to command,
　　The threats of pain and ruin to despise,
To scatter plenty o'er a smiling land,
　　And read their history in a nation's eyes,

Their lot forbade: nor circumscribed alone
　　Their growing virtues, but their crimes confined;
Forbade to wade through slaughter to a throne,
　　And shut the gates of mercy on mankind,

The struggling pangs of conscious truth to hide,
　　To quench the blushes of ingenuous shame,
Or heap the shrine of Luxury and Pride
　　With incense kindled at the Muse's flame.

Far from the madding crowd's ignoble strife,
　　Their sober wishes never learn'd to stray;
Along the cool sequester'd vale of life
　　They kept the noiseless tenor of their way.

Yet ev'n these bones from insult to protect
　　Some frail memorial still erected nigh,
With uncouth rhymes and shapeless sculpture deck'd,
　　Implores the passing tribute of a sigh.

Their name, their years, spelt by th' unlettered muse,
    The place of fame and elegy supply:
And many a holy text around she strews,
    That teach the rustic moralist to die.

For who to dumb Forgetfulness a prey,
    This pleasing, anxious being e'er resign'd,
Left the warm precincts of the cheerful day,
    Nor cast one longing ling'ring look behind?

On some fond breast the parting soul relies,
    Some pious drops the closing eye requires;
Even from the tomb the voice of Nature cries,
    Ev'n in our Ashes live their wonted Fires.

For thee, who mindful of th' unhonour'd dead
    Dost in these lines their artless tale relate;
If chance, by lonely contemplation led,
    Some kindred spirit shall inquire thy fate,

Haply some hoary-headed Swain may say,
    "Oft have we seen him at the peep of dawn
Brushing with hasty steps the dews away
    To meet the sun upon the upland lawn.

"There at the foot of yonder nodding beech
    That wreathes its old fantastic roots so high,
His listless length at noontide would he stretch,
    And pore upon the brook that babbles by.

"Hard by yon wood, now smiling as in scorn,
    Muttering his wayward fancies he would rove,
Now drooping, woeful wan, like one forlorn,
    Or crazed with care, or cross'd in hopeless love.

"One morn I miss'd him on the custom'd hill,
   Along the heath and near his fav'rite tree;
Another came; nor yet beside the rill,
   Nor up the lawn, nor at the wood was he;

"The next with dirges due in sad array
   Slow through the church-way path we saw him borne.
Approach and read (for thou canst read) the lay
   Graved on the stone beneath yon aged thorn."

The Epitaph

Here rests his head upon the lap of Earth
   A Youth to Fortune and to Fame unknown.
Fair Science frown'd not on his humble birth,
   And Melancholy mark'd him for her own.

Large was his bounty, and his soul sincere,
   Heaven did a recompense as largely send:
He gave to Mis'ry all he had, a tear,
   He gain'd from Heaven ('twas all he wish'd) a friend.

No farther seek his merits to disclose,
   Or draw his frailties from their dread abode
(There they alike in trembling hope repose),
   The bosom of his Father and his God.

Study Questions

1. What is the purpose of the first three stanzas?
2. What is the "narrow cell" of stanza 4?
3. Name the activities denied those in the grave. What was their daily life like?
4. Stanzas 8 and 9 are often quoted. What is the gist of each?
5. Which lines point out that splendid monuments cannot alter

the fact that all must die and that however different they may have been in life, all the dead are dead alike?

6. Note: Hampden was a squire who refused to pay the "tax of ship money", which eventually led to the Puritan Revolution. Whom does the poet suggest might lie in this graveyard? Gray implies there are also those who did not achieve great wickedness as well as those who did not realize great goodness. Why, according to the poet, didn't they achieve what they might have?

7. Stanza 14 is often quoted. What does it express?

8. Stanzas 17, 18, and 19 must be read together. If "to wade", "shut", "to hide", "to quench", and "heap" are all objects of the verb "forbade", what do stanzas 17 and 18 say?

9. What do you think about the view that both great men and greatly wicked men were prevented from achievement by poor circumstances?

10. Where does the poet say that even these poor graves have some sort of markers?

11. Where does Gray begin to write of himself? How can you tell?

12. What did Gray write for his own epitaph? What virtues did he claim? Where did he hope to end?

On the Morning of Christ's Nativity

by John Milton

I

This is the month, and this the happy morn,
Wherein the Son of Heaven's Eternal King,
Of wedded maid and virgin mother born,
Our great redemption from above did bring;
For so the holy sages once did sing,
   That he our deadly forfeit should release,
And with his Father work us a perpetual peace.

II

That glorious form, that light unsufferable,
And that far-beaming blaze of majesty,
Wherewith he wont at Heaven's high council-table
To sit the midst of Trinal Unity,
He laid aside, and, here with us to be,
   Forsook the courts of everlasting day,
And chose with us a darksome house of mortal clay.

III

Say, Heavenly Muse, shall not thy sacred vein
Afford a present to the Infant God?
Hast thou no verse, no hymn, or solemn strain,
To welcome him to this his new abode,
Now while the heaven, by the Sun's team untrod,
   Hath took no print of the approaching light,
And all the spangled host keep watch in squadrons bright?

IV

See how from far upon the eastern road
The star-led wizards haste with odors sweet!
Oh run, prevent them with thy humble ode,

And lay it lowly at his blessed feet;
Have thou the honor first thy Lord to greet,
   And join thy voice unto the angel choir,
From out his secret altar touched with hallowed fire.

The Hymn
I

   It was the winter wild,
   While the heaven-born Child
All meanly wrapt in the rude manger lies;
   Nature, in awe to him,
   Had doffed her gaudy trim,
With her great Master so to sympathize:
It was no season then for her
To wanton with the sun, her lusty paramour.

II

Only with speeches fair
She woos the gentle air
To hide her guilty front with innocent snow,
And on her naked shame,
Pollute with sinful blame,
The saintly veil of maiden white to throw;
Confounded, that her Maker's eyes
Should look so near upon her foul deformities.

III

But he, her fears to cease,
Sent down the meek-eyed Peace:
She, crownèd with olive green, came softly sliding
Down through the turning sphere,
His ready harbinger,
With turtle wing the amorous clouds dividing;
And, waving wide her myrtle wand,
She strikes a universal peace through sea and land.

IV

No war, or battle's sound,
Was heard the world around;
The idle spear and shield were high uphung;
The hookèd chariot stood,
Unstained with hostile blood;
The trumpet spake not to the armèd throng;
And kings sat still with awful eye,
As if they surely knew their sovran Lord was by.

V

But peaceful was the night
Wherein the Prince of Light
His reign of peace upon the earth began.

The Rhetorical Stage: Poetry Selections: Section III

The winds, with wonder whist,
   Smoothly the waters kissed,
Whispering new joys to the mild Ocean,
Who now hath quite forgot to rave,
While birds of calm sit brooding on the charmèd wave.

VI

The stars, with deep amaze,
   Stand fixed on steadfast gaze,
Bending one way their precious influence,
   And will to take their flight,
   For all the morning light,
Or Lucifer that often warned them thence;
But in their glimmering orbs did glow,
Until their Lord himself bespake, and bid them go.

VII

And, though the shady gloom
   Had given day her room,
The Sun himself withheld his wonted speed,
   And hid his head for shame
   As his inferior flame
The new-enlightened world no more should need:
He saw a greater Sun appear
Than his bright throne or burning axletree could bear.

VIII

The shepherds on the lawn,
   Or ere the point of dawn,
Sat simply chatting in a rustic row;
   Full little thought they than
   That the mighty Pan
Was kindly come to live with them below:
Perhaps their loves, or else their sheep,
Was all that did their silly thoughts so busy keep.

IX

When such music sweet
Their hearts and ears did greet
As never was by mortal finger strook,
    Divinely-warbled voice
    Answering the stringèd noise,
As all their souls in blissful rapture took:
The air, such pleasure loth to lose,
With thousand echoes still prolongs each heavenly close.

X

Nature, that heard such sound
Beneath the hollow round
Of Cynthia's seat the airy region thrilling,
    Now was almost won
    To think her part was done,
And that her reign had here its last fulfilling:
She knew such harmony alone
Could hold all Heaven and Earth in happier uniön.

XI

At last surrounds their sight
A globe of circular light,
That with long beams the shamefaced Night arrayed;
    The helmèd cherubim
    And sworded seraphim
Are seen in glittering ranks with wings displayed,
Harping loud and solemn quire,
With unexpressive notes, to Heaven's new-born Heir.

XII

Such music (as 'tis said)
Before was never made,
But when of old the sons of morning sung,

While the Creator great
His constellations set,
And the well-balanced world on hinges hung,
And cast the dark foundations deep,
And bid the weltering waves their oozy channel keep.

XIII

Ring out, ye crystal spheres,
Once bless our human ears,
If ye have power to touch our senses so;
And let your silver chime
Move in melodious time;
And let the bass of heaven's deep organ blow;
And with your ninefold harmony
Make up full consort to th' angelic symphony.

XIV

For, if such holy song
Enwrap our fancy long,
Time will run back and fetch the age of gold;
And speckled vanity
Will sicken soon and die,
And leprous sin will melt from earthly mould;
And Hell itself will pass away,
And leave her dolorous mansions to the peering day.

* * *

XXVI

So, when the sun in bed,
Curtained with cloudy red,
Pillows his chin upon an orient wave,
The flocking shadows pale
Troop to th' infernal jail;
Each fettered ghost slips to his several grave,

And the yellow-skirted fays
Fly after the night-steeds, leaving their moon-loved maze.

XXVII

But see! The Virgin blest
Hath laid her Babe to rest,
Time is our tedious song should here have ending:
Heaven's youngest-teemèd star
Hath fixed her polished car,
Her sleeping Lord with handmaid lamp attending;
And all about the courtly stable
Bright-harnessed angels sit in order serviceable.

Study Questions

1. What truths of the faith are mentioned in the first four stanzas?
2. What is the rhyme scheme of the prelude? What is the meter?
3. How does the author move from the prelude to the Hymn?
4. What is the rhyme scheme of the Hymn? What is the meter?
5. According to the poet, why was Christ born in winter?
6. What is the imagery of the second stanza of the Hymn designed to convey?
7. In stanzas III and IV, Milton suggests a reason why the historical time of Christ's birth was appropriate. What is it?
8. What is the meaning of: "The sun himself withheld his wonted speed,/ And hid his head for shame/ As his inferior flame/ The new-enlightened world no more should need"?
9. What is the thought of stanza 10? (Note: Cynthia is the goddess of the moon.)
10. In stanza XIII the crystal spheres of Ptolemaic astronomy are asked to ring out. What does the poem say would be the effect of such a song?
11. What is "Heaven's youngest-teemèd star" (stanza XXVII)?
12. What is the point of this ode? What effect is intended?

Ode to the West Wind

by Percy Bysshe Shelley

I

O wild West Wind, thou breath of Autumn's being,
Thou, from whose unseen presence the leaves dead
Are driven, like ghosts from an enchanter fleeing,

Yellow, and black, and pale, and hectic red,
Pestilence-stricken multitudes! O thou,
Who chariotest to their dark wintry bed

The wingèd seeds, where they lie cold and low,
Each like a corpse within its grave, until
Thine azure sister of the Spring shall blow

Her clarion o'er the dreaming earth, and fill
(Driving sweet buds like flocks to feed in air)
With living hues and odours plain and hill;

Wild Spirit, which art moving everywhere;
Destroyer and preserver; hear, O hear!

II

Thou on whose stream, 'mid the steep sky's commotion,
Loose clouds like earth's decaying leaves are shed,
Shook from the tangled boughs of heaven and ocean,

Angels of rain and lightning! there are spread
On the blue surface of thine airy surge,
Like the bright hair uplifted from the head

Of some fierce Maenad, even from the dim verge
Of the horizon to the zenith's height,
The locks of the approaching storm. Thou dirge

Of the dying year, to which this closing night
Will be the dome of a vast sepulchre,
Vaulted with all thy congregated might

Of vapours, from whose solid atmosphere
Black rain, and fire, and hail, will burst; oh, hear!

III

Thou who didst waken from his summer dreams
The blue Mediterranean, where he lay,
Lulled by the coil of his crystalline streams,

Beside a pumice isle in Baiae's bay,
And saw in sleep old palaces and towers
Quivering within the wave's intenser day,

All overgrown with azure moss, and flowers
So sweet, the sense faints picturing them! Thou
For whose path the Atlantic's level powers

Cleave themselves into chasms, while far below
The sea-blooms and the oozy woods which wear
The sapless foliage of the ocean, know

Thy voice, and suddenly grow gray with fear,
And tremble and despoil themselves: oh, hear!

IV

If I were a dead leaf thou mightest bear;
If I were a swift cloud to fly with thee;
A wave to pant beneath thy power, and share

The impulse of thy strength, only less free
Than thou, O uncontrollable! If even
I were as in my boyhood, and could be

The comrade of thy wanderings over heaven,
As then, when to outstrip thy skiey speed
Scarce seem'd a vision; I would ne'er have striven

As thus with thee in prayer in my sore need.
Oh, lift me as a wave, a leaf, a cloud!
I fall upon the thorns of life! I bleed!

A heavy weight of hours has chain'd and bow'd
One too like thee—tameless, and swift, and proud.

V

Make me thy lyre, even as the forest is:
What if my leaves are falling like its own!
The tumult of thy mighty harmonies

Will take from both a deep, autumnal tone,
Sweet though in sadness. Be thou, Spirit fierce,
My spirit! Be thou me, impetuous one!

Drive my dead thoughts over the universe,
Like wither'd leaves to quicken a new birth!
And, by the incantation of this verse,

Scatter, as from an unextinguish'd hearth
Ashes and sparks, my words among mankind!
Be through my lips to unawaken'd earth

The trumpet of a prophecy! O Wind,
If Winter comes, can Spring be far behind?

Study Questions

1. In the first section Shelley tells us the twofold character of the west wind. What is it? Give some example of each aspect.

2. In the second section the clouds are likened to four things. What are they? Which image links this stanza with the one before?

3. In the third section Shelley attributes a sympathy in the vegetation at the bottom of the sea with that of the land in the change of seasons. (That is, they are both affected by the seasons.) If this is so, why does the foliage of the ocean grow "gray with fear"?

4. The fourth stanza ties together the imagery of the previous sections. How does it do this? State in your own words the thought of this section.

5. Is Shelley young or old at the writing of this poem? He saw himself as a social reformer. Do you think his aspirations in this area were yet realized?

Ozymandias

by Percy Bysshe Shelley

I met a traveller from an antique land
Who said: Two vast and trunkless legs of stone
Stand in the desert. Near them, on the sand,
Half sunk, a shatter'd visage lies, whose frown,
And wrinkled lip, and sneer of cold command,
Tell that its sculptor well those passions read
Which yet survive, stamp'd on these lifeless things,
The hand that mock'd them, and the heart that fed;
And on the pedestal these words appear:
"My name is Ozymandias, king of kings:
Look on my works, ye Mighty, and despair!"
Nothing beside remains. Round the decay
Of that colossal wreck, boundless and bare
The lone and level sands stretch far away.

Study Questions

1. What is the theme of this sonnet? How does the poet convey his message?
2. Line 11 was written by the king to mean one thing, and now it means another. Express the two meanings.

On First Looking into Chapman's Homer
by John Keats

Much have I travell'd in the realms of gold,
    And many goodly states and kingdoms seen;
    Round many western islands have I been
Which bards in fealty to Apollo hold.
Oft of one wide expanse had I been told
    That deep-brow'd Homer ruled as his demesne:
    Yet did I never breathe its pure serene
Till I heard Chapman speak out loud and bold:
Then felt I like some watcher of the skies
    When a new planet swims into his ken;
Or like stout Cortez when with eagle eyes
    He stared at the Pacific—and all his men
Look'd at each other with a wild surmise—
    Silent, on a peak in Darien.

Study Questions

1. What are the realms of gold in which Keats has traveled? Is he talking about actual travel or travel he has taken through reading?
2. What are the western islands which bards in fealty to Apollo hold? Since the poem is about the wonders of reading Homer, who was, until this time, unavailable to those who did not read Greek, what has Keats been reading up until this time?

3. Chapman is a translator, who translated Homer into English. By virtue of the translation Keats is now able to enjoy the wide expanse that Homer ruled. What is that expanse?
4. How did Keats feel upon reading this translation? (Note: It was Balboa, not Cortez, who discovered the Pacific.)
5. The last line is very famous. Why are the men silent?
6. What is the rhyme scheme of this sonnet? Which kind of sonnet is it, Italian or Shakespearean?

Ode on a Grecian Urn
by John Keats

Thou still unravish'd bride of quietness,
    Thou foster-child of Silence and slow Time,
Sylvan historian, who canst thus express
    A flowery tale more sweetly than our rhyme:
What leaf-fringed legend haunts about thy shape
    Of deities or mortals, or of both,
        In Tempe or the dales of Arcady?
What men or gods are these? What maidens loath?
    What mad pursuit? What struggle to escape?
        What pipes and timbrels? What wild ecstasy?

Heard melodies are sweet, but those unheard
    Are sweeter; therefore, ye soft pipes, play on;
Not to the sensual ear, but, more endear'd,
    Pipe to the spirit ditties of no tone:
Fair youth, beneath the trees, thou canst not leave
    Thy song, nor ever can those trees be bare;
        Bold Lover, never, never canst thou kiss,
Though winning near the goal—yet, do not grieve;
    She cannot fade, though thou hast not thy bliss,
        For ever, wilt thou love, and she be fair!

Ah, happy, happy boughs! that cannot shed
　　Your leaves, nor ever bid the Spring adieu;
And, happy melodist, unwearièd,
　　For ever piping songs for ever new;
More happy love! more happy, happy love!
　　For ever warm and still to be enjoy'd,
　　　For ever panting, and for ever young;
All breathing human passion far above,
　　That leaves a heart high-sorrowful and cloyed,
　　　A burning forehead, and a parching tongue.

Who are these coming to the sacrifice?
　　To what green altar, O mysterious priest,
Lead'st thou that heifer lowing at the skies,
　　And all her silken flanks with garlands drest?
What little town by river or sea-shore,
　　Or mountain-built with peaceful citadel,
　　　Is emptied of this folk, this pious morn?
And, little town, thy streets for evermore
　　Will silent be; and not a soul, to tell
　　　Why thou art desolate, can e'er return.

O Attic shape! Fair attitude! with brede
　　Of marble men and maidens overwrought,
With forest branches and the trodden weed;
　　Thou, silent form, doth tease us out of thought
As doth eternity: Cold Pastoral!
　　When old age shall this generation waste,
　　　Thou shalt remain, in midst of other woe
Than ours, a friend to man, to whom thou say'st,
　　"Beauty is truth, truth beauty,—that is all
　　　Ye know on earth, and all ye need to know."

1. The first stanza describes a marble vase with a decorative band showing men and women going to offer a sacrifice. They were playing instruments and dancing as they went. The vase inspired this poem. Why would one call the vase the "unravished bride of quietness", a "foster child of silence and slow time", and a "sylvan historian"?

2. What is the purpose of the series of questions at the end of the first stanza?

3. How can one say that unheard melodies are sweeter than heard melodies? What ideas are advanced in the last six lines of the second stanza, and the whole of the third stanza?

4. In the fourth stanza the poet says the little town will be forever empty. Why?

5. In the fifth stanza "Attic shape" stands for the urn; "attic" means Athenian. "Attitude" here means something like bearing, posture, or air. "Brede" means decoration. What is the purpose of the first three lines?

6. Why does Keats say that the urn "dost tease us out of thought/ As does eternity"?

Break, Break, Break
by *Alfred Lord Tennyson*

Break, break, break,
  On thy cold gray stones, O Sea!
And I would that my tongue could utter
  The thoughts that arise in me.

O, well for the fisherman's boy,
  That he shouts with his sister at play!
O, well for the sailor lad,
  That he sings in his boat on the bay!

And stately ships go on
  To their haven under the hill;
But O for the touch of a vanished hand.
  And the sound of a voice that is still!

Break, break, break,
  At the foot of thy crags, O Sea!
But the tender grace of a day that is dead
  Will never come back to me.

Study Questions

1. Is this poem an example of an elegy? It was written after the sudden death of a close friend.
2. What is the purpose of the first stanza? What is its effect?
3. How does the poet express his sense of loss?
4. Which line most powerfully conveys the poet's loss?

The Young Neophyte

by Alice Meynell

Who knows what days I answer for today?
  Giving the bud I give the flower. I bow
  This yet unfaded and a faded brow;
Bending these knees and feeble knees, I pray.

Thoughts yet unripe in me I bend one way,
  Give one repose to pain I know not now,
  One check to joy that comes, I guess not how.
I dedicate my fields when Spring is grey.

O rash! (I smile) to pledge my hidden wheat.
  I fold today at altars far apart
Hands trembling with what toils? In their retreat

I seal my love to-be, my folded art.
  I light the tapers at my head and feet,
And lay the crucifix on this silent heart.

Study Questions

1. What is the form of this poem?
2. This poem was written on the occasion of the author's conversion to Catholicism. She was twenty years old at the time. How does the title fit the occasion?
3. What do the first two lines mean? Does the answer to the question give the theme of the poem?
4. "Giving the bud I give the flower" is the first of a series of metaphors that express the main idea of the poem. Give some of the others and explain the imagery in each.
5. What is the mood or tone of the poem?

How Do I Love Thee?

by Elizabeth Barrett Browning

How do I love thee? Let me count the ways.
I love thee to the depth and breadth and height
My soul can reach, when feeling out of sight
For the ends of Being and Ideal Grace.
I love thee to the level of every day's
Most quiet need, by sun and candlelight.
I love thee freely, as men strive for Right;
I love thee purely, as they turn from Praise.
I love thee with the passion put to use
In my old griefs, and with my childhood's faith.
I love thee with a love I seemed to lose
With my lost saints,—I love thee with the breath,
Smiles, tears of all my life!—and, if God choose,
I shall but love thee better after death.

Study Questions

1. When the poet says she loves "to the depth and breadth and height" her soul can reach, what is she saying? Which lines express love's kindness and consideration?

2. How does she express the freedom and purity of her love?

3. Grief tends to be a destructive emotion, using large amounts of energy. With this in mind, explain, "I love thee with the passion put to use/ In my old griefs".

4. Youth often feels a kind of adoration for certain people, amounting almost to worship. This is probably what the poem refers to as the "lost saints" of early life. What then is the poet saying in these lines, "I love thee with a love I seemed to lose/ With my lost saints"?

5. Compare this sonnet with "Let me not to the marriage of true minds admit impediments" (Shakespeare's Sonnet CXVI). Which is a more emotional approach? Which more intellectual?

The Kingdom of God

by Francis Thompson

O world invisible, we view thee,
O world intangible, we touch thee,
O world unknowable, we know thee,
Inapprehensible, we clutch thee!

Does the fish soar to find the ocean,
The eagle plunge to find the air—
That we ask of the stars in motion
If they have rumor of thee there?

Not where the wheeling systems darken,
And our benumbed conceiving soars!
The drift of pinions, would we hearken,
Beats at our own clay-shuttered doors.

The angels keep their ancient places;—
Turn but a stone, and start a wing!
'Tis ye, 'tis your estranged faces,
That miss the many-splendoured thing.

But (when so sad thou canst not sadder)
Cry,—and upon thy so sore loss
Shall shine the traffic of Jacob's ladder
Pitched betwixt Heaven and Charing Cross.

Yea, in the night, my Soul, my daughter,
Cry,—clinging Heaven by the hems;
And lo, Christ walking on the water
Not of Gennesareth, but Thames.

Study Questions

1. The first stanza has four examples of what poetic device?
2. Where does the poet tell us to look for God? How do the first two lines of the second stanza contribute to this thought? What does "The angels keep their ancient places;—/ Turn but a stone, and start a wing" mean?
3. Why are our doors "clay-shuttered"?
4. What does Francis Thompson say will move us to a recognition of the regular commerce between heaven and earth and of Our Lord?
5. What does "in the night" mean? Could it have two meanings?
6. To whom did Christ walk on the Sea of Galilee (here called Gennesareth)? How is the modern person like them?

The Hound of Heaven

by Francis Thompson

I fled Him, down the nights and down the days;
I fled Him, down the arches of the years;
I fled Him, down the labyrinthine ways
   Of my own mind; and in the midst of tears
I hid from Him, and under running laughter.
      Up vistaed hopes I sped;
      And shot precipitated,
Adown Titanic glooms of chasmèd fears,
   From those strong Feet that followed, followed after.
     But with unhurrying chase,
     And unperturbèd pace,
   Deliberate speed, majestic instancy,
     They beat—and a Voice beat
More instant than the Feet—
"All things betray thee, who betrayest Me."

     I pleaded, outlaw-wise,
By many a hearted casement, curtained red,
   Trellised with intertwining charities;
(For, though I knew His love Who followèd,
     Yet was I sore adread
Lest, having Him, I must have naught beside.)
But, if one little casement parted wide,
The gust of His approach would clash it to:
Fear wist not to evade, as Love wist to pursue.

Across the margent of the world I fled.
   And troubled the gold gateways of the stars,
Smiting for shelter on their clangèd bars;
    Fretted to dulcet jars

And silvern chatter the pale ports o' the moon.
I said to dawn: Be sudden—to eve:
    Be soon;
  With thy young skiey blossoms heap me over
  From this tremendous Lover—
Float thy vague veil about me, lest He see!
  I tempted all His servitors, but to find
My own betrayal in their constancy,
In faith to Him their fickleness to me,
    Their traitorous trueness, and their loyal deceit.
To all swift things for swiftness did I sue
  Clung to the whistling mane of every wind.
    But whether they swept, smoothly fleet,
  The long savannahs of the blue;
    Or whether, Thunder-driven,
  They clanged His chariot 'thwart a heaven,
Plashy with flying lightnings round the spurn o' their feet:—
  Fear wist not to evade as Love wist to pursue.

    Still with unhurrying chase,
    And unperturbèd pace,
  Deliberate speed, majestic instancy,
    Came on the following Feet,
    And a Voice above their beat—
"Naught shelters thee, who wilt not shelter Me."

I sought no more that after which I strayed
  In face of man or maid;
But still within the little children's eyes
  Seems something, something that replies;
They at least are for me, surely for me!
I turned me to them very wistfully;
But just as their young eyes grew sudden fair

With dawning answers there,
Their angel plucked them from me by the hair.

"Come then, ye other children, Nature's—share
With me" (said I) "your delicate fellowship;
    Let me greet you lip to lip,
    Let me twine with you caresses,
       Wantoning
    With our Lady-Mother's vagrant tresses,
       Banqueting
    With her in her wind-walled palace,
    Underneath her azured daïs,
    Quaffing, as your taintless way is,
       From a chalice
Lucent-weeping out of the dayspring."
    So it was done:
I in their delicate fellowship was one—
Drew the bolt of Nature's secrecies.
  I knew all the swift importings
  On the wilful face of skies;
  I knew how the clouds arise,
  Spumed of the wild sea-snortings;
  All that's born or dies
  Rose and drooped with; made them shapers
Of mine own moods, or wailful or divine;
  With them joyed and was bereaven.
  I was heavy with the even,
  When she lit her glimmering tapers
  Round the day's dead sanctities.
  I laughed in the morning's eyes.
I triumphed and I saddened with all weather,
  Heaven and I wept together,
And its sweet tears were salt with mortal mine;
Against the red throb of its sunset-heart

I laid my own to beat,
    And share commingling heat;
But not by that, by that, was eased my human smart.
In vain my tears were wet on Heaven's grey cheek.
For ah! we know not what each other says,
    These things and I; in sound *I* speak—
Their sound is but their stir, they speak by silences.
Nature, poor stepdame, cannot slake my drought;
    Let her, if she would owe me,
Drop yon blue bosom-veil of sky, and show me
    The breasts o' her tenderness
Never did any milk of her once bless
    My thirsting mouth.
    Nigh and nigh draws the chase,
    With unperturbèd pace,
Deliberate speed, majestic instancy;
    And past those noisèd Feet
    A Voice comes yet more fleet—
"Lo! naught contents thee, who content'st not Me."

Naked I wait Thy Love's uplifted stroke!
My harness piece by piece Thou hast hewn from me,
    And smitten me to my knee;
    I am defenseless utterly.
    I slept, methinks, and woke,
And slowly gazing, find me stripped in sleep.
In the rash lustihead of my young powers,
    I shook the pillaring hours
And pulled my life upon me; grimed with smears,
I stand amid the dust o' the mounded years—
My mangled youth lies dead beneath the heap.
My days have crackled and gone up in smoke,
Have puffed and burst as sun-starts on a stream.
    Yea, faileth now even dream

The dreamer, and the lute of the lutanist;
Even the linked fantasies, in whose blossomy twist
I swung the earth a trinket at my wrist,
Are yielding; cords of all too weak account
For earth with heavy griefs so overplussed.
  Ah! Is Thy love indeed
A weed, albeit an amaranthine weed,
Suffering no flowers except its own to mount?

  Ah! must—
  Designer infinite!—
Ah! Must Thou char the wood ere Thou canst limn with it?
My freshness spent its wavering shower i' the dust;
And now my heart is as a broken fount,
Wherein tear-drippings stagnate, spilt down ever
  From the dank thoughts that shiver
Upon the sighful branches of my mind.
  Such is; what is to be?
The pulp so bitter, how shall taste the rind?
I dimly guess what Time in mists confounds:
Yet ever and anon a trumpet sounds
From the hid battlements of Eternity:
Those shaken mists a space unsettle, then
Round the half-glimpsèd turrets slowly wash again.
  But not ere him who summoneth
  I first have seen, enwound
With glooming robes purpureal, cypress-crowned;
His name I know, and what his trumpet saith.
Whether man's heart or life it be which yields
  Thee harvest, must Thy harvest-fields
  Be dunged with rotten death?

  Now of that long pursuit
  Comes on at hand the bruit;

That Voice is round me like a bursting sea:
     "And is thy earth so marred,
      Shattered in shard on shard?
Lo, all things fly thee, for thou fliest Me!
     Strange, piteous, futile thing!
Wherefore should any set thee love apart?
Seeing none but I makes much of naught" (He said),
"And human love needs human meriting:
     How hast thou merited—
Of all man's clotted clay the dingiest clot?
     Alack, thou knowest not
How little worthy of any love thou art!
Whom wilt thou find to love ignoble thee,
    Save Me, save only Me?
All which I took from thee I did but take,
    Not for thy harms,
But just that thou might'st seek it in My arms.
    All which thy child's mistake
Fancies as lost, I have stored for thee at home:
    Rise, clasp my hand, and come!"
     Halts by me that footfall:
    Is my gloom, after all,
Shade of His hand, outstretched caressingly?
    "Ah, fondest, blindest, weakest,
    I am He whom thou seekest!
Thou dravest love from thee, who dravest Me."

Study Questions

1. Francis Thompson was in a minor seminary as a boy but found
   he did not have a vocation. He then tried medical school, but
   failed at that. While in medical school he was sick and given
   laudanum as a pain reliever. He became addicted to the sub-
   stance. Deciding to try writing as a career, he left home for

London and lived for a period of time on the streets, begging for food. He was a homeless drug addict. Eventually the Meynells befriended him, recognizing his great talent. Mr. Thompson recovered his health and became a Catholic writer, the "poet of the return to God". "The Hound of Heaven" is the story of Francis Thompson's life. Read the text and try to divide it into the following sections:

(a) Introduction of theme: Man's attempt to flee God and the consequent discovery that, without God, there is nothing else.

(b) Recourse to human loves: (Note: "Wist" means "knew". The idea is that God in His love knew better how to pursue than the sinner, in his fear, knew how to evade.) What reason is given for fleeing from God's love?

(c) Recourse to the heavens: What lesson was the poet taught by the stars and planets? Is a study of the universe going to reveal a regularity and constancy in nature? Which lines reveal this? What is the figure of speech used in, "I said to dawn: Be sudden—to eve: Be soon"? And why is this phrase used here? What are "skiey blossoms"? What effect does the refrain at the end of this section have?

(d) Recourse to innocence: In the next section the poet recounts his resort to the innocence and love of children. In this section there is an implied restatement of the theme of the poem. What is it?

(e) Turning to nature: This section recounts the poet's attempt to find solace in nature. What figure of speech is employed in calling nature "our Lady-Mother"? Find other examples of this figure within this section. What is "her wind-walled palace"? "her azured daïs"? Did this unity with nature satisfy the poet's need? Why not? There is a change in the refrain each time it is used. In this section it becomes "Lo! naught contents thee, who content'st not Me." How is this appropriate to the preceding lines?

(f) Analysis of the situation: The sixth section contains a review by the poet of his position vis-à-vis God. What is his judgment? To whom is the poet comparing himself when he says, "I shook the pillaring hours"? By "linked fantasies" the poet is referring to his poetry, which has also failed him. Why has it failed?

After describing his own situation, the poet goes on to recount his view of God's methods. What does he say about this? (Note: The amaranthine weed is an imaginary plant that absorbed all the water from the area around it, thus killing all other plants near it.) Can you find a metaphor in this section? Can you find a simile? Whom does the poet see in the battlements of Eternity? Is this an additional complaint against God? (g) God's answer: This last section is God's answer to the poet. Write this answer in your own words. (Note: "Bruit" is an archaic word for sound, clamor, din, or for a report or a rumor. A "shard" is a piece of a brittle substance.)

God's Grandeur

by Gerard Manley Hopkins, S.J.

The world is charged with the grandeur of God.
　　It will flame out, like shining from shook foil;
　　It gathers to a greatness, like the ooze of oil
Crushed. Why do men then now not reck his rod?
Generations have trod, have trod, have trod;
　　And all is seared with trade; bleared, smeared, with toil;
　　And wears man's smudge and shares man's smell: the soil
Is bare now, nor can foot feel, being shod.

And for all this, nature is never spent;
　　There lives the dearest freshness deep down things;
And though the last lights off the black West went
　　Oh, morning, at the brown brink eastward, springs—
Because the Holy Ghost over the bent
　　World broods with warm breast and with ah! bright wings.

Study Questions

1. What is the problem laid out in the octet? What is the poet's attitude toward man's use of nature? What is the resolution offered in the sestet?
2. Can you find at least four examples of alliteration or assonance?
3. What is the rhyme scheme of the poem? And what is the sonnet form?

Spring

by Gerard Manley Hopkins, S.J.

Nothing is so beautiful as spring—
    When weeds, in wheels, shoot long and lovely and lush;
    Thrush eggs look little low heavens, and thrush
Through the echoing timber does so rinse and wring
The ear, it strikes like lightning to hear him sing;
    The glassy peartree leaves and blooms, they brush
    The descending blue; that blue is all in a rush
With richness; the racing lambs too have fair their fling.

What is all this juice and all this joy?
    A strain of the earth's sweet being in the beginning
In Eden garden.—Have, get, before it cloy,
    Before it cloud, Christ, Lord, and sour with sinning,
Innocent mind and Mayday in girl and boy,
    Most, O maid's child, thy choice and worthy the winning.

Study Questions

1. What images are used to call to mind the springtime?
2. What is springtime compared to?
3. Can you give an example of alliteration or assonance found in the poem?
4. What is the rhyme scheme? Is this a sonnet form?

Invictus

by William Ernest Henley

Out of the night that covers me,
   Black as the Pit from pole to pole,
I thank whatever gods may be
   for my unconquerable soul.

In the fell clutch of circumstance
   I have not winced nor cried aloud.
Under the bludgeonings of chance
   My head is bloody but unbowed.

Beyond this place of wrath and tears
   Looms but the Horror of the shade,
And yet the menace of the years
   Finds, and shall find, me unafraid.

It matters not how strait the gate,
   How charged with punishments of scroll,
I am the master of my fate;
   I am the captain of my soul.

Study Questions

1. What seems to be the ultimate virtue, as portrayed by this poem? Is supernatural faith or hope expressed? What do you think about the point of view here communicated?
2. What is the meter of the poem? What is the rhyme scheme?

Lead, Kindly Light

by John Henry Newman (before becoming a cardinal)

Lead, kindly Light, amid the encircling gloom,
    Lead Thou me on!
The night is dark, and I am far from home—
    Lead Thou me on!
Keep Thou my feet; I do not ask to see
The Distant scene,—one step enough for me.

I was not ever thus, nor prayed that Thou
    Shouldst lead me on;
I loved to choose and see my path; but now,
    Lead Thou me on!
I loved the garish day, and, spite of fears,
Pride ruled my will: remember not past years!

So long Thy power has blest me, sure it still
    Will lead me on
O'er moor and fen, o'er crag and torrent, till
    The night is gone;
And with the morn those angel faces smile
Which I have loved long since, and lost awhile!

Study Questions

1. Compare the message of this poem to that of "Invictus". How do they differ? Who is the captain of Newman's soul?
2. What is the rhyme scheme? What is the meter?
3. What is the plea of the first stanza?
4. The second stanza contrasts two periods of Newman's life. How are those periods characterized?
5. In the third stanza what figure of speech portrays a struggle in the heart of the author? Why does he continue on a path that is so difficult?

Cadgwith

by Lionel Johnson

My windows open to the autumn night,
In vain I watched for sleep to visit me:
How should sleep dull mine ears, and dim my sight,
Who saw the stars, and listened to the sea?

Ah, how the City of our God is fair!
If, without sea and starless though it be,
For joy of the majestic beauty there,
Men shall not miss the stars, nor mourn the sea.

Study Question

1. What is the thought of the first stanza? How does that lead to
   the second stanza?

Answers to Study Questions

"Edward, Edward"   *p. 370*

1. This poem is a ballad, a short narrative poem originally composed to be sung. As is typical of the ballad there is a single episode of an extremely dramatic nature presented. The action of the poem is revealed in a dialogue; motives for the action are suggested and implied rather than directly expressed. Further, there is not much in the way of characterization or description.

    There is a refrain in every stanza of this poem that displays "incremental repetition", a stanza that repeats the preceding stanza with the variations necessary to continue the story. The first and third lines of every stanza are the same, as are the fifth and seventh. The second line of every stanza is "Edward, Edward", and the sixth is always "Mither, mither", indicating the ongoing dialogue. The fourth line varies from the second in a way that advances the story, and similarly the eighth line differs from the sixth.

    There are some differences in "Edward, Edward" from the typical ballad as characterized in the definition at the beginning of this section. The characters are of the nobility rather than of commoners, for Edward has a "hawk", and a "red-roan steed"; their "fair" home has a "hall" and "towers" as well. The supernatural does not figure largely in the poem, though the "curse of hell" is certainly significant in understanding what happened. This particular ballad is not about physical courage, but it is about love in a certain respect. Evidently Edward has followed his mother's suggestion in killing his own father. The natural love between father and son and between husband and wife has been perverted, and, as a result of this action, the love of mother and son has been destroyed as well. All of the stanzas, up to the last, are intended to reveal, little by little, what happened and why. They are not divided into two stanzas that identify the hero, two that tell the story, and remaining stanzas that give the action; however, the first two stanzas do reveal certain of Edward's attributes (he has both a hawk and a horse of which he is fond), the next two tell the central previous action (that he killed his father) and that a dire consequence is expected, and the remaining stanzas reveal the extent of those consequences.

2. Edward has killed his father. His mother counseled him to do this deed. Probably, he didn't immediately tell what he had done because he was overcome with shame and horror at the deed he had committed, as well as anger against his mother.

3. The mother is selfish and callous; her response to the news of her husband's death reveals this, as does her response to Edward's self-imposed penance. She is not sad or concerned about Edward or remorseful for her part in the patricide. She just asks what penance Edward will perform (not volunteering to bear part of the burden), and when she hears that he plans to leave all that is his and never return, she asks what he'll leave to her. It would seem that the relationship of Edward and his mother has been one of passivity on the son's part and dominance on the mother's, since he has killed his father on his mother's advice.

4. The climax of the story occurs in the last four lines, when we learn that the mother incited the murder and that the son now hates her for it.

"Get Up and Bar the Door" *p. 372*

1. Once, about the time of the feast of Saint Martin, a wife had made puddings and was boiling them, when the weather became windy and blew into the house. The woman's husband told her to go and bar the door to keep out the wind. She re-

plied that she was busy with her household tasks, and that she wasn't going to bar the door, not if it remained open for a hundred years. Then husband and wife made a firm pact that whoever spoke first would have to go and bar the door. In the middle of the night two men came into the pitch-black house. The strangers looked around and wondered aloud whether this was the house of a rich man or a poor man, but neither husband nor wife would speak because of their bet. Then, in front of the silent couple, the strangers ate both the white puddings and the black, but still neither husband nor wife would speak, though the wife thought much. Next the strangers decided to cut off the husband's beard and kiss the wife. One of the men then pointed out that there was no water in the house to be used for shaving, but the other replied that they could use the pudding broth instead. At this suggestion the husband jumped up and protested angrily, "Would you kiss my wife in front of my eyes, and scald me with pudding-broth?" Immediately the wife jumped up and skipped gaily, telling her husband that he lost the bet by speaking the first word, and that he now had to bar the door.

Much of this action is implied rather than explicitly stated. It is never specifically said that the strangers came into the house, and into the presence of the couple, but it is implied in the sixth stanza, where the poem notes that the couple refused to speak. Also, one stranger tells the other to take his knife for the purpose of shaving the husband, but there is no description of the action of handing the knife over, or of the subsequent search for water, which must have taken place, ending with the suggestion to use the pudding broth instead.

2. This ballad is composed in the **ballad stanza**—quatrain rhyming *abcb*, with alternating iambic tetrameter and iambic trimeter lines. (See the second section of poetic terms.)

> The **wind**/ sae **cauld**/ blew **south**/ and **north**,
> And **blew**/ in **to**/ the **floor**;

Quoth **our**/ good **man**/ to **our**/ good **wife**,
"Gae **out**/ and **bar**/ the **door**.

"The Burning Babe" p. 374

1. This is a Christmas poem because it is about the Infant Christ. However, it is not the usual picture of Christmas, with its joy in the Incarnation. Rather, this poem anticipates the Passion and crucifixion of Our Lord, and our redemption, which is the result. Christ came to earth to save us from our sins, so His Incarnation is fulfilled in the Cross. In this poem Father Southwell has included both the promise and the fulfillment of the Incarnation.

2. A metaphor is a comparison between two things that does not employ "like" or "as". There are numerous such comparisons in the poem. In the fifth stanza Our Lord's breast is compared to a furnace, the thorns that wounded Him to the fuel of the furnace, love to the fire of the furnace, sighs to the smoke of the fire, and shame and scorn to the ashes in the furnace. In the sixth and seventh stanzas men's sinful souls are compared to the metal wrought in the furnace, then melted down into a bath to be washed.

   The third stanza contains a "conceit". The Infant Christ, scorched by the heat of the fire, sheds a flood of tears, and these tears, which might have been expected to quench the fire, did not do so. This is a striking and unexpected image. The fire is Christ's love for man, and the tears are a sign of the sorrow of Our Lord that no one comes to Him to warm themselves at the fire of His love. It might be expected that the neglect suffered by Our Lord would quench His love for sinful man, but, in fact, His sorrow and His love were bred together.

   There is personification in the sixth stanza: both Justice and Mercy are spoken of as if they had human characteristics.

3. Two instances of alliteration are found in the fifth stanza,

"My faultless breast the furnace is,
The fuel, wounding thorns;
Love is the fire, and sighs the smoke,
The ashes, shame and scorns.

4. The rhyme scheme is *abcb*, and the meter is iambic tetrameter alternating with iambic trimeter.

As I/ in **hoa**/ ry **win**/ ter's **night**
Stood **shive**/ ring **in**/ the **snow**,
Sur **prised**/ I **was**/ with **sud**/ den **heat**
Which **made**/ my **heart**/ to **glow**;

"To the Memory of My Beloved Master, William Shakespeare" p. 375

1. Section 1 is from the beginning to line 14. This is the introduction to the poem; here Jonson indicates what he is *not* doing in this poem. He is not writing to draw envy upon Shakespeare. Further, he is not merely going to say in general that Shakespeare's writings are such that no man or muse could praise them too much, though this is true. Such general praise might proceed from ignorance or blind affection, or from crafty malice. In fact, however, even crafty malice would be ineffective against Shakespeare's greatness.

   The second section begins in line 15 and goes to line 44. This section starts by stating that Shakespeare is the soul of the age; but the conclusion is that he is more than that—he is not of an age, he is for all time. His poetry is better than even the greatest of previous poets. It is better than that of any other English poet living or dead; in fact, it is so great that he lives yet, as long as his book lives. Further, Jonson would call forth even the great Greek and Roman poets to give homage to Shakespeare.

   The third section begins at line 45 and continues to line 52. This part of the poem says that Shakespeare was richly gifted by nature, more so than Aristophanes or Terence or Plautus.

The fourth section, lines 53 to 68, qualifies the previous section. It points out that art is also part of the picture. However richly gifted by nature one is, there must be both work and art involved in the final product.

The fifth section, from line 69 to the end of the poem, is a conclusion mourning Shakespeare, but then stating that Shakespeare is a star, influencing the stage still. This stage has mourned his passing and would despair ever seeing daylight again, except for the work Shakespeare left behind.

2. The central thought in this poem is praise of Shakespeare, but informed praise, from one who knows and can compare Shakespeare's work to the work of others. Such a one may praise not only the work but also see its greatness and its lasting excellence.

3. "But these ways/ Were not the paths I meant unto thy praise" is the sentiment expressed at the beginning of the poem. Mr. Jonson is saying that he does not wish to praise Shakespeare in terms that are too general or vague because they might then be taken as coming from ignorance, affection, or malice.

"Thou art a monument without a tomb" is said after the poet tells us that he will not compare Shakespeare to Chaucer, Spenser, or Beaumont. Jonson does not think Shakespeare needs a fancy tomb to be memorialized, or to live on. He says that Shakespeare is a monument in himself, through his work, and it is through his work that he lives still.

"Yet I must not give Nature all; thy art,/ My gentle Shakespeare, must enjoy a part" points out that art is also responsible for greatness of Shakespeare's work. Nature may give wonderful gifts, but there must still be both work and art involved in the final product.

4. The meter is iambic pentameter, and the whole poem is in couplets.

Sonnet LXI from the Amoretti

p. 379

1. It calls to mind the passage in Scripture where God says, "Let us make man in Our image. . . . So God created man in His own image, in the image of God He created him; male and female He created them." This scriptural passage refers primarily to man's having an intellect and will, for we are made in God's image in that way. But it is also true to say that men were created with sanctifying grace, wherein we share in the divine life. The poet here alludes to these verses to suggest the interior beauty of his beloved and to tell us the source of that beauty.

2. The rhyme scheme of the sonnet is *ababbcbccdcdee*. The first twelve lines are of a piece, expressing one thought, the transcendence of the beloved, and the last two lines contain a reflection that comes from the preceding thought. These are characteristics of the English sonnet.

3. The central idea is the perfection of this woman, and the distance between her and the men who might love her. She is a glorious image of God's beauty, divinely wrought, like an angel, adorned with the gifts of the saints.

Sonnets by William Shakespeare

XVIII

p. 380

1. Shakespeare says that the one of whom he writes is more beautiful and moderate than a summer's day, because a summer's day does not last, "summer's lease hath all too short a date", it is sometimes too hot, and often it is not sunny. In fact, "every fair from fair sometime declines", but his friend will not decline, not even in death, for "thy eternal summer" and "that fair thou owest" are immortalized in this sonnet.

2. He means that his friend has the beauty of soul that will not fade, and that beauty is immortalized in these lines.

The Rhetorical Stage: Poetry Selections: Section III

447

3. The basic thought of the sonnet is to compare the limited existence of the beauty belonging to a summer's day with the eternity of true beauty. The couplet adds the idea that so long as men can see and read, the beauty and goodness of the one here spoken of will be remembered.

XIX

1. Time is personified as one who devours and moves quickly. Time blunts the lion's paw, plucks the teeth from the tiger, burns the phoenix, and makes the seasons pass in swift succession.
2. The "heinous crime" is making his friend grow old and dimming his beauty by drawing lines in his fair brow.
3. The poet will defeat Time by immortalizing the youth and beauty of his friend in his verses.

XXXVI
p. 382

1. The speaker is acknowledging that his guilt, the blots upon his character, make it necessary for these two friends to stop seeing and talking to each other, at least publicly. He says that it will not alter their concern for each other, but it will keep them apart. Otherwise his faults will dishonor his friend, by reason of their association.
2. In the couplet the poet urges his friend not to besmirch name and honor by associating with someone who is guilty of some wickedness, but to realize that by preserving his own character, he makes it possible for his friend to share in it.
3. The rhyme scheme is *ababcdcdefefgg*; the meter is iambic pentameter.

CXXXVIII
p. 383

1. He doesn't tell her that what she says is untrue, because he wants to act as though he were some untutored youth, innocent of the world's false subtleties.

2. No, he knows that what she says is untrue, but he wishes it were true. Passionate love usually belongs to the young, so when one is older and in love, one's age is something of an embarrassment; for this reason the poet says, "age in love loves not to have years told".

3. The poet says that love's best habit is in seeming trust, but in fact, love's best habit is in real trust. The imitation, by the fact that it is an imitation, shows that the genuine article is better.

4. The conclusion of this sonnet is that it is their mutual faults that are being flattered by this lying: "And in our faults by lies we flatter'd be". This does not seem to be good for one's character. Sonnet CXVI, in contrast, says that true love doesn't need to ignore the realities of life; it is not shaken by the passage of time and the coming of old age. It is constant and fixed, and thus a real help in the vissitudes of life.

CXVI   p. 384

1. A sword is said to be made of "true" steel when it does what it is supposed to do, without buckling or breaking. "True minds" may be understood in a similar sense. True minds belong to those who are loyal, trustworthy, dependable.

2. Love is not Time's fool because the changes that Time brings will not mislead true love. Time is often personified as an old man with a sickle; the sickle is a sign of the way time eventually cuts down even the most hale and hearty. C. S. Lewis, in *The Silver Chair* and *The Last Battle*, has a character he calls Father Time, who rests underground until the end of Narnia and then emerges to call all creatures home.

3. The theme of the sonnet is that those who are loyal and true are capable of a lasting love.

Shakespeare says that true love does not alter with alterations in the beloved, because it is not dependent on the external appearance. It is steadfast and can weather the storms of life without failing; it is like a light or a beacon that guides the wanderer.

4. Time is personified, and there are similes: love is said to be "an ever-fixed mark" and a "star to every wandering bark".

XXX   p. 385

1. The remembrance of the past is summoned.
2. This is an example of the English or Shakespearean sonnet. The two basic thoughts are that in memory the speaker lives again many sorrows, fresh again in the remembrance, but when he thinks of his friend, his sadness is gone, and the losses he has suffered are as though they were not. The first quatrain recalls the many things the poet has worked to acquire but that he has failed to obtain. Then he is sad both because he doesn't have the things and because he wasted all that time trying to get them. The second quatrain recalls the friends who have died, who will never be seen again in this world, and the sorrows associated with those friends when they were alive. The third quatrain recalls complaints from the past, reviewing the situations and moaning about them again as if they had just happened.
3. Some examples of alliteration are "**s**essions of **s**weet **s**ilent thought,/ I **s**ummon", "**w**ith old **w**oes new **w**ail my dear time's **w**aste", "**d**eath's **d**ateless night", "**l**ove's **l**ong since cancell'd woe", "**g**rieve at **g**rievances", "**w**oe to **w**oe".
4. "Old woes new wail my dear time's waste", "drown an eye", and "death's dateless night" are conceits.

XXIX   p. 386

1. The first eight lines are very unhappy, even despairing.
2. It is the thought of his friend that changes his mood.
3. "And trouble deaf heaven with my bootless cries,/ And look upon myself and curse my fate" are the opposite of the ending of the sonnet.

4. It has the rhyme scheme of an English sonnet, *ababcdcdefefgg*, but it is divided in thought into an octet and sestet, like the Italian sonnets, rather than three quatrains and a couplet, as is usually considered the English form.

5. The lark arising at dawn from the earth to the sky is the image used by the poet to characterize his change in mood.

LV
p. 387

1. The poet's friend is the "you" that is addressed here.

2. "These contents" are the content of these lines, that is, the thought that is contained and immortalized in this sonnet.

3. The first quatrain says that nothing material is going to outlast this poem. His friend will continue to shine brightly in a poem, even if the "gilded monuments of princes" will eventually crumble. The second quatrain says that war will remove all monuments but not the remembrance of love in those who live. The third quatrain says that when death and other calamities happen, the friend will still come forth and be praised in the eyes of all, even to the end of time and the last judgment, for, says the couplet, the friend will live in this sonnet and in the eyes of those who love.

4. Great literature is not affected by time, in the sense that it freezes a moment in time, as does a painting, for once written it will always stay as it was when written. But great literature also is said to be eternal because it conforms to reality. It is an expression of the real world and how it works, what its nature is. This means that it continues to be true as long as reality remains the same, that is, forever.

LXXIII
p. 388

1. Sleep is death's second self.

2. Line 12, "Consumed with that which it was nourished by", is a conceit. It is a poetic metaphor, pointing, in a startling

juxtaposition, to the thought that the ashes, which now con-
sume the person, once nourished him.

3. Yellow leaves hanging on nearly empty branches, the twilight of
the day, as sunset fades in the west, and the glowing of the ashes
of a fire that was once vigorous. These are the images that are
here used to signify old age.

4. The couplet reflects on the strength of the love that can see the
end approaching and yet continue to love.

Sonnet 41, by Philip Sidney   *p. 389*

1. This is an English sonnet, though it has some of the characteris-
tics of the Italian sonnet. The first two quatrains employ the
abbaabba rhyme scheme, as do the Italian sonnets. However, the
first wave of thought in the poem ends in the twelfth line, with
the last two lines providing the answer to the question posed by
the rest of the sonnet.

2. The first thought is that people speculate on why the poet has
done so well in feats of arms. The second thought is the answer
to that question: it is because Stella looked on.

3. The rhyme scheme is *abbaabbacdcdee*.

4. These lines give the speculation of some that his prowess is due
to his natural heritage, to the fact that on both his maternal and
paternal sides there are those who excelled in such contests.

Two Sonnets from Divina Commedia   *p. 390*

1. Dante's work is compared to a cathedral, and those who read it
to the laborers who come to the cathedral to pray.

2. The subject of the *Paradiso* is the saints and martyrs of the
Church, the Church Triumphant, those who have persisted and
won the crown.

3. The first sonnet is one of faith and of looking for help in the
burdens of life. The second sonnet is one of triumph, of hope
fulfilled.

4. In "The Day Is Done" the poet says he turns to poems of peace in times of sadness, and in these sonnets he certainly indicates that the *Divine Comedy* brings peace. However, he also says that it is not to the old masters that he turns for peace, and Dante is one of the great masters.

5. The rhyme scheme is *abbaabbacdcdcd* in the first sonnet, *abbaabbacdecde* in the second.

"The Owl Critic" p. 391

1. This is an example of narrative poetry.
2. The rhyme scheme used is couplets.
3. The point of the poem is that sometimes "experts" don't know what they think they know. The expert in this story is evidently only familiar with dead owls that are supposed to look like living ones. Apparently they don't, and certainly this man doesn't know a live owl when he sees one.

"To Lucasta, Going to the Wars" p. 394

1. It appeals to both; the figurative language appeals to the emotions, while the message is primarily an appeal to the intellect.
2. First stanza: Don't tell me that I am unkind in leaving you to go to war. Second stanza: It's true that now the thing closest to me is the war. Third stanza: But you should be pleased that I do so, since my love for you is greater because I love honor as much as I do.
3. In the first stanza there is a juxtaposition of the images of a nunnery with war and arms; in the second there is the contrast between "embrace", which is confining, and "free"; while in the third there is the dissimilarity of "adore" to "inconstancy".
4. Yes, because if a love is by nature subordinate, then it won't be what it should be unless it is subordinated. The poet is telling his lady that the love with which he loves her is better than it would otherwise be, because he loves honor even more than he loves her. Would she want his love if he were a dishonorable

person, offering dishonorable love? She would not. But this love of his, since it is subordinate to honor, has certain consequences that are hard.

"At the Aquarium" p. 395

1. Both the people and the fish have a kind of wonder in their eyes, they are pale and wan, they watch with cold surprise. They also share a lack of purpose in their lives; the fish "have no pathway where they go, they flow", and the peering people "wander also to and fro,/ And know not why or where they go".

2. The first hint one receives of the twist in the poem is with the line, "The level people in the air".

3. Answers to this question may vary, but it seems clear at least that the aimless wandering of many people reminds Mr. Eastman of fish, and that such folk are, in certain important respects, no better than fish.

4. The rhyme scheme is that of couplets.

"To a Waterfowl" p. 396

1. The poet is reminded, and comforted by the thought, that he is like the waterfowl. He, too, is on his way, alone, to a particular goal. He, like the waterfowl, has dangers to face, and, again like the bird, will be lead by God safely to his destination.

   In prose the poem says something like this: While watching a glowing sunset the poet sees a bird flying, by itself, high up in the sky. He wonders where it is going and notes that the bird is so far above the earth that a fowler would be unable to bring it down. He reflects that God has instructed the waterfowl in the right way to take, so that the bird, though alone, is not lost, even though his way is not marked. The bird will continue on his course, not stopping for rest until he finds his summer home. There he will stop, then build a nest. The poet reflects that the same is true for himself and that watching the waterfowl has impressed this lesson upon his heart. God, who teaches and protects the waterfowl, will also teach and protect him in the long way that he must tread alone.

The theme of the poem is proposed in the last sentence, but may be universalized to include us all. It reminds one of Scripture, where it is said, "Consider the lilies of the field . . ."

2. There are several instances of alliteration in the poem. "**M**ight **m**ark", and "**f**igure **f**loats" in the second stanza, the many words beginning with *s* in the sixth stanza, the five words beginning with *h* in the seventh stanza, as well as "**z**one to **z**one" in the last stanza. Some examples of assonance are: "h**a**ve f**a**nned,/ **A**t th**a**t . . . **a**tmosphere" in the fifth stanza, "**A**nd soon th**a**t toil sh**a**ll end" in the sixth stanza.

3. The references to color in the poem are "rosy" in the first stanza and "crimson" in the second. The poet mentions the dark night, which might also be construed as a color—black.

4. The pattern is 3,5,5,3; there are three accented syllables in the first line, five in each of the two next lines, and three in the last.

"To Althea, from Prison"   *p. 398*

1. It is iambic tetrameter, alternating with iambic trimeter.
   > When **love**/ with **un**/ con **fin**/ èd **wings**
   > **Ho** vers/ with **in**/ my **gates**,

   The rhyme scheme is *abab*.

2. First stanza: When Althea, because of her love, comes to visit him in prison, and they embrace through the grate, he feels freer than the birds in the air.

   Second stanza: When he and his comrades who are loyal to the king drink wine, even in their grief they are more free than the fish drinking freely in the deep.

   Third stanza: When he sings of the glories of the king, he'll be freer than the wind, even though he may be put to death for treason.

Fourth stanza: Walls do not make a prison, nor do bars make a cage. What is necessary for freedom is love and purity. In fact, the confinement of a prison can, for such a person, become a hermitage.

The first three stages lead up to the fourth, each of them detailing a way in which the prisoner finds himself to be free—more free than unconfined animals. In this stanza he gives the reason: what is essential for freedom is an innocent, quiet mind, love freely chosen, and allegiance bestowed without constraint. His soul is his own, and thus, though his body be confined, his soul is not. The angels share this freedom, the freedom of the rational person, and animals do not.

"Repentance" *p. 399*

1. The rhyme scheme is interesting. You may think it is *abcaacba dedeff*, with the second four lines being a mirror images of the first four. However, pronunciations often change over time. The original rhyme scheme was probably *abbaabba cdcdee*. The word "infinities" was most likely pronounced so as to rhyme with "advise".

2. The first wave of thought describes the general resurrection at the end of the world. The two types of people are those who have died and are now called forth from the dead, and those still living at the time of the resurrection.

3. It means that the angels are blowing their trumpets at the four corners of the earth, that is, throughout the whole world.

4. The second wave of thought is the poet's request for a little more time before the resurrection. He says that it will be late to ask for the grace of repentance once the resurrection happens; he'd prefer that God should teach him to repent here and now, for if He does that, the poet's pardon is assured.

"Batter My Heart"

p. 400

1. The harsh sound of the repeated *b* gives the physical impression of breaking or battering.
2. The first metaphor is that of the usurped town. (This figure of speech uses the word "like", but it is extended beyond the usually limited likeness of a simile.) The poet likens himself to an usurped town, which tries to admit the rightful ruler, but is not able to do so, due to a defect in the one who is supposed to represent, and work for, the ruler. The second metaphor is that of love and marriage. The poet likens his love for God to that of a person who is betrothed to one but loves another. He asks that his betrothal to God's enemy be broken by God. Further, he asks that God should take him by force, imprison him, for then he will be free.
3. The last two lines contain two examples of a conceit. The poet says freedom is found in subjugation, and chastity is found in forced love.
4. The following elements of metaphysical poetry are seen in this poem: it treats of the great concerns of man: God, love, sin, suffering, and death. It contains serious philosophic truths. Its emphasis is on thought rather than feeling. It also uses dramatic speech and words and expressions from everyday speech, has a logical structure, uses sensual imagery for religious experience, and finds points of similarity between widely differing things.

"Why So Pale and Wan?"

p. 401

1. Cavalier poetry is characterized by a keen, clever, sometimes flippant attitude. It also often exhorts one to make the most of today, for the material world will not last. These characteristics are found in this poem; it is very clever, rather flippant, and tells the young lover not to spend time vainly: it's a waste of a precious commodity and will not achieve the desired end.

2. The rhyme scheme of the poem is *ababb*. The meter is trochaic, until the end. The last stanza changes to iambic. The change emphasizes and calls attention to the advice of the last stanza.

> **Why** so/ **pale** and/ **wan,** fond/ **lov** er?
> **Prith** ee,/ **why** so/ **pale**?
> **Will,** when/ **look** ing/ **well** can't/ **move** her,
> **Look** ing/ **ill** pre/ **vail**?
>
> Quit, **quit**/ for **shame**!/ This **will**/ not **move**;
> This **can**/ not **take**/ her.
> If **of**/ her **self**/ she **will**/ not **love**,
> **Noth** ing/ can **make**/ her:
> The **dev**/ il **take**/ her!

3. Suckling's advice is that if the one you love doesn't return your love, don't pursue the relationship. You can't make her love you, so forget it. He suggests that it's unmanly, unworthy behavior.

"Elegy Written in a Country Churchyard"   p. 402

1. These first three stanzas set the mood of the poem. Visually they call to mind the evening dusk, and they establish a sense of loneliness and the end of things.
2. The narrow cell is the grave.
3. They arose early, worked hard in the fields, and enjoyed the evening return to home and hearth.
4. Stanza eight says that those with more worldly ambition and splendor should not ridicule the simple life of the poor and obscure. Stanza nine gives a reason: whether one is rich or poor in life, the end is the same: everyone dies.
5. "Can storied urn or animated bust/ Back to its mansion call the fleeting breath?/ Can Honour's voice provoke the silent dust,/ Or Flatt'ry soothe the dull cold ear of Death?"
6. The poet suggests that some potentially great men may lie in the graveyard, men who could have changed the course of his-

tory, as did Hampden, Milton, and Cromwell, had they been educated ("But Knowledge to their eyes her ample page/ Rich with the spoils of time did ne'er unroll"), and wealthy ("Chill Penury repress'd their noble rage,/ And froze the genial current of their soul").

7. It also expresses the idea that some of the great-souled and beautiful are born, live, and die in circumstances that conceal their qualities.

8. The poet, in these stanzas, suggests that not only were good and virtuous actions and habits not allowed to grow in the impoverished circumstances of the poor, but those circumstances also prevented many sinful actions as well.

9. What do you think?

10. "Yet e'en these bones from insult to protect/ Some frail memorial still erected nigh,/ With uncouth rhymes and shapeless sculpture deck'd,/ Implores the passing tribute of a sigh."

11. He starts talking of himself when he says, "For thee, who mindful of th' unhonour'd dead/ Dost in these lines their artless tale relate;/ If chance, by lonely contemplation led,/ Some kindred spirit shall inquire thy fate".

12. Gray's epitaph claims obscurity and poverty, and a melancholy nature. However, he says, he was generous and sincere, giving to the unfortunate all that he had (viz., his pity). God repaid him for these virtues by giving him a friend. He hopes to end in the bosom of God the Father.

"On the Morning of Christ's Nativity" p. 408

1. The virginity of Mary, Mother of God, is referred to in "Of wedded maid and virgin mother born"; original sin, the need for redemption, and the promise of God to send a Redeemer are referred to in "That he our deadly forfeit should release,/ And with his Father work us a perpetual peace." The Incarnation of the second Person of the Blessed Trinity and His birth

are the subjects of the second and third stanzas. The visit of the magi to the stable in Bethlehem is mentioned in the fourth stanza.

2. The seven-line stanzas of the prelude have *ababbcc* as the rhyme scheme. The meter is iambic pentameter for the first six lines and iambic hexameter for the last line (a stanza form known as **rime royal**).

3. In the prelude he asks the heavenly muse to help him write a song in honor of the birth of the Christ Child. The Hymn is that song.

4. The Hymn has eight-line stanzas with ending rhymes in this pattern, *aabccbdd*, for its rhyme scheme. The meter is complex, by reason of the variations in feet per line. It is iambic rhythm, with 3,3,5,3,3,5,4,6 as the regular pattern of feet per line.

5. Christ was born in winter because He was born in poverty and Nature in winter is impoverished, so she sympathizes with her Master. Also in winter there is snow, which covers the sinful state of Nature, so that her deformities should be hidden from her Maker.

6. It doesn't really mean that Nature is sinful; it can't be, because it doesn't have choice. But the frozen, empty, unproductive earth is compared to a sinner hiding his guilt. This is a metaphor.

7. There is peace throughout sea and land.

8. The sun is here personified, that is, given human characteristics. He recognizes the great light that has come into the world, a spiritual light much greater than his own physical light.

9. Nature hears such glorious music coming from the sky (the region of the moon), that she almost thinks that the end of the world as she has known it has come.

10. He says that "Time will run back and fetch the age of gold", a suggestion that with such sound a new and better age, like that of Paradise at the beginning of time, would occur. Vanity would die, and sin be gone; hell itself would pass away.

11. It is the star of Bethlehem.

12. The point of the ode seems to be just what Milton says at the beginning. It is his gift to the Christ Child, a recognition and celebration of the great gift God has given us in the Incarnation. The effect, in the verses we have here, is primarily joyful and grateful.

"Ode to the West Wind" p. 415

1. The autumnal west wind is characterized as wild, a destroyer, driving all before it. The west wind of spring, his "azure sister", is mild and encouraging, a preserver. The wild west wind drives the seeds to their dark wintry bed, where they lie as though dead until the west wind of spring blows over the earth and fills both plain and hill with beautiful living colors and sweet springtime odors.

2. The clouds are likened to earth's decaying leaves, angels, bright hair, locks, the vaults of the sepulcher's dome. The decaying leaves provide a link with the previous section, where the dead leaves are mentioned in the second through fourth lines.

3. They know that the wild west wind brings the cold winter climate.

4. The first three lines of the fourth section mention the dead leaves of the first section, the clouds of the second section, and the waves of the third section. They are all brought to mind and seen as different images of the same idea, all objects that share in the strength and power of the wild wind. In this section the poet wishes that he, like these objects, could participate in the attributes of the west wind. In his youth he thought he could, but the thorns of life have taught him otherwise. Now he asks in prayer that he might be lifted like the wave, the leaf, the cloud. He now sees himself as chained, even though he is meant to be tameless, swift, and proud, as is the west wind.

5. He seems to be old because he says, "What if my leaves are falling". It also seems that he has not yet seen the effects of

his reform, for he asks that this poem will spread throughout the "unawakened earth". But he has hopes still, because he says, at the very end, "If Winter comes, can Spring be far behind?"

"Ozymandias" *p. 418*

1. The sonnet recounts what has come of the boastful and powerful Ozymandias. He was at one time in a position of power in the world, and he triumphed over those around him, proclaiming his supremacy. Yet there is nothing now left of his works or rule. The theme of the sonnet is that human power and dominion do not endure, especially those based on cruelty. As Gray indicates in his "Elegy", the dead are dead alike, and immortality is not granted to human authority.

2. Line 11 is "Look on my works, ye Mighty, and despair!" Ozymandias meant to boast to the mighty of the world that they could never equal his achievements and that they should despair of trying. The meaning now conveyed, however, is that the mighty should look at the destruction of all Ozymandias' works and realize that their own accomplishments will also disappear without a trace.

"On First Looking into Chapman's Homer" *p. 419*

1. The realms of gold here mean the places he has visited by his reading of the great literature of the world.

2. The western islands refers to the British Isles, where there have been many great authors who have been true to the ideals of song and music. These are the authors that Keats has been reading until now.

3. The "expanse" is great epic poetry, of which the *Iliad* and the *Odyssey* are the prime examples.

4. Keats felt as though he had just discovered a new, heretofore unsuspected, planet or a new ocean. The discovery of Homer's

works was so astounding, so great, that it was like looking into a whole new area of life.

5. Some discoveries are so great that there are no words adequate to express them. One even wonders if it can really be as it appears, or if that is hoping for too much.

6. The rhyme scheme is *abbaabbacdcdcd*. The sonnet is Italian; it has the Italian form, and there is a division of thought between the octet and the sestet. In the octet Keats describes his past situation. The last line of the octet is pivotal, providing the connection between this previous sitiuation and the present. The sestet is a description of the state of mind of the poet now that he has been introduced to Homer.

"Ode on a Grecian Urn" *p. 420*

1. It is the unravished bride of quietness because it has retained, through the centuries, its original purity and beauty. It is the foster child of silence and slow time because though silence and slow time did not produce it, they did preserve it. And it is a sylvan historian because it records a wooded scene.

2. To give the reader, in an interesting way, an undestanding of what is depicted on the vase.

3. The suggestion is that unheard songs can be whatever you imagine them to be, whereas heard songs will always fall short in some way from perfection. The unheard, but imagined, song sings to the spirit of the viewer, who invests it with his ideals. The rest of this stanza, and the whole of the next, point out the advantages and the disadvantages of the lack of change found in works of art. The goal is never attained, yet the beauty will never fade. The love depicted, though it will not be fulfilled, will never become a cause of sorrow or weariness.

4. The inhabitants of the town have all gone to the sacrifice, and since the scene depicted will never change, they will never be anywhere other than where they are at the moment of the picture.

5. The first three lines of the fifth stanza are a description of the urn, to bring its image before the reader.

6. The picture on the urn brings to our minds the same aspects of reality that are clear to us when we think about eternity. The urn will persist, through our generation and beyond, always calling to mind the truth that is found in beauty.

"Break, Break, Break" *p. 423*

1. An elegy has death or mourning as its theme. It is quiet in mood and tends to be contemplative in nature. This poem has these characteristics, though there is more anguish in it than, say, in Gray's "Elegy in a Country Churchyard".

2. The first stanza, both in terms of the visual image and the repeated harsh *b* sound, has a sense of loneliness and sorrow.

3. The poet expresses his loss in these words, "But O for the touch of a vanished hand./ And the sound of a voice that is still!" and "But the tender grace of a day that is dead/ Will never come back to me."

4. Perhaps the first of the statements given above is most powerful, because it is the most explicit.

"The Young Neophyte" *p. 424*

1. The rhyme scheme is *abbaabbacdcdcd*. It has two quatrains followed by a sestet (though it is arranged in two groups of three). The rhyme scheme is that of an Italian sonnet.

2. The author is both young and new to Catholicism. She is just beginning a lifelong commitment to a faith that will inform every part of her life.

3. The first line is a question, "Who knows what days I answer for today?" Except for God, no one knows the answer to that clearly and explicitly. Nonetheless, the poet is aware that though she cannot see the days ahead with the clarity of the present, she is still able to offer the whole of her life to God. What the days

ahead hold in particular makes no difference to this giving of self. In "giving the bud", that is, herself in her youth, she recognizes that she is "giving the flower", herself as an adult as well. She goes on to say that she is now bowing both her unfaded brow and the faded brow which will belong to her in old age. She is bending her knees both in their present condition and as they will be in later life. The whole of this poem is intended to say that today, in making this committment, she permanently submits the whole of her to life to God and His Church, right up to the day of her death when "I light the tapers at my head and feet,/ And lay the crucifix on this silent heart."

4. "Thoughts yet unripe in me I bend one way", "I dedicate my fields when Spring is grey", and "to pledge my hidden wheat" are all one extended metaphor. They say again what the first metaphor said, that she is giving all of her life, even what is not yet actually present but only potential.

5. The mood is solemn and earnest, imparting a feeling of intelligent conviction.

"How Do I Love Thee?"

p. 425

1. She means that her love is limited only by her own limitation. She loves with her whole being, as completely as she is able. The kindness and consideration of love are expressed in "I love thee to the level of every day's/ Most quiet need, by sun and candle-light."

2. She says that she loves as freely as men strive for right, and as purely as they turn from praise. In other words, her love is given as men give love to the things they know are good, and it is without self-interest.

3. In her grief she wasted her passion, but now that same energy is being put to a better use.

4. This intense adoration, or hero worship, is usually grown out of as one leaves childhood. Here Mrs. Browning says she feels that

kind of intensity of love, which she had thought was gone forever.

5. This poem is a more emotional approach, while Sonnet CXVI is more intellectual. That doesn't mean there isn't some of both in each, but the primary thrust of this is an appeal to emotion, calling to mind the feelings evoked by intense love. Shakespeare's sonnet is more a discussion of the quality of permanence found in true love. There is a dispassionate sense, an objectivity that is not present in "How Do I Love Thee?".

"The Kingdom of God" p. 426

1. There are four conceits in the first stanza.
2. The poet tells us to look for God immediately around us. Would a fish have to soar to find his natural element? Or an eagle have to plunge down to find the air? No, in both cases the animal is surrounded by what he needs. Similarly, we are surrounded by God's presence, if we but have the eyes to see. "The angels keep their ancient places;—/ Turn but a stone, and start a wing!" means that the angels are as much a part of our lives as they were in Jacob's time, when in a vision he saw their constant traffic between heaven and earth. If we turn over a stone we will find an angel.
3. Our doors are said to be clay shuttered because our bodies are made of clay, and the soul and the spiritual world it needs must meet through the "door" of the body.
4. Our cry of sadness and loss will move us to the recognition of the spiritual world around us.
5. "In the night" can mean in the physical night, when the sun has gone down, but it can also mean in the darkness of the lost and lonely soul.
6. Christ walked to the apostles on the Sea of Galilee. They had trouble believing that it was truly the Lord; this poem is about how hard it seems for modern man to believe that Christ is truly present in the daily events of his life.

(a) The introduction of the theme is found in the first fifteen lines.

(b) The second section is the next nine lines, starting with "I pleaded, outlaw-wise" and ending with "as Love wist to pursue." The poet says that he's afraid that if he has God, he won't be able to have anything else as well.

(c) This section starts with "Across the margent of the world I fled" and ends with "Naught shelters thee, who wilt not shelter Me." The lesson of the stars and planets was that their constancy and regularity showed them to belong to God, to His plan. Recourse to them inevitably led the sinner back to God. Their beauty is a created beauty, and their order is a created order, so contemplation of them directs one to their Creator. The lines "I tempted all His servitors, but to find/ My own betrayal in their constancy,/ In faith to Him their fickleness to me,/ Their traitorous trueness, and their loyal deceit." The figure of speech used in "I said to dawn: Be sudden—to eve: Be soon" is personification, and it is used here to convey the sinner's desire that time move swiftly. "Skiey blossoms" mean the stars, which are the blossoms of the sky. The effect of the refrain is to give an image of the unhurried, but unfaltering, pursuit of the sinner by God.

(d) This section begins with "I sought no more that after which I strayed" and ends with "Their angel plucked them from me by the hair." The poet restates the theme when he says, "*They* at least are for me, surely for me!" He is trying to find goodness that is directed to him, without reference to God. But there is no such good thing. All goodness comes from and leads to God.

(e) This section begins with the line "Come then, ye other children, Nature's" and ends with "Lo! naught contents thee, who content'st not Me." Nature is personified as "our Lady-Mother", who has "tresses", a "palace", and a "daïs". She drinks from a chalice and lights candles. The "wind-walled palace" is the earth, and the "azured daïs" is the blue sky. Unity with nature did not satisfy the poet's need, because though he responded to nature, she was unable to respond to him. He wanted something from nature that nature was unable to give; he wanted it to be more than it is capable of being. The ending refrain, "Lo! naught contents thee, who content'st not Me", reflects the poet's lack of fulfillment and gives the reason for it. He is himself wrongly ordered, so he is not able to be satisfied with letting things be themselves. He wants them to conform to his wishes, but his wishes are wrong, because of the wrongness in him.

(f) The sixth section starts with "Naked I wait Thy Love's uplifted stroke!" and ends with "Be dunged with rotten death?" The poet views the mess he has made of his life and realizes that without God there is nothing. But he still does not rightly understand his relationship to God; he still thinks that God demands all that he has to give and allows no other loves. The poet compares himself to Samson of the Old Testament, who destroyed the Philistines by pulling down the pillars of the house in which they were banqueting, thus killing himself as well. The "linked fantasies" have also failed him, because the fragile cords of poetry cannot hold the heavy griefs of earth.

The poet describes God as an amaranthine weed, absorbing all love and thus killing any other possible loves. He thinks God purifies man by subjecting him to suffering and breaking his heart. There is a metaphor in the line "Ah! Must Thou char the wood ere Thou canst limn with it?": the wood is compared to the soul, which is made suitable by suffering, and thus able to be used by the designer and artist, who is compared to God. There is a simile in "now my heart is as a broken fount". The poet sees Death (personified) in the battlements of Eternity. The poet now makes his final complaint, that God should require death as a prelude to eternity.

(g) The last section starts with "Now of that long pursuit". God says

to the sinner, "So, have you found earth unsatisfactory, your ide-
als shattered? Try to understand, these things have left you, be-
cause you have left Me. You want to love and be loved, but why
would anyone love you? No one but I can or will make much of
nothing, for human beings love where love is merited. You have
not merited love, and thus you will not find anyone to love you,
except Me. I took that which I took from you, not to hurt you,
but so that you would come to me for it. You have thought all
that you desired was lost, but in fact I have stored it for you in
heaven. Come with Me now. I am all that you sought; in driving
Me from you, you drove all that you desired away."

"God's Grandeur"

p. 436

1. The problem is that men are not aware of the grandeur of God,
which is to be found in Nature. For years now, men have
worked in trade, in an artificial environment, which has re-
moved them from contact with nature and destroyed the agri-
cultural lifestyle. The resolution offered in the sestet is that
nature can't be submerged entirely, for there is within things
themselves a freshness, which will emerge, because the Holy
Ghost takes care of the world.
2. There are examples in every line:
"**g**randeur of **G**od"
"**sh**ining from **sh**ook foil"
"It **g**athers to a **g**reatness"
"**r**eck his **r**od"
"have **t**rod, have **t**rod, have **t**rod"
"And all is s**ear**ed with trade; bl**ear**ed, sm**ear**ed, with toil"
"And wear**s** man'**s s**mudge and share**s** man'**s s**mell: the **s**oil"
"Is bare now, nor can **f**oot **f**eel, being shod"

"**n**ature is **n**ever spent"
"d**e**ar**est** fre**s**hne**ss d**eep **d**own things"

"last lights"

"**br**own **br**ink"

"**B**ecause the Holy Ghost over the **b**ent/ **W**orld **br**oods with **w**arm **br**east and **w**ith ah! **br**ight **w**ings."

3. The rhyme scheme is *abbaabba cdcdcd*. The sonnet form is Italian.

"Spring" *p. 437*

1. The weeds growing "long and lovely and lush", thrush eggs and songs, the blooms of the glassy peartree, the rich blue of the sky, and the racing lambs all call to mind the spring.

2. It is compared to the garden of Eden before the fall.

3. "**Wh**en **w**eeds, in **wh**eels", "**l**ong and **l**ovely and **l**ush", "**l**ook **l**ittle **l**ow heavens", "**thr**ush/ **Thr**ough", "echoing **t**imber does so **r**inse and **wr**ing/ The ear, **i**t strikes **li**ke **li**ghtning", "**bl**ooms, they **br**ush/ The descending **bl**ue; that **bl**ue is all", "**r**ush/ With **r**ichness; the **r**acing lambs", "**f**air their **fl**ing", "**j**uice and all this **j**oy", "**b**eing in the **b**eginning", "**cl**oy,/ Before it **cl**oud, **Chr**ist", "**s**our with **s**inning", "**m**ind and **M**ayday in girl and boy,/ **M**ost, O **m**aid's child", and "**w**orthy the **w**inning" are examples.

4. The rhyme scheme is *abbaabba cacaca*; it is the Italian sonnet form.

"Invictus" *p. 438*

1. The ultimate virtue appears to be a kind of (rather irrational) courage, maintaining control in the face of unending horror, being the master and captain of one's actions. The poet praises the subject's refusal to bow to circumstance, even the circumstance of everlasting death. It seems that the *lack* of supernatural faith and hope forms the occasion of the praise in the poem.

2. The meter is iambic tetrameter, and the rhyme scheme is *abab* in each stanza.

"Lead, Kindly Light"   *p. 439*

1. The messages of the two poems are very different. In "Lead, Kindly Light" Newman acknowledges that he is not the captain of his own soul, at least not a fit captain, and that he needs guidance, and for that reason he asks God to enlighten him and show him the path to follow. This is very different in tone and thought from "Invictus", where the poet praises the soul who goes alone, walking without fear into the darkness.

2. The rhyme scheme is *ababcc*, and the meter is iambic pentameter in lines 1, 3, 5, and 6 and iambic dimeter in lines 2 and 4.

3. The poet's plea in the first stanza is that God, the kindly Light, should continue to show him where to put his next step. He says that he doesn't ask to see the whole of the path he is to follow, just the next step.

4. The first period was when Newman wanted to choose his own path, when he loved the showy and gaudy (probably he liked being the best or being noticed), and pride ruled his will. (It's worth noting that when God was not leading, Newman did not think that he was master of his own soul. Rather, he thought his vices ruled him.) Now he asks for guidance and is willing to follow step by step as he is led.

5. Newman uses a metaphor to characterize the struggle he expects. He calls them "moor and fen" and "crag and torrent". But he persists in spite of difficulties because he expects to find what he loves at the end of the path.

"Cadgwith"   *p. 440*

1. The first stanza says that the world is so full of beauty that the poet doesn't want to sleep and miss a moment of the splendor. Yet, in heaven we will be happy without the natural beauties we are now accustomed to. In that case, heaven must be incredibly wonderful.

Acknowledgments

The author and publisher wish to acknowledge special permission to reprint the following:

"There Once Was a Puffin", by Florence Page Jacques, has been reprinted by permission of The Nature Conservancy.

"Pocahontas", by Rosemary Carr Benét, from *A Book of Americans*, by Rosemary and Stephen Vincent Benét (Holt, Rinehart and Winston). Copyright 1933 by Rosemary and Stephen Vincent Benét. Copyright renewed 1961 by Rosemary Carr Benét. Reprinted by permission of Brandt & Brandt Literary Agents.

"Benjamin Franklin", "Captain Kidd", "Christopher Columbus", and "George Washington", by Stephen Vincent Benét, from *A Book of Americans*, by Rosemary and Stephen Vincent Benét (Holt, Rinehart and Winston). Copyright 1933 by Rosemary and Stephen Vincent Benét. Copyright renewed 1961 by Rosemary Carr Benét. Reprinted by permission of Brandt & Brandt Literary Agents.

"At the Zoo", by A. A. Milne, from *When We Were Very Young*, by A. A. Milne, illustrations by E. H. Shepard. Copyright 1924 by E. P. Dutton, renewed 1952 by A. A. Milne. Reprinted by permission of Dutton Children's Books, a division of Penguin Putnam Inc.

"The Christening", by A. A. Milne, from *When We Were Very Young*, by A. A. Milne, illustrations by E. H. Shepard. Copyright 1924 by E. P. Dutton, renewed 1952 by A. A. Milne. Reprinted by permission of Dutton Children's Books, a division of Penguin Putnam Inc.

"Furry Bear", by A. A. Milne, from *Now We Are Six*, by A. A. Milne, illustrations by E. H. Shepard. Copyright 1927 by E. P. Dutton, renewed 1955 by A. A. Milne. Reprinted by permission of Dutton Children's Books, a division of Penguin Putnam Inc.

The dictation selections from the works of Hilda van Stockum, Mary Arnold, Ethel Pochocki, Merial Trevor, Leonard Wibberly, Barbara Willard, and Kathryn Worth are used with the permission of Bethlehem Books, Bathgate, N.D.

The author and publisher are grateful to all the poets, other writers, and publishers whose work is represented in this book. It is our hope that this book will contribute to the formation of a new generation who will appreciate literary excellence.

Index of Poets

Index of Poets

Index of Poets

Index of Poets

Index of Poems

Index of First Lines

Index of First Lines

Index of First Lines

Index of Dictation Selections

Index of Selections to Memorize